Freethoughts

Freethoughts

Atheism – Secularism – Humanism

Selected Egotistically from the *Freethinker*

Barbara Smoker

Freethoughts

by Barbara Smoker

Each item was first published in the *Freethinker* on the date shown and first published collectively as a book in 2002.

Copyright © Barbara Smoker 2002

The moral right of Barbara Smoker to be identified as the author of this work is hereby asserted in accordance with the Copyright, Designs and Patents Act. However, she gives general permission for quotation from any part of it, provided its intent is not distorted and it is clearly attributed to her and to the *Freethinker*.

She is indebted to Jim Herrick, as chairman of the board of G W Foote & Co, for facilitating this production, to Herem and associates for computerisation from the printed page, to Andrew Philippou for his practical assistance, to Barry Duke for electronic versions of the more recent items, and to Rona Gerber for the cover illustration.

Published by

G W Foote Ltd   25 Red Lion Square   London   WC1R 4RL

Printed in England   ISBN 0 9508243 5 6

Contents

Introduction

THIS selection of snippets written by me for the *Freethinker* over a period of more than 35 years is, I must admit, something of an ego-trip – designed, in old age, to give me a voice beyond the crematorium. But I would not have bothered with it unless I thought there were items here of lasting secularist significance, and of general historical interest. If the book makes me enemies, I only hope they are the right enemies.

The three-and-a-half decades covered by this auto-selection, from 1966 to 2002, begin with the final emergence of my mature views on religion and bio-ethics, and continue into my eightieth year. The contemporary scene on which I comment from that perspective includes unprecedented scientific progress, a remarkable transformation of the supposedly immutable RC Church, the rise of New Age cults, and the growing threat of multicultural extremism in Britain.

Future campaigns against new religious encroachment will need to spell out the same principles as those I promulgate. I often worked them out for myself when I might have found them on tap in freethought writing of the past, if only they had not been buried in large tomes of small print. This volume, being less formidable, might prove to be of some practical use as well as a diverting read – and there is no copyright, of course, in ideas.

I plead Guilty in advance to charges of repetition. The ephemeral nature of periodical publication has always tempted journalists to recycle their earlier material, and the advent of word-processors has, of course, increased the temptation. In mitigation, there is little point in rephrasing unless one can improve on the original.

While eliminating some of the duplication, I have preferred to retain most of the echoes, rather than refer the reader back and forth. Besides, the repetitions may serve to underline the need for secular humanist campaigners to keep hammering away, year by year, decade by decade, at the same stubborn unreason and the same social ills stemming from religious mind-sets.

Though I have written for a number of other journals over the decades, I am confining myself here to items culled from the *Freethinker* – a deliberate limitation that enables me to coin the title *Freethoughts* and to use, with gratitude, the imprint of G W Foote & Co, publishers of the paper.

Founded in 1881 by G W Foote, who became president of the National Secular Society in 1890, the *Freethinker* has always worked hand-in-hand with the NSS, of which I myself was president for quarter of a century. The journal's survival for so long with the same title and in the same ownership – without ever missing an issue, even when its premises were reduced to rubble on 10 May 1941 by one of Hitler's bombs – makes it unique in the ephemeral world of journalism.

As Jim Herrick wrote in his history of the paper, *Vision and Realism* (1982), 'it has exerted influence out of all proportion to the circulation it has enjoyed'. And it has never lost sight of Foote's original free-speech ethos or of his specific bold aims – the irreverent deflation of religious pretensions and the exposure of social intrusion instigated by Christian pressure groups – though the style has naturally been updated.

When I first began writing for it, the *Freethinker* was still a weekly, and it was a sad decision to reduce it to monthly publication; but that was inevitable in the modern world of rising costs – and, somehow, of fewer hours in the day than there seem to have been a hundred years ago. But my rummaging through back issues to put this book together has produced more items bearing my name than I ever imagined I had written. And I am also including a few by other writers reporting on my activities or reviewing my writing.

Instead of providing an index, I have added explanatory sub-titles throughout and included them in the list of contents so that every theme covered can be easily located, while the chronological arrangement facilitates historical research.

There have been six or seven *Freethinker* editors in my time, and I am grateful to them all, especially when they not only encouraged me in what I wanted to write but gave me books to review and persuaded (even bullied) me to investigate and write on topical subjects that I would not otherwise have tackled.

BARBARA SMOKER

Freethoughts

Atheism - Secularism - Humanism

Humanism on a Postcard

'HUMANISM' is based on the conviction that human experience is the sole source of man's knowledge and of his standards of desirability and morality. So the humanist way of reaching conclusions and deciding on practical action is the 'scientific method' – that is, study of all the available facts rather than reliance on preconceived ideas.

Having rejected all doctrinaire systems of belief based on alleged supernatural revelation and infallible authority, humanists feel that human life, here and now, is worth making as happy as possible. It is up to human beings to improve the world in which they find themselves, for there is no god to do it for them and no future life in which the wrongs of this one will be redressed. However, this does not mean 'I'm all right, Jack'. Man, as a social animal, should be concerned with the whole human environment, achievement, fulfilment, and dignity.

[23 September 1966]

[Though not my first contribution to the *Freethinker*, this item makes an appropriate opening to the book, on the Socratic principle of beginning with a definition of one's basic terms.]

What is a Humanist?
[Letter]

IAIN McGregor suggests that, though we know what a *humorist* is, we do not know what a *humanist* is. What, he asks, does a humanist eat and drink? And how does he vote? But humorists are no more homogeneous in such irrelevant matters than humanists are.

A humanist is one whose primary concern is this world and the people in it – unlike most religions' adherents who put God in his heaven before people on earth, and, equally, unlike governments and financiers, who put the gross national product before either people or the earth.

This humanist concern is expressed in a two-word slogan being used by the British Humanist Association for a campaign to be launched in April: 'People First'.

[26 February 1972]

People First
[Letter]

I AM appalled by D. C. Taylor's letter objecting to the humanist principle that 'all people are entitled to a decent home, enough food, etc.' Assuming that *he* has a decent home, enough food, etc., I should like to know if he will be one of the first to relinquish them and die of exposure and/or famine. Humanists believe that we must drastically reduce the number of babies born, but that, once born, they all have the right to the necessities of life.

The slogan 'People First' does not, of course, imply the total exclusion of other species from 'the scheme of things entire': on the contrary, the quality of human life would be greatly impoverished if we did not share the earth with a wide variety of animals. We could certainly do with fewer pet dogs (for whose food kangaroos and whales are slaughtered), though I would not cull dogs, even, by starvation.

[18 March 1972]

Determinism
[Letter on Monod and Causation]

TREVOR Morgan seems to base his refutation of Monod's *Chance and Necessity* on the fallacious belief that determinism must eliminate chance. Whenever separate chains of causation converge and the convergence causes something else, this is surely what we mean by chance.

For example: all the biochemical compounds which, coming together, produced DNA, presumably came to be in the same place at the same time as a result of separate chains of causation, their final meeting being a chance meeting, in the everyday sense. Even if there were enough of all the required chemicals around at the same time to make contact between them a statistical certainty, the particular contacts were still *determined by chance*; and so with every event in the universe.

[2 September 1972]

Chance, Causality and Design
[Letter]

THE letter from M A Forsyth (16 September) betrays a misunderstanding of the concept of 'chance' as defined by Jacques Monod, and of the arguments put forward by Brian Khan and myself (Letters, 2 September) in support of Monod's thesis.

As Mr Khan explained, chance refers not to the absence of causation but to the absence of design. Mr Forsyth thinks this is tantamount to saying that 'the automatic boiling of water, on being heated, is an act of chance'. But the mere fact that water boils when in contact with sufficient heat is a matter of cause and effect – based, at the molecular level, on statistical certainty. If someone deliberately brings the water and heat together in order to boil the water, this is an act of purpose; if they come together fortuitously (for example, because the house is on fire), this is chance. But even the act of purpose always has innumerable chance factors behind it – for instance, the chances determining the very existence of a human being with the desire and the wherewithal to boil water at that particular time and in that particular place.

As for Mr Forsyth's reference to games of chance, no one denies that 'all kinds of factors' determine the outcome: it is in the random bringing together of the variable factors into a particular relationship that chance resides. Where players are able to control some of the variable factors, an element of skill reduces the element of chance.

Since, says Monod, happenings at the molecular level are completely random – though often statistically certain – *everything* is ultimately determined by chance. Moreover, in such unique events as the 'creation' of a particular planet, a particular animal species, or a particular individual, even the certainty that is inherent in large numbers is absent. There is thus no room left for the religious concepts of ultimate purpose and divine will – nor. similarly, for Lady Luck or dialectical materialism! Hence the unease that Monod has caused among theologians on the one hand and Marxists on the other. (Believers in lucky charms are less likely to have read Monod.)

Some of the up-to-date theologians are now reduced to saying, 'Yes, perhaps God is, so to speak, just playing dice – but might he not have *loaded* the dice?' Oh, God of my youth, how low hast thou fallen!

[30 September 1972]

The Greatest Abortionist of All

[Editorial Report by Christopher Morey]

BARBARA Smoker concluded her presidential address at the annual general meeting of the National Secular Society, in London on Sunday 30 June, by reciting a prayer for use by campaigners against the 1967 Abortion Act. Miss Smoker, a former Roman Catholic and ex-member of the Legion of Mary, said: 'Nobody, of course, likes abortion. Nobody likes vaccination or dentistry either. But they are often the lesser of two evils. The National Secular Society does not approve of using abortion as a lazy method of birth control. But it approves of abortion where the alternatives would be worse, and therefore supports the 1967 Act.

'The Lane Committee, after two years of collecting and considering evidence, unanimously concluded that the beneficial effects of the Act far outweigh its disadvantages. Their Report had been eagerly awaited by the anti-abortion lobby, organised by mainly Catholic front groups, in confident expectation that it would come out against the 1967 Act and give them ammunition for their campaign. Disappointed and infuriated by the Report, they have renewed their efforts to sabotage the Act. We all uphold the right of doctors and nurses to opt out of any involvement in abortion on grounds of conscience. But the opponents of the 1967 Act, not content with safeguarding the rights of those with conscientious objections, want to impose their wishes on everyone.

'Who are these busybodies? They are Roman Catholics (including celibate priests and nuns) and fundamentalist Protestants who have no scruples about herding school-children to anti-abortion rallies. Absolute opposition to abortion, even when the foetus is known to be seriously defective, can have no possible justification apart from religious dogma. It can be justified only by putting the supposed will of a supposed deity before humanitarianism.

'Ironically enough, however, the God that Christians worship and obey is, according to their own beliefs in his power, the greatest abortionist of all time, being deliberately responsible for spontaneous abortion (miscarriages), the incidence of which far exceeds that of induced abortion, even today.'

Miss Smoker then concluded: 'I suggest that the anti-abortion lobby adopts this prayer: "0, thou great Abortionist! Thine is the monopoly of righteous abortion, for ever and ever. Amen".'

[July 1974]

Religious Chain-Letters

> Freethinkers may regard chain-letters simply as an irritation, and consign them to the nearest rubbish-bin, where they belong. But gullible and superstitious people do not treat them so flippantly, and many fear that breaking the chain may have serious consequences.

IF there is one thing worse than an ordinary chain-letter, it is a religious chain-letter. I have recently received one – probably sent by someone who saw my name and address in the correspondence column of a newspaper and, perhaps, noticed that my theme was religion!

Purporting to have originated with St Antoine de Sedi, a South-American missionary, the letter contains several case-histories of former recipients who allegedly won huge lottery prizes and the like within a few days of receiving the chain-letter, only to lose them again if they failed to pass on twenty more copies of it. Others are said to have met with sudden death for the same crime. ('General Walsh received the letter in the Philippines and received $775,000.00, but six days later lost his life because he failed to circulate the chain.') The kernel of the letter reads: *'Trust in the Lord with all your heart, and all will acknowledge that he will light the way. This prayer has been sent to you for good luck.'*

An elementary grasp of geometrical progression would save people from wasting time and postage on such absurdities. At the foot of the letter are listed the last 29 names in this particular chain. If each of the twenty people to whom the first of the 29 sent his copies had obeyed the peremptory injunction to do likewise, and their twenty had too, and theirs, and theirs, and theirs, then within a month every man, woman and child in the United Kingdom would have received copies, with no more than seven names on any one list. By the ninth name, everyone in the world would have received copies. Long before my particular copy, with its 29 names, had been reached, the enterprise would have used up all the paper in the world and all the trees, and would have employed all the world's population non-stop in the manufacture of paper, the copying of the letter, and attempts to deliver it to people already up to their necks in copies.

The letter does, however, contain one true statement: it says 'This is not a joke.' Unfortunately, it is not. Many people are superstitious enough to spend their last few shillings on postage stamps to avoid breaking the chain, while some, physically incapable of copying the letter, will worry themselves to death over it.

A few years ago, visiting a friend in hospital, I was horrified to see one of these religious chain-letters on his bedside locker, and took it away in the hope he would forget about it. He was lying in a coma, caused by hypertension, and he died a few days later. He was superstitiously religious, and would certainly have worried about breaking the chain through being too ill to make copies of the letter. It is quite likely that this did in fact hasten his end. The perpetrators of the chain, had they known about his death, might well have claimed it as a consequential fulfilment of their prophecy. No joke, indeed.

[March 1976]

'The Golden Rule'

[Letter on Reciprocity]

IN his article 'Reciprocity and Neighbourliness in Jesus' Teaching' (*Freethinker*, February), G A Wells seems to credit Jesus with initiating the positive form of the Golden Rule (in modern parlance, 'Do as you would be done by'); but in fact it appears in many pre-Christian philosophies. Indeed, even the words of Jesus quoted in the article (Matthew 7:12) continue 'for this is the law and the prophets', which seems to disclaim it as something new; while Jesus' second formulation of it, 'Thou shalt love thy neighbour as thyself' (Matthew 19:19), is a direct quotation from Leviticus (19:18).

In any case, however, is the busy-body positive form really morally superior to the live-and-let-live negative form? I tend to agree with Bernard Shaw: 'Do not do unto others as you would that they do unto you. Their tastes may not be the same.'

I also question Wells's dismissal of reciprocity as a worthy incentive for morality. As long as its application is general, and not confined to those individuals likely to be in a position to reciprocate, it is in fact the basis of humanist utilitarian ethics. I do agree with Professor Wells, however, that morality for the sake of a vastly inflationary reward in a future life smacks of Big Business.

[March 1976]

The Pope is Now a Protestant

> Is the Roman Catholic schismatic movement, led by the arch-conservative archbishop, Monsignor Marcel Lefebvre, no more than a 'storm in a chalice'? That is what spokesmen for the Church would have us believe. But Barbara Smoker, president of the National Secular Society and herself a former Roman Catholic, is convinced that it is a crisis of major proportions and could well prove to be of great historical significance.

'THE new rite of the Mass is a bastard rite, the sacraments are bastard sacraments, and the priests who emerge from the seminaries are bastard priests'. The words of an Evangelical fanatic, perhaps? Not at all. These are the words of a 71-year-old Roman Catholic prelate, who, until 1970, was one of the most eminent pillars of the Church.

The quotation is taken from a statement made to the press by Monsignor (alias Archbishop) Marcel Lefebvre a few weeks ago, when, before a fervent assembly of some 7,000 Catholics in the sports stadium at Lille, he celebrated Mass in the old Tridentine rite.

Referring to himself, in traditional pastoral terminology, as 'a shepherd', he also dared to call the Pope 'a wolf'. And, worse still: the Pope is, he declared, no longer Catholic, but Protestant.

Having been brought up as a Roman Catholic myself, with a soul-stirring convent education from 1927 to 1939, I cannot but agree with Lefebvre's accusation that the Pope has (however reluctantly) turned Protestant. And with him, almost the whole College of Cardinals; most bishops and priests; practically every community of monks or nuns (in

18

which the remaining adherents to pre-conciliar tenets are mostly elderly and easily overruled); and practically the whole laity, world-wide. And this second Reformation, even more sweeping than the first, has, amazingly, been effected almost entirely within the past fifteen years.

My convent education left me with the firm impression that there were two main categories of religion: on the one hand, the true religion, ensconced in the Roman Catholic Church; and on the other, every other religion and sect, from Shintoism to the Plymouth Brethren, united in their common attribute of error. This arrogant certainty is now a thing of the past – except for Lefebvre and his supporters.

What do I (and Lefebvre) mean by Protestantism? A number of things. The final arbiter in matters of faith is now more likely to be the Bible, freely interpreted, than the authority of Catholic tradition, and the final arbiter in matters of morals is more likely to be the individual conscience than the authority of the hierarchy. The mystique of a priest with his back to the congregation, muttering Latin prayers and incantations and making secret gestures over the altar has given place to a participant congregation. Decisions are no longer made authoritatively by the Pope or bishop or parish priest or abbot or mother superior, as the case may be, but democratically, in committee. And, though there is much to be said for committees, they rarely exude the same aura of finality as the single authoritative voice – especially when, in the case of *ex cathedra* papal pronouncements, that voice is directly monitored by the Holy Ghost. But papal infallibility has given place to collegiate infallibility – and even that now keeps a low profile.

As for modern vernacular liturgies, compiled in committee under democratic procedures, they can hardly compete in terms of poetry and mystery with the medieval hocus-pocus they have superseded. And when the language group to be catered for, in identical wording, includes such linguistically disparate cultures as those of Britain and the United States, the resulting compromise is often excruciatingly banal.

In my Catholic youth, no women, even nuns, were permitted to set foot in the sanctuary during Mass, while grubby little boys were drilled in the Latin responses and recruited as Mass servers. For unpriestly hands to touch the consecrated host was utterly taboo; but now, communicants

– even female communicants – are encouraged to receive the host in their hands, instead of on the tongue as before.

I was taught consistently at school that the souls of unbaptised infants spent eternity in Limbo – a humanitarian advance, at least, on consigning them to the eternal punishment of hell-fire for something outside their control. But now Limbo has gone; even Purgatory (without which, indulgences and requiem Masses lose their *raison d'être*) is very much played down, and apparently on the way out; and Hell itself has lost its terrors in nebulous metaphorical interpretation.

In my Catholic days it was mandatory at every Benediction in this country for the Prayer for the Conversion of England to be recited. Such an insult to other Christian sects would be unthinkable in today's ecumenical climate.

In recent months, Lefebvre and his schismatic traditionalist movement have obtained for the Roman Church an unprecedented amount of secular reportage and comment – which the Church authorities would have much preferred to do without. The Roman Catholic press in Britain had been trying (in accordance with Vatican policy) to play down the crisis, but suddenly the *Observer* of 8 August devoted 30 column inches to a report on it from their Paris correspondent; the next morning, it was the subject of the first leader in *The Times,* which, in addition to an article by its religious affairs correspondent the following week, devoted most of its readers' letters space to the subject for almost a fortnight; and on 13 August the *Guardian* chipped in with an article on it by their man in Paris. Then BBC radio made it the subject of an item in 'From Our Own Correspondent'. The media had obviously decided that the rift in the Roman Church had become significant.

But in all the talk of forbidden medieval rites, rebel priests and prelates, and illicit ordinations, the underlying motives of the leading personalities of the traditionalist movement have been obscured. Most readers have probably been left with the impression that, despite its aspirations for *aggiornamento,* the Roman Church is, after all, being true to its historical insistence on total obedience, permitting no deviation from the post-conciliar forms of worship, and employing all the pre-conciliar heavy-handedness of censure, indict, suspension *a divinis* from priestly activity, and even threats of excommunication, against those whose only sin is nostalgia. But it is not quite like that.

Freethinkers, and liberals generally, who have expressed sympathy with Lefebvre as a rebel against the Vatican's dictatorial refusal to allow deviant forms of worship have failed to understand the sort of ecclesiastical feudalism that he stands for. On the other hand, I would not waste any tears over the plight of the Church – except, possibly, tears of merriment, as I watch their past teachings come home to roost. Ultimately, the secularist interest would probably be best served if neither side made any concession, so that the rift widens and becomes permanent. 'And if a house be divided against itself...'.

The breakaway movement was started with the financial backing of wealthy French families, who have always been the mainstay of the Church in France. Lefebvre himself comes from this establishment background: from a family with an industrial fortune in northern France – the stronghold of Catholic authoritarianism. His second-in-command is 78-year-old Monsignor Francois Ducaud-Bourget, known to be an admirer of Mussolini and Franco.

Having bought five priories in France with his French donations and opened hundreds of Tridentine Mass centres in that country, Lefebvre and his cabal reached out into Switzerland, Germany, Britain and the United States. Wealthy Catholic families in America are now pouring money into their coffers – presumably with an eye to social and political, rather than supernatural, dividends.

In Britain, the movement is led by the ample figure of Father Peter Morgan, a fanatical convert from Anglicanism, who was re-ordained by Lefebvre. He has been reported as saying that Franco was 'too liberal'.

During the Vatican Council, Lefebvre opposed many of the new provisions – especially those devolving power from the Apostolic See to (of all things!) regional conferences – and, indeed, as a known conservative, he was expected to do so. However, when these provisions were carried, he did sign the documents approving them. So when, between 1968 and 1970, he founded the Fraternity of St Pius X (named after the pope responsible for a famous encyclical against Modernism in 1906) and opened two theological study centres in Switzerland, no one took much notice. Then it was discovered that, not only was Lefebvre continuing to use the superseded Tridentine liturgy himself, but he was training his students in the old rite, preparatory to ordaining them in the diaconate (which had been abolished by Vatican II), and later as full priests.

The Church could afford to close an eye to a few elderly clerics persisting in using the Pius V Missal, but the ordination of young men to carry on the schism was another matter – so Lefebvre was ordered by the pontiff to close his seminary at Ecône, together with its subsidiary houses that had by now sprung up in France, Britain, Germany, the United States, and even Rome itself. But the archbishop continued to defy the Vatican.

For another three years the Church played a waiting game – though Lefebvre's seminarists now numbered over a hundred. Then a special Cardinalate Board was set up to confer with him – the outcome being his now famous 'profession of faith' in November 1974, when he declared (in Latin, of course):

> With all our heart and with all our soul we will adhere to Catholic Rome, custodian of the Catholic Faith and of the traditions needed to preserve this faith, to Rome Eternal, Master of Wisdom and Truth. But we refuse, and have always refused, to follow the Rome of neo-modernistic and neo-Protestant tendencies so clearly shown in Vatican Council II... No authority, not even the highest hierarchy, can force us to abandon or to weaken our Catholic faith clearly expressed and professed by the magisterium of the Church over nineteen centuries...

Again the Vatican held its hand – for another 18 months.

Only in May this year, during the consistory at which the nineteen new cardinals were created, did Pope Paul make a solemn declaration, calculated to chill the spine of any son of Holy Mother Church – the declaration that Lefebvre had placed himself outside the Church. But Lefebvre's spine is not easily chilled – he is too confident of the rightness of his cause: 'The good God wishes that I should ensure the survival of the Catholic ministry.'

It is paradoxical in the extreme that a man who has always stood for ecclesiastical authority as against the claims of private conscience should now himself oppose the ecclesiastical authority he has always acknowledged – but, as he sees it, only his movement is now in step with the will of God and with the whole history of the Catholic Church.

He has suggested, in fact, that Pope Paul's pontificate is bound to be retrospectively nullified when the Church eventually comes to its senses.

Oh, yes – he accepts papal infallibility all right; but no pronouncements made by the present pope have unequivocally fulfilled the conditions prerequisite for infallibility. Besides, how can a pope who is obviously in heresy be exercising the divine protection from error that is on offer to him?

Lefebvre and his supporters claim that, since Pope Pius V promulgated the Tridentine Mass as unchangeable for all time, it is obvious that no subsequent pontiff could legitimately substitute another rite. The official reply is that the Church, being a living entity, must, whatever Pius V thought to the contrary four centuries ago, be subject to development. A Protestant line of argument if ever there was one!

Pope Paul is by no means a Protestant at heart; nor are many of the cardinals, especially those of the Vatican secretariat. The reactionary (not to say panicky) encyclical, *Humane Vitae,* showed them in their true colours. But Protestantism has been forced on them by the strength of the modernist movement in the Church, brought to the surface – and, moreover, given executive power – by the Second Vatican Council: the legacy, ironically enough, of the 'stop-gap' pontiff, Pope John.

Not that the recommendations of the Council were themselves wholeheartedly Protestant. It was mainly the unexpectedly thorough implementation of those proposals that wrought such a change. For instance, it was generally assumed that Mass in the vernacular, as recommended by the Council, meant more or less straight translations from the Latin rite crystallised by Pius V after the Council of Trent; but in the event, very significant changes were made. There is even one optional post-consecration form of English wording in which the consecrated bread and wine are referred to not as body and blood but as 'the bread of life' and 'this cup' – obviously with an eye to eventual communion with Protestant churches – and I was interested to note that this was the wording chosen for a Mass recently broadcast by the BBC.

From our utilitarian standpoint, the liberalisation brought about in the Roman Church by Vatican II has been almost entirely for the better

– not least, for the mental health of millions of its people and for a more humanistic outlook on the rest of the world – but there is no denying that the Roman Church has lost not only much of its mystique, after which many people hanker, but also the certainty which comforted those born into the faith and attracted many a convert to it. Hence the appeal of the traditionalist movement.

Preservation of the Tridentine liturgy is not, as many commentators have assumed, what the fuss is all about. But making it the visible symbol and rallying point of his movement was Lefebvre's stroke of genius. Thousands of nostalgic Catholics have been attracted to his illicit Masses, mostly unaware of the élitist sociological and political ethos behind the ritual. Thousands more would attend these Masses if this were geographically feasible, and probably hundreds of thousands would do so but for their ingrained horror of disobeying the Pope.

Most Catholics find it difficult to understand why the Apostolic See cannot allow the old rite to exist alongside the new. They point to the paradoxical situation that, whereas dire warnings about attending non-Catholic services are no longer to be heard in any Catholic church, such warnings are constantly given against attending a Tridentine Mass – the very rite which, until ten years ago, it was compulsory for all Catholics to attend on Sundays and Holidays of Obligation. How absurd that what used to be compulsory should suddenly be forbidden!

The fact is, however, that had the choice of rite been left to the personal preference of priests and laity, not only would it have been difficult to get the new Normative Mass established, but each of the two rites would have tended to have its own following – resulting in a division within the Church, rather like the Church of England division into High and Low churches. The solid liturgical unity of the Roman Church, its greatest source of strength for the past four centuries, would thus have been lost.

However, now that the Normative Mass is well established, the Church could probably afford to relax the ban on the old rite, at least for a certain proportion of the Masses in each parish. (At present, the official ration for Britain is one public Tridentine Mass a year, and that only in Westminster Cathedral!) Confronted by the alternative of imminent large-scale schism, the Holy See may well be preparing some face-saving formula to allow a few Tridentine Masses in every church, and so steal Lefebvre's thunder. In that event, most of his popular Tridentine support would very likely drop away.

The schism of the remaining out-and-out reactionaries would then be no more serious for the Church than that of the Old Catholics, who broke away from Rome over the doctrine of papal infallibility after the (First) Vatican Council in 1870. There are still a number of Old Catholic congregations in Germany and the United States, and at least one in London, but they have never posed any really serious threat to Mother Church.

Like the traditionalist movement today, the Old Catholics were able, a century ago, to claim that it was the Papalists who were heretical, in their newly defined doctrine, while they themselves could not be accused of any heresy – only, at most, of schism. (Rejection of authority is schismatic, whereas the promulgation of false doctrine is heretical.)

Since the Old Catholics obtained their episcopal orders from a Dutch Jansenist bishop, the Roman Church has never been able to deny their claim to the 'apostolic succession'. Thus, Old Catholic priests – unlike those of the Church of England, however 'High' – have always been credited by the Roman Church with all the supernatural powers (though not, of course, the legality) of their own priests.

Recent references to this in the RC press highlight the concern of believers with the magical powers conferred on a priest at ordination and with whoever may have these powers outside the one true fold of their own Church. It seems that, in recent years ecumenism (combined, no doubt, with declining congregations) has brought about a merger between the Old Catholics and Anglo-Catholics (i.e. High C of E) – and, as Old Catholic bishops (wearing red gowns with a sort of Lutheran ruff at the neck) have been officiating at the consecration of some of the new Anglican bishops, it is being seriously debated by RC theologians whether the apostolic succession may not have infiltrated back to some sections of the Church of England in this way.

One of the doctrinal 'facts' repeatedly taught in my convent school was: 'Once a priest, always a priest.' Even a heretical priest who denied the true faith, or a schismatic priest who left the Church, or a wicked priest who (horror of horrors!) took unto himself a wife, could never lose the supernatural power of saying Mass – that is, the power of changing bread and wine into the 'body, blood, soul and divinity' of Christ.

God, it is understood, is bound by his own promises to obey the command of the renegade priest, much as a High Court Judge is bound by his own past decisions. Perhaps a more apt simile, being in the realm of magical myth, is that of Aladdin's lamp, whose genie is bound to obey whoever rubs the lamp, even the wicked uncle. A universal folk-myth underlies all priest-craft, from that of the primitive witch-doctor to the latest ordinand.

Thus, one of the practicalities I was taught at school was that though one should never, under any circumstances, participate in Protestant worship, since the Protestants, having broken away from the 'apostolic succession', had no valid orders, it would actually be better to attend a Mass of the Greek/Russian Orthodox Church than to miss Sunday Mass altogether, since Orthodox priests were in the unbroken line of apostolic succession and, being validly (though unlawfully) ordained, were empowered to effect the transubstantiation of bread and wine into the godhead.

Since transubstantiation remains a firmly entrenched part of Catholic doctrine and is still the essence of the Mass, of whatever rite, no suspicion of doubt can be cast on the validity of Lefebvre's priestly powers, conferred by his ordination way back in 1929, nor on his subsequently acquired powers, dating from his episcopal consecration, to ordain new priests with the same supernatural powers. This means that the Church is faced with a self-generating schism – the first such break since that of the Old Catholics, who, in terms of numbers, have proved a negligible threat. And whereas the appeal of the Old Catholics was to academic restraint, the appeal of the Tridentists is to popular sentiment, which could prove highly infectious.

Needless to say, for those who believe in magic, the question of who is able and who is allowed to perform it is of prime importance. In any other sphere of human endeavour, the proof of the pudding would be in the eating: but it is an article of Catholic faith that the fundamental change that occurs in the bread and wine at the Consecration makes no difference to the 'accident' of appearance or taste. There can therefore be no tangible test that the magic has taken place. In other words, it is on the same level of confidence trickery as the Emperor's new clothes.

And when the magic formula is put into plain English, or French, the trickery loses much of its confidence.

[October 1976]

Demonologists are the True Christians
[Editorial Report by William McIlroy]

'WHILE religion, as far as popular adherence in this country is concerned, has dwindled rapidly in the past few years, we cannot claim this as a total victory for freethought', Barbara Smoker declared in her presidential address at the annual general meeting of the National Secular Society, which took place in London on 12 December.

'Unfortunately', she went on, 'its place has largely been filled by a sudden upsurge in occultism, covering a wide range of superstitious beliefs and practices, some of which are far more dangerous than the general run of orthodox religion was – at least, since it gave up burning heretics and terrifying children with lurid descriptions of hell.'

Miss Smoker told the meeting that superstition declined in the 18th century, but had a surprising revival in the late 19th century, with all the nonsense of astrology, hauntings, séances, clairvoyance, automatic writing, ouija boards, numerology, faith-healing and so on. It declined at the turn of the century, but has suddenly become fashionable again in the past decade, and all the same old nonsense has come back (except for such completely discredited frauds as table-rapping and muslin ectoplasm), but with pseudo-scientific additions such as ufology and the 'Geller effect'.

The NSS president continued: 'The mainstream Christian churches, having played down Satan and Hell since the turn of the century, have destroyed their *raison d'être* and seen their congregations melt away, while the fundamentalist and charismatic wing of the Protestant churches has retained its hold on more people. Being now proportionately the strongest wing of Protestantism, the evangelicals have become more influential than formerly, and have forced the hierarchy to condone more primitive practices and beliefs.

'The orthodox Christian churches, which stood aloof from spiritualism and Christian Science during their Victorian heyday, have now started jumping on to the present bandwagon.

'A Church of England clergyman, the Rev Trevor Dearing, who recently published a book on demonic possession and exorcism, combines what he calls "the two ministries" of exorcism and faith-healing.

'He was eager to demonstrate both in a Birmingham television studio last month. I was invited to appear on the programme with him, as token opposition, and I found his performance, at a distance of three or four feet even more sickening than I had expected.

'In the hospitality room before the programme began, I listened to his female disciples chattering about him like lovesick schoolgirls. In the studio, I was amused to see that the camera crew had marked the floor not only with Mr Dearing's standing position but also with the spot on which the exorcisee, in a re-enactment, was to writhe and the candidates for faith-healing, in actuality, were to swoon.

'Mr Dearing has the advantage of good looks, which he enhances with eye-catching clothes and a carefully casual hairstyle. But his greatest asset is his long, sexy fingers. While he presses the forehead of a client with the fingers of one hand and the back of her neck with the other hand, his congregation, well represented in the audience, sing, to an affective tune, "He touched me, he touched me!" No doubt, if asked, they would insist that "He" is Jesus. But the sexual connotation could hardly be more explicit.

'During the past few years the entry of many clergymen, of various denominations, into the demon business has given considerable impetus to belief in demonic possession, and is the chief cause of recent tragedies, the most publicised of which have been two horrific murders.

'There was the murder of Christine Taylor by her husband after he had been subjected to a night of mind-bending medieval ritual presided over by C of E and Methodist clergymen. More recently, there was the murder of eight-year-old Samantha Read by her father, while her mother and five-year-old brother looked on – because they believed that she was possessed by a devil that threatened the salvation of mankind as the end of the world drew near. A similar case occurred in 1891, and was reported in the *Freethinker* at the time.

'Although 65 leading theologians last year denounced the practice of exorcism today, there was only one bishop among them, and most C of E bishops merely counselled stricter rules for carrying out exorcisms. This implicit endorsement by the Established Church fans the flames of popular credulity.

'The cinema may also bear some measure of responsibility, with such films as *Rosemary's Baby*, *The Exorcist* and *The Omen*. Films, however, would be unlikely to be accepted as anything more than spine-chilling entertainment if they were not backed up by institutional Christianity, which people may still take for real.

'It should not be forgotten that, despite the denials of more sophisticated theologians, belief in demonic possession is crucial to the Christian faith. The one justification for Christianity is its fight against the wiles of Satan and his wicked angels, from whose power souls must be redeemed by baptism and faith in order to gain eternal bliss.

'The demonologists are really the consistent, true Christians. So, perhaps, after all, it is still religion in its most basic forms that is the chief enemy of rationalism and of humanity.'

[December 1976]

Good God!

[Preview of Anti-Theological Book of Verses]

In her forthcoming copiously illustrated book, Barbara Smoker turns to verse to plunge into weighty questions concerning the existence of God – using rhyme, rhythm, and plenty of reason in this 'string of verses to tie up the deity'.

When I refer to God as 'her',
    your senses all but fail;
but if, being God, 'he' has no bod-y,
    why must he be male?

God's proved (I'm told) since life is splendid;
  yet (with logic equal)
Life's so unjust that when it's ended
  it must have a sequel!

I strove in vain, abused my brain,
  to square a God of Love
with what I found the world around.
  Speak not of joys above:
for how could any future gain –
  even eternity –
wipe out the anguish and the pain
  in temporality?

'The ground of being' has a grand
  and philosophic ring –
but theists who would take their stand
on abstract 'ground' tread shifting sand:
  it doesn't mean a thing.

'Blaspheming atheist!' So you deem?
  Submit it to your reason.
How can atheists blaspheme?
  (Can aliens talk treason?)

If churchmen fear lest things I say
  against their childish creed
should harm their god in any way –
  that's 'blasphemy', indeed!

[August 1977]

Enough to Make You Swear

[Affirmation in Court]

> Under the Administration of Justice Act 1977, 'Any person who objects to being sworn shall be permitted to make his solemn affirmation instead of taking an oath in all places and for all purposes where an oath is or shall be required by law, which affirmation shall be of the same force and effect as if he had taken the oath' (Section 8). But how does it work out in practice? Barbara Smoker, President of the National Secular Society, here gives an account from recent first-hand experience.

BEING called for jury service at the Old Bailey in October gave me personal experience of this swearing-in business, and I have to report that the recent theoretical reform of the law regarding secular affirmation has made little practical difference so far.

A two-page explanatory leaflet about jury service is sent to prospective jurors when they are first notified of their summons – which may be many weeks before their actual attendance at the Court – and the mention of affirmation in that leaflet, amounting only to the three words 'or to affirm' put in brackets after 'to take an oath', is probably the only attempt that will be made to bring the right of affirmation to their attention.

Under the Administration of Justice Act of this year, it is no longer necessary to state the reason for wishing to affirm. This is certainly a step forward, for there is little doubt that some judges (and some juries) do not have the same respect for atheists as they do for Quakers (the main religious group that has traditionally affirmed). My own recent experience, however, shows that we cannot be content with this minor reform. We must continue to press for a complete reversal of the present system in which the oath is still the norm and affirmation is something peculiar.

In the present climate of religious scepticism there is no reason at all why secular affirmation should not be the form of wording automatically provided for jurors and witnesses, though the old religious oath could remain permissible for those who specifically request it. Like religious worship in schools, the oath ought to be opted into, not opted out of.

The first time that my name was called in the courtroom ballot, I made my way to the jury bench, where I found there was a printed card with the wording of the oath for each juror. I turned my card over, thinking that the form of affirmation would be on the other side, but it was not. 'Take the bible in your right hand!' I was commanded, a small black-bound book being thrust in front of me. Firmly ignoring the proffered testament, I turned to the judge and said 'I wish to affirm.' Before the affirmation card was located, the defending counsel called out 'Challenge!' and I was told to stand down. Afterwards, a number of my fellow jury-panellists asked me what I had said and what it meant. None of them seemed to have any idea that one did not have to take a religious oath.

Of the dozens of juries that I saw sworn-in that week, almost every juror took hold of the closed book – which is surely a 'closed book' indeed to most of them – and either gabbled or stumbled over the printed wording of the oath in a way that indicated it meant no more to them than an archaic ritual and they found it almost incomprehensible. Only two jurors apart from myself took a personal stand with regard to the oath – a Jew, who asked for, and was provided with, an Old Testament, and a Muslim, who said he did not wish to take a Christian oath, and was at first told he could affirm but was then challenged and asked to stand down.

Perhaps I should explain here the right of peremptory challenge. Both the defence and the prosecution are allowed to demand the replacement of up to seven of the jurors who are picked by ballot, without stating any reason. The accused or his counsel exercise this right with the word 'Challenge!' and the prosecuting counsel with the pretentious phrase 'Stand by for the Crown'. In both cases, the challenge has to be made as the prospective juror is taking his or her place on the jury bench, and before the juror is sworn. Since there is normally nothing to go by but the appearance of the juror, it is obviously a gamble. But defending counsel seem to operate a rule-of-thumb by which they accept all young people, nearly all black and brown people, and most men, but challenge some middle-aged white men who also look middle-class, and almost all middle-aged white women unless dressed in unconventional style.

Deducing this during the first day of my service on the Old Bailey jury panel, and being very reluctant to sit in judgment on anyone, I took care to keep my hair tidy, wear my most conformist clothes, and put on a severe facial expression every time I was picked in the ballot for a case. And, sure enough, it worked: I was immediately challenged by the counsel for the defence – every time except twice, and even in those two cases I was belatedly challenged.

One of those two occasions I have already mentioned: as soon as I said I wished to affirm, the challenge was made. This I found (and find) rather puzzling, for I would have thought that opting for affirmation suggested, primarily, an independent mind, and that independent minds are more likely to be favourable to the defence. However, the barristers in question apparently did not think so.

On the other occasion, I got even further before being challenged. Indeed, I had given up all hope this time of a reprieve, for the statutory period allowed for the peremptory challenge had expired by a long chalk, and in other cases I had seen judges disallow any slightly belated challenge.

What happened, however, was this. I asked, as before, to affirm. Then the judge, to my astonishment, questioned me as to whether affirmation would be binding upon my conscience.

Needless to say, he had asked no such question of the ten jurors who had already been sworn-in for the case, nor did he ask it of the two who followed me. His obvious assumption, therefore, was that no one, or almost no one, would dare defy religious superstition by breaking a bible oath, whereas secular affirmation – though, for the past two centuries, just as binding in law as the oath – might well be a trick to escape divine wrath! That an educated man of high standing could, in the last quarter of the twentieth century, have such medieval ideas is amazing; but then the whole legal profession is weighed down with just such amazing anachronistic concepts.

In questioning me in this way, not only was the judge letting the medieval straws in his wig show; not only was he in clear contravention of the law by failing to put affirmation on the same footing as the oath; he actually went beyond what he would have been empowered to do even before the new Act, for the only questions he was allowed to ask then (but no longer) in relation to affirmation were to ascertain whether it was religious belief or unbelief that made one unwilling to take the usual oath. He was never permitted to ask whether affirmation would be binding on one's conscience. Ever since the right of affirmation as an alternative to the oath in courts of law was first introduced in 1749 (mainly for Quakers) and extended to atheists (largely as a result of one of the National Secular Society's first big campaigns) under the Evidence Amendment Acts of 1869 and 1870, affirmation has had the same legal force as an oath, and to break the affirmation has constituted the crime of perjury, just as much as breaking the oath. Besides, to ask jurors or witnesses whether, virtually, they intend to commit perjury is as foolish as it is offensive, since anyone who has this intention would hardly jib at the far less serious falsehood of denying it!

Had the judge thought it through beforehand, he could hardly have failed to see the absurdity of his question. So it seems likely that it was a spontaneous reaction to the sudden realisation that under the new law he was no longer permitted to ask a question about religious beliefs, as he was accustomed to do, whilst feeling that he ought to ask something to justify allowing me to affirm instead of meekly taking the oath like everyone else.

I, too, however, was caught on the hop. I had thought of the possibility of a judge being ignorant or forgetful of the new law, and, had he asked me about my religious beliefs, I was ready with my answer, referring him to the Act. But it had not occurred to me that I would be asked something else. So taken aback was I by the unexpected question that I merely answered 'Yes!' – though the degree of astonished indignation in my face and tone of voice almost amounted to contempt of court. Only afterwards, unfortunately (or perhaps fortunately, since I would not have wanted to spend several days in the cells), did I think of the reply 'Do you wish to put me under affirmation before I answer that question?'!

After my contemptuous 'Yes!', the affirmation card was found and handed to me, and I began to read from it – slowly, and with meaningful emphasis, in contrast to the meaningless way in which the other jurors had mumbled the oath. I was about three-quarters of the way through the form of words when the sound of 'Challenge!' from the body of the court pulled me up short. I looked enquiringly at the judge, and he looked indecisively at the defending counsel. 'That challenge was rather late', he said sternly; 'the juror had already begun to affirm.' The barrister said he had called 'Challenge!' before, but had not been heard the first time. (A likely story!) The judge looked at me, and perhaps was thinking that I might prove a liability on the jury. Or perhaps he felt uneasy about my reaction to his erroneous question. Anyway, for whatever reason, he suddenly decided to allow the challenge, and asked me, politely, to stand down.

Trying not to show my delight, I walked up the courtroom with all the dignity I could contrive, until past the sight-lines of all the lawyers and officials, and then winked at the remainder of the jury panel awaiting the next name to be called. Knowing, of course, that my aim was to avoid jury service altogether, they all grinned back at me.

The following week, my challenge record still intact, I left the Old Bailey, a free woman exempt from jury service for the next two years.

[December 1977]

The Need to Chew Up Bishops!

[Editorial Report by Jim Herrick]

BARBARA Smoker, President of the National Secular Society, has said in defence of her devouring of bishops, that this is a small price to pay for preventing the delay of social reforms.

At the AGM of the National Secular Society at Conway Hall on Sunday, 4 December (the feast of St. Barbara!), Barbara Smoker was re-elected President – being only the ninth president in its 112 years. Thanking the members for this implicit vote of confidence, she said that having a woman as its president was just one indication that the NSS is socially far in advance of all the main institutionalised religions in this country. Not one of them yet permits women to occupy key positions in its hierarchical structure.

'Had I remained in the Catholic Church', remarked Miss Smoker with an ironic smile, 'I could never have become a priest, let alone a bishop or cardinal – though I hasten to add that that was not my reason for leaving the Church.

35

'Somehow, in the intervening years, I seem to have acquired the reputation of devouring bishops – probably fried for breakfast. This is gross slander. I merely bite their heads off; and then only when they really deserve it. Which is, I'm sorry to say, all too often.

'Continuing to refuse equality of opportunity to their own women members and perpetuating anti-feminism in society at large (four centuries after Luther coined the phrase 'A woman's place is in the home') is just one of many social issues on which the churches (not to mention the mosques and temples) are dragging their holy feet and keeping everyone else's feet in shackles as long as possible.

'The legalisation of voluntary euthanasia, the preservation of legal (and therefore safe) abortion, and the abolition of censorship, whether censorship through the revival of blasphemy law or any other means, are examples of current issues on which the opposing pressure groups divide almost exactly along religious lines. Thus, religion still pursues its age-old mission, as a satellite of the ruling power, of slowing down the rate of social progress in terms of human welfare.

'During the past two centuries, the pioneering "infidels" – who campaigned for the abolition of the slave trade, for the promulgation of family planning, for the legal equality of women, for the rights of religious and ethnic minorities, for democratic rights, for the right of non-believers to affirm instead of taking a religious oath, for the introduction of cremation, for the legalisation of homosexual acts between consenting adults, for the legalisation of abortion, for the reformation of divorce laws, and so forth – have generally been opposed by the whole Bench of Bishops, both in the House of Lords and with their wider authority through the pulpit. But once these reforms have been achieved, in spite of them, and have become part of modern civilisation, most of the churchmen have come to welcome them, and even claim credit for them. Some of these claims have been made so often that almost everyone believes them.

'What is far more crucial, however, is the effect of the long delays on people's lives. Even if history is on the side of secularism (and that is by no means certain), delays in furthering human welfare cannot but mean more human misery for those individuals and groups living during the period of the delay. And since, as freethinkers, we are convinced that this life is all that there can possibly be for each person, it is that much more important that it should be made as good a life as possible.

'If chewing up a few bishops helps in this, just a little, it is but a small price to pay – however distasteful it may be to us.'

[January 1978]

The Holy Family

Has any theologian ever tried to disentangle the threads of relationship in the 'holy family'?

Leaving poor old Joseph out of it (as merely the Christ child's foster-father) we find some strangely incestuous relations between God and the so-called BVM. If the first person of the Trinity is her father, the second her son, and the third the sire of her son – to put it politely, her ghostly husband – then, according to the doctrine that these three persons are one God, this one God must be, simultaneously, her father, son and husband.

It follows that Mary is her own step-mother. Also her mother-in-law, sister-in-law, daughter-in-law, aunt, niece, half-sister, step-daughter, step-grandmother, step-granddaughter...

[January 1978]

Juror's Responsibility

[Letter on the Penal System]

FRANCIS BENNION upbraids me (February *Freethinker*) for dodging jury service at the Old Bailey, seeing this as a rather reprehensible abdication of social responsibility – because 'someone has to decide the guilt or innocence of persons accused'. As if there were any clear-cut division between guilt and innocence!

Mr Bennion apparently assumes (as befits a lawyer) that, if I did serve on a jury, I would dutifully 'find according to the evidence' – even if this pointed to a verdict of Guilty, the probable consequence of which would be a prison sentence. To do so, and simply to leave the outcome to the judge, would, in my view, be an 'abdication of social responsibility' indeed, since experience shows that judges and prisons do far more harm than good. (For eight years I had a part-time job with the Institute for the Study and Treatment of Delinquency, which confirmed my view that imprisonment is likely to aggravate the prisoner's anti-social tendencies and damage his family, as well as costing far more in public resources than any other course of action.)

The whole notion that punishment somehow wipes out guilt or repays a debt to society is based on religion, not on reason. Not only do I reject this religious notion, I also reject the authoritarian attitude that credits judges with superior wisdom in the matter of penology – or, say, bishops in the matter of eschatology. That is why I am a member of Radical Alternatives to Prison (the inaugural meeting of which, in 1969, I chaired), as well as a member of the National Secular Society.

Maybe it would have been better if I were to take the opportunity of achieving a few perverse acquittals. However, as this would entail deliberately breaking my affirmation, it posed something of a moral dilemma. It occurred to me to take the bible oath, tongue-in-cheek, as I would have felt happier about breaking that than breaking the secular affirmation; but I also wanted to test the new law on affirmation, and, by affirming, possibly to cause a few people to think. Next time, perhaps, I will opt for the perverse acquittals. Will that satisfy Mr Bennion?

[March 1978]

No Shroud of Evidence

[The Turin Hoax]

Are we living at the start of a new Dark Age, with science selling out to superstition? At the turn of the century, the future seemed to be with rationalism. Now, much of the academic world has sunk into a morass of mindless occultism: astrology, spiritualism, witchcraft, exorcism, the revival of blasphemy trials, the 'Bermuda Triangle', and Uri Geller; culminating this year in a great resurgence of belief in the Holy Shroud – stirred up by a vast international public-relations exercise in time for its celebration this autumn of 400 years' sojourn in Turin. Here, the president of the National Secular Society investigates the investigations into this fantastic relic.

WHEN your one true God incarnate not only rises from the dead but even ascends bodily to heaven, what future is there for the relics industry? Unlike his contemporary, John the Baptist, whose severed head was at one time proudly exhibited in at least six churches simultaneously, JC left not a toe behind. But reliquarians are nothing if not resourceful.

Was there not, after all, the foreskin from the circumcision? Divine foreskins turned up all over the place. And what about the navel-cord? At least six churches boasted the authentic one. Milk-teeth, of course, abounded. And speaking of milk, 'Specimens of the Virgin's milk', says Joseph McCabe (in *A Rationalist Encyclopaedia)* 'were held in honour in various Spanish churches until the materialistic nineteenth century'.

Beyond these few items, however, they had to make do with secondary relics: the swaddling clothes, thorns from the crown, whole crowns of thorns, the crucifixion nails, and enough splinters from the one true cross to keep a chip-board furniture factory in production for months on end. Most popular of all, however, were the Veronica towel (on which JC had left a miraculous image of his face) and the burial cloths. The true shroud of Jesus was in such demand that it was preserved in hundreds of shrines throughout Christendom.

Gradually, in the interest of plausibility, all the shrouds were eliminated except one – the best one: the *Santa Sindone,* or Holy Shroud of Turin, still kept in the Royal Chapel of Turin Cathedral. This relic went one better than the Veronica, as it boasted an image of the whole body of the Saviour, front and back – not just the face. And it has continued to attract a good annual catch of pilgrims whose piety is surpassed only by their gullibility. But now that McCabe's 'materialistic nineteenth century' has given way to the pseudo-scientific occultism of the latter half of the twentieth century, the pilgrims have been joined by eminent scientists and intellectuals, who might have been expected to know better.

Physicists, forensic experts, a blood-analysis specialist, a chemist, an expert in early textiles, head of a radiological laboratory, an art expert, historians, and a television team, all converged on the Cathedral of Turin in 1973 to bring their expertise to bear on bolstering the credibility of the 'shroud'. Five years later, perfectly timed to boost the 400th-aniversary celebrations this autumn of the cloth's arrival in Turin, a book about it – *The Turin Shroud* by Ian Wilson – is being published this month by Victor Gollancz Ltd, and a film about it, *The Silent Witness,* has had eleven showings a day for five weeks at the Piccadilly Hotel Cinema. (In spite of some horrible torture scenes, the film was not given an X certificate, and many parents took their children to see it.)

For the sake of *Freethinker* readers, I have ploughed through the book and sat through the film. The genre of both might be described as science fiction posing as fact – the genre associated, for instance, with the name Von Däniken. Millions of apparently reasonable people will swallow the most incredible hypotheses if these are supported by pundits presenting half-truths couched in scientific jargon. This book and this film have pundits, half-truths, and jargon galore.

The day before the film opened – with obvious significance, on Easter Sunday – a reputable newspaper, *The Sunday Times,* devoted most of its colour supplement to 'Christianity's most controversial relic', and, since the author of the article was none other than the author of the book, it consisted of the same special pleading, though in mercifully smaller compass. Two weeks later, the Religious Affairs Correspondent of *The Times,* no less, devoted the whole of his weekly article to an equally mystical assessment of 'the most curious object in the world'.

Meanwhile, a question about the shroud predictably cropped up on the BBC radio programme 'Any Questions?' The complementary programme 'Any Answers?' included a letter from me in which I pointed out that, while it would be impossible to devise any scientific test that could conclusively prove the Turin cloth to have been the burial shroud of a particular person, there were tests which, if carried out, could prove it to be a fake – and the most relevant of these was radio-carbon dating (such as was carried out on the Piltdown Skull a quarter-of-a-century ago), which could establish, within 50 years or so, when the flax was grown from which the linen was made.

The late Archbishop of Turin steadfastly refused permission for this test to be carried out, ostensibly because it would entail the destruction of too large a fragment of the cloth. So refined has the carbon-dating technique now become, however, that the fragments already removed for other tests would suffice for it, so the new Archbishop is left with no excuse to withstand the increasing demand (from believers and sceptics alike) to allow fragments of the shroud to be dated by the carbon-14 method, and it seems likely that this will be done during, or shortly after the International Shroud Congress in Turin in October.

As a result of my letter on 'Any Answers?', I received a lengthy telephone call from an executive member of the British Society for the Turin Shroud, in the course of which I asked him how the members of his Society would react if carbon dating were carried out and it revealed that the material from which the cloth was made could not possibly have existed as long ago as the alleged life-time of Jesus. 'Oh', came the staggering reply, 'we don't expect the date to come out right: you see, the Resurrection would entail a burst of radioactivity, which would nullify the tests completely.' So they have their excuse ready in advance.

The article in *The Times* also prompted a letter to that paper from me and, to my knowledge, letters from several other freethinkers, but none were published, and I was told by the Letters Editor that he did not want to start up a lot of correspondence on the subject. My abortive letter read as follows.

How on earth can your Religious Affairs Correspondent claim (April 10) that, were the Shroud of Turin 'any other object from antiquity, the chances are very high that by now its authenticity would have been accepted beyond question'? Having seen the film and read most of what has been published about the alleged relic, I am certain that no other object with an unbroken chronicled existence of only six or seven centuries would, without scientific dating, be accepted by educated people as being almost two-thousand years old, let alone as a particular legendary object.

The nature of the image suggests that it was formed by the cloth's being placed over a corpse or a life-size figure of a man, and then subjected to scorching in some way. But it is a rather big jump from that conclusion to the pseudo-scientific hypothesis that the scorching was caused by the burst of radioactivity that 'might be expected' when a dead man suddenly rises from the dead! (What observations, I wonder, have been carried out on radioactive resurrections, and what data compiled on them?)

When the linen was tested for the presence of blood and sweat, none was found: had there been some, this would no doubt have been hailed as evidence of its authenticity; as it was, the conclusion drawn was that the image must have been produced miraculously. The marks that appear to corroborate the scourging and the spear-thrust of tradition are taken as positive evidence; on the other hand, the marks that seem to indicate a cap (rather than the traditional circlet) of thorns and the apparent nail wounds through the wrists (rather than the traditional palms) are taken as ruling out a medieval forgery, since the forger would naturally have kept more closely to tradition! (Heads I win, tails you lose.)

In the film, the Los Angeles pathologist, Dr Robert Bucklin, says there seem to be abrasion marks on the shoulders as though a heavy object had been carried on them, and an abrasion mark on the nose (or was it the knees?) as though caused by a fall. Why not suppose a fall on the shoulders and a heavy object carried on the nose? (Or knees?)

The scientists guilty of such unfounded interpretations must have a strong emotional desire to believe in a miraculous resurrection so that, no doubt, they can believe (by extension) that they themselves, unlike the rest of nature, will live for ever.

At one time there were many hundreds of objects venerated as the one true shroud of Jesus; but all the other shrouds were eventually eliminated in favour of this one. And still, in an age supposedly of science, it brings a lot of money into Turin, as well as lending spurious authenticity to the gospel story – but now with the connivance of a number of scientists who are prepared to betray science.

'Belief in the shroud', writes Clifford Longley, 'requires only belief in the integrity of scientific method, not faith.' What it seems to me to require is a most unscientific faith in the integrity of scientists.

I would not dispute Mr Longley's contention that 'Either the shroud is indeed the very wrapping in which Jesus's body was buried, or it is a stupendously clever fabrication meant to deceive' – but there have always been 'stupendously clever' forgers.

Since writing that letter, I have been wondering whether the 1931 photographer, the late Commander Giuseppe Enrie, was not even more 'stupendously clever' than the anonymous medieval forger of the original image. After all, the amazingly detailed medical descriptions of the wounds depicted in the image (e.g. 'Each bled in a manner which corresponded to the nature of the injury' – Dr R. Bucklin; and 'They have been caused by independent puncture wounds of the scalp' – Dr D. Willis) are based not upon examination of the impressionistic smudges on the cloth itself, but upon the far clearer photographs taken of the cloth, either in negative or positive.

There can be no doubt that the reverse image, as seen in photographic negative, has a far more realistic appearance – as was discovered by the first photographer of the relic, Secondo Pia, in 1898. But it needed more than that to revive the kind of medieval credulity we see today. The medicos could hardly have based a convincing diagnosis on the Pia photograph as Ian Wilson describes it:

> Today the Pia negative, which caused such excitement, is rarely reproduced. It is of the whole cloth, with the face a mere detail, and by modern standards it is of poor quality and seems distorted by the cloth having been under glass at the time. It has been totally superseded by far more professional photographs taken in 1931.

Certainly, the vast improvement in photographic equipment during the 33 years from 1898 to 1931 would account for there being so much more clarity in the later photographs that they have 'totally superseded' the earlier one. But why have photographic improvements in the next four decades not produced even better results, to supersede in turn those of 1931? In June 1969, there was another sequence of photographs taken (again with no covering glass between) by a young photographer, Gioanni Battista Judica-Cordiglia.

'Although he used more advanced photographic equipment', comments Ian Wilson, disparagingly, 'his photographs turned out to be in many instances inferior to those taken by Enrie in 1931.' That is an understatement – as can be seen by comparing the reproductions in the *Sunday Times* colour supplement: the sensational black-and-white photographs by Enrie alongside the blurred colour photographs by Cordiglia. The book itself does not provide any such comparisons, as – significantly enough – it uses only Enrie's photographs. But the best direct comparison can be made between a positive print of the back-of-body image photographed by Enrie which is reproduced only in the book, and a positive colour-print of the same image, photographed by Cordiglia, which is reproduced only in the colour supplement.

Whereas the peripheral marks on the cloth – scorch-marks from the known fire incident of 1532 and earlier damage apparently made by a hot poker – are shown in much greater precision in the later photograph, the central image is much clearer in the earlier one. What possible explanation for this can there be, other than some retouching of the Enrie photograph?

Although Ian Wilson can hardly have failed to notice this discrepancy, I can find no reference to it by him (or anyone else, for that matter) in all the irrelevant verbiage on the subject. And it is difficult to avoid the suspicion that there is an element of deliberate reticence, not only in his failing to raise this question but in the fact that the two prints have appeared only in different publications. (The editor of a colour supplement would doubtless make it a condition of publication that some, at least, of the illustrations should be in colour.)

Wilson describes Enrie as 'a widely accredited professional photographer who worked in the presence of some hundred scholars and other dignitaries, including the then septuagenarian Pia'. And, later, referring to Enrie's best negative (which Enrie himself egotistically called 'my perfect plate'), Wilson declares:

> There can be no question regarding the authenticity of the phenomenon reproduced on it. Among those who watched Enrie working was a specially appointed commission of expert photographers who checked every stage and issued a notarised statement that his work was free from any kind of retouching.

This somehow reminds me of all those earnest scientists who, having carried out observations of Mr Uri Geller at work, have declared that (though he was known as a clever entertainment magician in his youth in Israel, and has actually been caught using magicians' trickery during some of his supposedly 'paranormal' feats) he could not possibly have fooled them. Educated people, especially those educated in the exact sciences, are often the easiest to fool. And it would most likely have been even easier for Giuseppe Enrie than for Uri Geller, since the 'specially appointed commission of expert photographers' did not, presumably, keep him under observation day and night, in his bath and in his bed.

When a man is under observation to prevent him from cheating, he is all the more likely to do so if he can see how to get away with it. Besides, Enrie seems to have been motivated by a childish vanity. In Walsh's translation of his book *La Santa Sindone rivelata dalla fotografia,* Enrie describes what his sensational success meant to him in these words:

> I well remember as one of the most beautiful moments of my life, certainly the most moving of my career, the instant in which I submitted my perfect plate to the avid look of the Archbishop and that select whole group of people.

My theory is that Enrie secretly retouched his glass plates, and then made new high-contrast plates from them – after which, he would have destroyed the originals. If I am right, he was a twentieth-century accessory- after-the-fact to a medieval forger!

Of course, I cannot produce conclusive proof to substantiate the theory; I merely say that to my mind it seems more probable than the main alternative 'scientific' theory: that, nearly two thousand years ago, a man who had been dead and buried from a Friday afternoon till Sunday morning (usually counted as the prophesied three days) suddenly jumped to his feet, with a burst of nuclear energy, leaving a radioactive imprint of his body on the linen sheet that had covered it – and that that same sheet turned up in France some fourteen centuries later, after a lengthy Mediterranean tour, plausibly traced by Ian Wilson.

To be fair, many churchmen and theologians are sceptical about the origins of the 'shroud' and have warned their flocks against basing their faith on a mere material object. Roman Catholics and evangelical Protestants are mostly at one on this – though the RCs are, as ever, trying to have it both ways, by publicising alleged cures vouchsafed to Holy Shroud pilgrims, but stressing at the same time that whether the relic is genuine or not, the essence of its veneration by the pilgrim is 'spiritual'.

However, one piece of medical evidence cited by Ian Wilson does raise a rather awkward question for Catholics. This is the factual evidence that the body weight of a crucified man could not be held by nails driven through the palms of the hands, but only through the wrists. While this is good news for the shroud promoters – since they are able to claim that it could not have been known by a medieval forger, and yet the apparent wounds left by the nails are shown on the shroud at the wrists – it is not so good for belief in stigmata. There is a long, entrenched tradition in the RC Church that certain saints are impressed with facsimiles of the wounds of Jesus, as (in the pious view) a divine favour. The fact that miraculously impressed facsimile wounds in the palms are incompatible with the new wrist theory prompted me to write a letter to the RC papers, asking:

> What, then, is the revised Catholic view of the stigmata of Francis of Assisi and all the other revered stigmatists (some within living memory) who 'miraculously' received wounds in the wrong place?
>
> Freethinkers have always put the phenomenon of stigmata down to medical hysteria and/or fraud. Catholics must surely now agree with us.

Ironically enough, acceptance of the shroud as a genuine relic has been more wholehearted among some of the supposed 'progressive' Anglicans than among Catholics – possibly because Anglicans have less experience of this sort of thing. The most notable of these gullible 'progressives' is Dr John Robinson (of *Honest to God* fame), who is not only cited in the Wilson book and in the *Sunday Times* magazine as a convert to belief in the authenticity of the shroud, but who also appears in the film, where he has the gall to state that the evidence for the cloth's being the genuine Jesus shroud is so overwhelming that 'the burden of proof' has now shifted to the sceptic.

But what does he mean by 'proof'? If the 'proofs' put forward by Ian Wilson are anything to go by, any interpretation, however far-fetched, is admissible in support of the shroud, and will be accepted without critical analysis by people who ought to know better. If further examination of the cloth were to reveal some Roman numerals in one corner, they would surely be assumed, without question, to be Joseph of Arimathea's laundry-mark.

[May 1978]

The Fallibility of Popes

The late Pope Paul VI will be remembered above all as the pope who refused to sanction the contraceptive Pill and who thus brought about the rapid decline of ecclesiastical authority. Here the president of the National Secular Society assesses Paul's pontificate and the problems facing his successor.

DESCRIBING, in an Italian radio interview, the death of Pope Paul VI, the Vatican's Assistant Secretary of State used a strange though significant turn of phrase when he said that 'an electrocardiograph made by the doctors confirmed that *unfortunately* the Holy Father had left this earth to enter paradise' (my emphasis). If the man genuinely believed that this life is merely a prelude to a better one, why describe the transition as unfortunate – especially for a soul whose salvation might be assumed and whose earthly sojourn had in any case well exceeded the biblical span?

Roman Catholics the world over were then urged by their bishops and priests to pray for the repose of their late pontiff's soul. Even if no more than 10 per cent of the world's seven-hundred-million RCs responded to this appeal, the aggregate of prayers recited to reduce his purgatory must have far exceeded those said for most of the faithful departed. Is this an extension of the unfairness of life into the next world? Or does the pope need so many more prayers than anyone else?

Logic, however, is hardly to be expected from religious quarters. It is more important, if less amusing, for us to consider the effect of the pontificate just ended upon the Church and upon the world.

From a personal viewpoint, Paul VI deserves some sympathy. Known in his pre-papal years as an intellectual progressive, keen on social justice, and groomed to succeed the equally intellectual (though less liberal) Pius XII, he had to wait, in the event, for another four-and-a-half years before he ascended the papal throne – and those four years radically changed the whole tenor of his subsequent pontificate and his place in history. The rustic, avuncular Pope John, whose reign intervened, opened the floodgates of ecclesiastical reform, and for the next fifteen years his liberal successor found himself forced into a conservative role, in a desperate attempt to stem the flood.

He struggled loyally to make sense of John's wild ideas, to reconcile them with the 'infallible' statements of the past, and to keep the erstwhile monolithic structure of Roman Catholicism from complete disintegration. That he did, in fact, manage largely to do so was all but miraculous. He also achieved considerable modernisation of the papacy, in such matters as his unprecedented globe-trotting, elimination of much of the medieval pomp, and deletion of many legendary characters from the universal calendar of saints. However, the thing he will inevitably be remembered for is his refusal to sanction the contraceptive Pill.

The committee of enquiry set up by Pope John to consider the whole question of birth control gave Pope Paul a unique opportunity to pronounce the Pill OK without betraying the banning by his predecessors of mechanical methods of contraception. But this would have entailed some less than honest reinterpretations of the grounds given in earlier pontificates for such condemnation, and unfortunately, as well as unexpectedly, the Pope put his intellectual integrity and the apostolic continuum before a compassionate concern for the quality of life of millions of human beings.

Perhaps he lacked the imagination to envisage the unremitting child-bearing, the drudgery, the squalor, the malnutrition, the physical suffering to which he was condemning so many of his 'flock'. He also manifestly failed to realise that in the developed areas of the world most Catholic women had jumped the gun in the belief that he was about to sanction the Pill, and, having started, most of them would simply go on using it, often with the connivance of their priests, in spite of his prohibitory encyclical, *Humanae Vitae*. And more and more would follow their example.

This, above all else, has weakened the authority of the Vatican – this one great blunder undermining Pope Paul's efforts to keep the magisterium intact through all the theological, liturgical, collegiate, and ecumenical changes of his fifteen-year reign.

In a letter published in the *Guardian* (August 9), a Catholic monk actually asserts that it is possible to accept this papal ruling without living by it. (And he is not a Jesuit, either!) But this is blatant whistling in the dark, and will fool nobody.

Humanae Vitae, though by far the greatest blunder of Paul's reign, was by no means the only one. There was also, for instance, his parallel rigidity on the celibacy of priests. And there was his apparent connivance at the Vatican's fraudulently obtaining EEC subsidies by openly importing, secretly exporting, and then re-importing (several times over) EEC surplus butter, between Italy (member of the EEC) and the Vatican (outside the EEC) – but perhaps the only blunder in this was being found out and creating a scandal.

It is generally considered to be in bad taste, however, to speak out too forthrightly in assessing the record of a public figure immediately after death – especially a religious public figure – as the LBC radio news commentator Ian Gilchrist discovered, to his cost. It is easy enough to understand how, in his unscripted chat show, he came to refer to Pope Paul as a 'silly old fool who has caused misery to millions of gullible people'. Not surprisingly, however, thousands of Catholic listeners immediately protested and succeeded in getting the poor man suspended from the show – though most of them were themselves doubtless proclaiming, in the conduct of their lives, the very same opinion.

At the other extreme was the absurd spectacle of Anglican churches flying their St George's flags at half-mast for six days, mourning the late Pope. One almost expected an earthquake with all those Protestant churchmen of the past four centuries turning in their graves! And there is added irony in that St George was one of the saints dismissed by Paul VI as mere legend so as to make Christianity more credible in the modern world.

But what of the future of the Roman Church and the papacy? The new pontiff is faced with daunting problems largely created by his predecessor. Either he must condone the widespread flouting of *Humanae Vitae*, and with it papal authority, or he must explicitly contradict its teaching and thus undermine the supposedly immutable magisterium.

Sooner or later the latter course will have to be taken, and the pope who takes it may at last breathe a sigh of relief that Paul VI was modest enough to refrain from putting the seal of infallibility on the encyclical. Even so, nothing can now halt the decline of ecclesiastical authority, whether the late Pope's ruling is formally rescinded or simply disobeyed. It therefore looks as though the cause for which centuries of freethinkers have worked, struggled, been imprisoned, and suffered torture and death has finally been brought about by the papacy itself – by the incompatible sequence of the impetuous John and the uneasy Paul.

The name John Paul, chosen, as we go to press, by the newly-elected heir to the papacy, is presumably intended to appeal to progressives and conservatives alike. But it could prophesy a falling between stools.

If the next few occupants of Peter's chair play their cards cleverly enough, they may, by concentrating on Christian unity, expand their empire once more to virtually the whole of Christendom. But never again will they rule as autocrats over the lives of the people.

Thank God for the fallibility of popes!

[September 1978]

Pope Without a Crown
[John Paul I]

> The unexpected death of Pope John Paul I, after only 34 days in office, has brought characteristic explanations from believers in divine guidance. Here Barbara Smoker looks at some of these responses and sees the funny side of the situation. She also looks ahead, for the second time in five weeks, to the ways in which the new incumbent of the See of Rome is likely to wield the considerable feudal power that he still holds in the modern world.

'ONE of the shortest papal reigns in modern times' was the cautious comment on BBC radio in the early news bulletins that Friday morning only 34 days after Albino Luciani had become Pope John Paul. One of? And even at that, only in modern times? Obviously no one had got around to checking the historical records; but they need not have been quite so cautious.

They would have had to trace back almost 400 years, to 1605, to find a shorter pontificate – that of Leo XI, who, though aged only 50, caught a chill during his coronation on the seventeenth day of his reign and died ten days after that. Fifteen years earlier, there had been an even shorter papal reign – that of Urban VII, who reigned from September 15 to 27, 1590. The shortest reign of all, however, seems to have been that of Stephen II, lasting a mere four days, in 752 AD. He was never crowned, and for this reason it has been disputed whether he could be counted as a pope at all, though in fact a reign begins on acceptance of the office, not on coronation. However, John Paul I had already made the decision not to be crowned....

According to official Catholic reckoning, he was the 263rd pope – making the average reign, down the centuries, seven-and-a-half years each.

Whether the very brief reigns of Stephen II, Urban VII, and Leo XI gave rise to puzzlement and questioning and superstitious explanations we do not know, but probably not, for it is only in the present century that sudden death from natural causes has become a matter for speculation. In the case of John Paul I, the response on all sides has been the insistent question 'Why?'

Cardinal Confalonieri, Dean of the Sacred College, himself twenty years older than the late pope, threw wide his arms, in Italian fashion, asking 'Why did he go? Who knows what is the design of God?' And Cardinal Florit, Archbishop of Florence, echoed 'I have been shaken by this sorrowful event, which convinces me of one thing: that the intentions up there – I mean God's – are inscrutable. We wonder why God has permitted this death ...'.

Not all of the faithful, however, have been content to leave it at that. In the twentieth century, people expect the cause of death to be discovered, if necessary, by *post-mortem* examination – but it is contrary to the Vatican's Constitution to carry out such an examination, and, since the late Pope Paul VI refused to relax this ruling, no one can be sure what killed John Paul I, though a coronary seems most likely. Not surprisingly, however, the uncertainty has led to rumours of foul play – possibly because this pope promised to be a bit too liberal in some directions.

But for every person who suspects the hand of an assassin in this death, there are thousands who see the hand of God in it – for one reason or another. One of the most widespread theories among the die-hards in the Church is that John Paul I, had he lived, would have rescinded his predecessor's encyclical against contraception, *Humanae Vitae*, and that this would not have been in accordance with the divine will; so, for the sake of the Church's teaching and in order to preserve papal infallibility, God had no option but to prevent the pope from living long enough to carry out this terrible intention. (Why God did not prevent the conclave of cardinals from electing him in the first place is a little obscure.) What adds weight to this theory is that John XXIII, who set up the commission that investigated the whole question of birth control, was expected to accept their recommendation that the Pill should be permitted – and he died just before the commission made its report, which his successor, Paul VI, rejected. It seems that some of the cardinals have themselves been thinking along these lines, resolving to steer clear of any candidate likely to be soft on contraception, if only for the sake of his expectation of life.

Certainly some of them suggested, after John Paul's death, that they thought the brevity of the reign indicated that they had somehow misinterpreted the Holy Spirit's intentions and elected the wrong man. Was it a fault in transmission, or reception?

Other people, captivated by John Paul's engaging smile and his apparently simple and humble character, have declared that the good die young. 'We wanted him so much, but God wanted him more,' said the *Universe* editorial, ostensibly quoting 'a blind old lady'. (Secular papers traditionally quote a man on a Clapham omnibus, but the religious press generally have an old lady on hand, preferably blind.)

Taking the too-good-to-live line of thought a step further, a number of the devout have suggested that God would in fact have taken Albino earlier but had deliberately spared him long enough to reward his humility with the honour of the highest title the Church can bestow on a living man. (It would not be surprising if they soon proceeded to bestow on him beatification, to be followed by canonisation, in response to popular emotion.)

Explanations for this sudden death have also been found in less religious superstitions. For instance, he was the first pope to choose a double-barrelled name, and such names, it is said, are unlucky. Then, no coronation! As was asked of Stephen II, twelve centuries ago, how can a pope be pope without a coronation?

A more sophisticated explanation that I was given while carrying out a little market-research among Catholics was that God wanted the cardinals to get to know one another better, and he therefore arranged it so that they would have to hold two conclaves instead of one.

Then there was the progressive, though superstitious, Catholic from Nigeria – where Catholicism is tinged with the old tribal beliefs, and where Catholics pay little attention to popes, especially in such personal and practical matters as birth control – who told me that the Pope's death was a sign from God that he did not want there to be any more popes ruling over his Church.

The purely philosophical reaction to this death sees it as a reminder that all humans, even popes, are mortal. The ultimate rationalist reaction, complete with useful lesson, was expressed in a letter to *The Times* that is worth quoting.

> Cardinal Hume and other leading RCs ask what the meaning is of the untimely death of Pope John Paul I ... For an unbeliever, there is no astonishment when a confirmed cigarette smoker in his sixties has a fatal heart attack ... Although I do not see any sign of the Holy Spirit playing a part in these matters, it would undoubtedly be of enormous benefit to mankind if every Catholic were to begin campaigning vigorously against the use of tobacco.

As a non-smoker (despite my name), I am ready to use any opportunity to campaign against the noxious weed: but in all honesty I cannot think it was the major factor in the late pope's sudden demise. The most likely trigger was the unexpected and unaccustomed pressure of the responsibilities of a head of state, prime minister, religious leader and pop idol, rolled into one. For a man who had spent most of his life as a simple priest, with no experience of affairs of state, to be thrust suddenly into such a position in his 66th year – an age at which most men have gone into retirement – it must all have been a quite intolerable strain, especially as he seems to have been the sort of person who really believed in all the Catholic fairy-tales, including his own infallibility, and therefore must have been literally worried to death when he found himself out of his depth.

His brother, Eduardo Luciani, says that when they had lunch together at the Vatican after the election, Albino confided in him: 'I was shocked and terrified when they told me I had been elected'. And Fr Mario Senigaglia, who, as secretary to Luciani when he was Patriarch of Venice, knew him well, has commented simply, in contrast to all the superstitious theorising, 'He had to suffer efforts and tensions he could not stand'.

In fact, with hindsight, the election of such a man to the papacy appears not only lacking in imagination and common-sense on the part of the cardinals (let alone their divine guide) but an act of unconscious cruelty.

However, we need not feel too sorry for Albino Luciani, alias Pope John Paul I. His was the rags-to-riches story to cap them all; and, instead of ending his life with, say, five weeks of a terminal illness, he had five weeks of glory, actualising a schoolboy fantasy, and then died in his sleep. Moreover, his posthumous reputation is unassailable, for he had no time to blot his copybook. The only universally esteemed pope is a dead pope.

Besides, he did achieve something in his brief reign that it will be difficult for the future to undo: he went further than either of his immediate predecessors in eliminating much of the traditional pomp of the papacy, thus improving and modernising its image. For that very reason, secularists and others who are aware of the dangers of organised religion should maintain their eternal vigilance with even more vigour in the immediate future.

As I wrote in the September *Freethinker,* one of the major decisions facing the papacy at this time is whether to go along with Pope Paul's hard line on birth control, as set out in his encyclical *Humanae Vitae* – and inevitably condone its widespread flouting, even by staunch Catholics, and with it the flouting of papal authority in general – or to repudiate some of that encyclical. Even though Paul refrained from putting the seal of infallibility on it by issuing it *ex cathedra,* for a pope to make an explicit repudiation of any of it is bound to undermine the allegedly immutable magisterium, however ingenious the face-saving formula with which the repudiation be made.

It was probably the responsibility of this decision facing him that was largely responsible for John Paul's early death. Was he really about to give his blessing to the Pill, as so many of the esoteric theories for his death suggest? The die-hards, who tend to identify their views with the divine will, are ready to see the restraining hand of God in the fatal heart-attack; while, among the liberals, are those who have been voicing suspicions of assassination. In each case because, they believe, John Paul was about to sanction the Pill. Whether he had in fact reached a final decision about it we shall probably never know.

Now a second John Paul (not, as proposed by *Private Eye,* John Paul George Ringo) has ascended the papal throne. The name chosen by (or, probably, for) a new pope has traditionally indicated his main policy line by reference to predecessors of the same name, and on this occasion it was odds-on that it would be John Paul again unless the cardinals had changed their minds fundamentally over the type of man required.

In the event, the only important criteria that seem to have changed between early September and mid-October were the age and physical fitness of the prospective pontiff. And, of course, the 450-year-old criterion that the pope must be Italian. The choice of Luciani to become John Paul I had got away from the tradition of a curial pope, and the choice of Karol Wojtyla as his successor goes a big step further in getting away from Italian birth – so far away as a country in the Eastern bloc.

After the conclave, the cardinals tried to play down the political significance of this, preferring to stress the man's pastoral credentials for spiritual leadership. But Russian reaction has been very wary – in contrast to the rejoicing in other socialist countries, not only in Poland but also, less predictably, in China (possibly for no better reason than the discomfiture of the USSR).

We have to hand it to the cardinals – they seem to have made a most astute choice this time, with or without divine guidance. Poland is probably the most Catholic country in the world, and Catholicism there is at the same time an expression of patriotism and a focus of dissidence against the communist regime. Wojtyla's past record is one of give-and-take with the regime but of insistence on civil rights – primarily, of course, for religionists, but generally too.

John Paul II is apparently a far more decisive man than Paul VI, and has already made it clear where he stands on theology and liturgy (firmly middle-of-the-road), on church authority (for strong discipline within the fold, tolerance for those outside it), and on Christian unity (cautiously progressive). But he has not breathed a word so far on the burning social issue of birth control. He can hardly delay doing so for long.

In the unlikely event of his suffering an untimely death, the superstitions would rise with irresistible force. He, like his predecessor, has refused a coronation; he has the same double-barrelled name; and – who knows? – the Holy Ghost might want yet another get-together of cardinals.

For the Vatican, however, it would mean the expenditure of another million-or-so pounds. Already they have something of a cash-flow problem, with two expensive conclaves in seven weeks, and have issued a new stamp to help them out. This time they have taken care to choose a man renowned for his physical fitness.

[November 1978]

[Subsequently it became clear that the death of John Paul I was unlikely to have been from natural causes at all.]

C.K. Ogden
[Book Review]

[*C. K. Ogden: A Collective Memoir*, edited by P Sargant Florence and J R L Anderson (Elek/Pemberton, £8.00, paperback £4.00).]

IF posthumous fame were any guide to a person's greatness and the influence of his or her life, the name of C K (never Charles Kay) Ogden would be better known than, say, Teilhard de Chardin, Chesterton, Tolkien, T S Eliot, Hemingway, Stanley Baldwin, or Montgomery (to cite a random few of his more celebrated male contemporaries), instead of being all but forgotten by the elderly and unknown to the young.

Considering all the variety of his life and importance of much of his work, not to mention his quirks of character (his often wearing masks, for instance), it is amazing that Ogden has so far – more than twenty years after his death – attracted no biographer. Apart from the radio 'portrait' of him put out by the BBC in 1962, there has been nothing. All the more welcome, then, to this symposium; all the more praise to its editors and publishers for enabling some of his surviving friends (including Dora Russell and Lord Zuckerman) to record their memories of him and pay tribute to his life and achievements.

Readers who know nothing about Ogden, or nothing except that he was the inventor of Basic English, will find the book an eye-opener; and even his most knowledgeable admirers must discover in it new facets of this many-sided man. Besides, any light thrown on Ogden helps to illuminate half of the present century and many of its important thinkers.

One of the reasons for his posthumous neglect is doubtless his tendency to hide behind the names of the many scientists, psychologists, philosophers, mathematicians, historians, and others, whose writings he encouraged and published. For instance, Wittgenstein, whose *Tracatus Logico-Philosophicus* Ogden co-translated: without Ogden, Cambridge would never have given Wittgenstein the recognition and the Chair of Philosophy that enabled him to influence the whole of modern philosophical thinking.

The chief reason, however, for Ogden's underrating is that he was a polymath in an age of specialisation. J R L Anderson puts it well.

What was Ogden – philosopher, psychologist, linguist, editor, art critic, antiquarian bookseller, antique dealer, expert on musical boxes? Look at a list of his publications, and one's instinct is to say (in bewilderment, or exasperation, depending on one's cast of mind), 'I don't believe it'. It seems inconceivable that a single lifetime can have produced not merely so much, but so much of real importance in so many fields. For Ogden was no dilettante – his multifarious knowledge had depth as well as breadth, and he had only to touch a subject to illuminate it. This is naturally unpopular. We like our chess players to play chess, not to be goalkeepers of international standard as well.

In addition to all his intellectual pursuits, Ogden espoused many social causes in advance of his time, such as women's rights, family planning, workers' control, world peace and secular humanism. He was founder of the *Cambridge Heretics* and the *Cambridge Magazine*. And he was a serious athlete until a rheumatic illness forced him to give up the running-track. He also had a great sense of fun, which comes through in his writing. Even his female nom-de-plume was a pun: Adelyne More.

Above all, however, he invented and developed Basic English – a great invention, as undeservedly neglected today as Ogden himself. As he explained to the War Cabinet in 1943, 'Basic English is a selection of 850 English words, used in simple structural patterns, which is both an international auxiliary language and a self-contained first stage for the teaching of any form of wider or Standard English.'

It was as a by-product of writing the philosophical work *The Meaning of Meaning* (jointly with I A Richards, who is one of the contributors to this 'collective memoir') that Ogden hit on the astonishing discovery that there are in English these key words, to which the whole language can be reduced. That a list of 850 words (plus short supplementary word-lists for the various sciences) could prove so versatile is almost incredible. Only 18 of the 850 words are verbs – yet these, through combination with non-verbs (e.g. 'put together' for assemble, compile, combine, juxtapose, etc.) replace some four-thousand Standard English verbs.

In the book under review, two of the contributors write entirely in Basic English – but I do not think anyone could guess the fact from the writing style, except perhaps for its extra-lucid readability.

In addition to its two main uses, mentioned by Ogden above, Basic English is an invaluable educational tool, since students attempting to translate any passage (whether factual or literary) into Basic will immediately reveal any lack of comprehension.

Why, then, is it now in the doldrums? Until 1943, it was promulgated by the Orthological Institute, which was funded by several foundations (mostly American) and to which Bernard Shaw, among others, was planning to leave his money. President Roosevelt wrote that 'Basic English has tremendous merit in it,' and Winston Churchill, in his 1943 Harvard speech, said '… Here you have a very carefully wrought plan for an international language, capable of very wide transactions of practical business and of interchange of ideas ….'

Then Churchill persuaded the British Government to take over the promotion of Basic – and it was the kiss of death. The American foundations withdrew their aid, support in other countries fell away, and Shaw changed his will. The agencies charged with the job proved unbelievably incompetent, and all activity dwindled, coming to a complete halt with Ogden's death in 1957.

It may, however, be no more than a temporary halt. Today we need Basic English even more than in Ogden's lifetime, for not only is the demand for English as an international language stronger than ever, but computers also need a limited vocabulary and simplified grammar and syntax.

Let us hope that this book may inspire long-overdue biographies and critical studies of C K Ogden in the near future, to revive interest in the man and his work, and particularly in Basic English.

[February 1979]

The Pope's Manifesto

What is to be expected from the pontificate of John Paul II, which could easily see the twentieth century out? The Pope has given some unmistakable clues in his first encyclical and two subsequent documents, scrutinised for *Freethinker* readers by the president of the National Secular Society. She looks at what he has said, how he has said it, and, not least, what he has left unsaid.

POPE John Paul II has now shown his hand, in three official letters published during Lent. They reveal that he is disappointingly conservative in many ways, and indicate a pontificate of Catholic consolidation rather than the liberalism we had hoped for.

The first and longest of these three documents is his first encyclical – that is, a letter addressed to the whole body of Roman Catholics throughout the world – which was published in mid-March. The other two, published a month later (on Maundy Thursday, traditionally the feast of priests) are a 33-page message to RC priests and a five-and-a-half page message to their bishops.

The first two words of the Latin version of the encyclical are *Redemptor Hominis* (the Redeemer of Man). By tradition, the opening words of a papal encyclical are carefully chosen to form a suitable title for it and to sound the keynote of its theme. Furthermore, the keynote of a new pope's first encyclical is to be taken as a clue to his prevailing concerns and the political direction of his reign. From the opening of this encyclical ('The Redeemer of Man, Jesus Christ, is the centre of the universe and of history') we can see that John Paul II is other-worldly, doctrinaire, and theologically conservative, and that his pontificate is unlikely to give the progressive theologians their head. This pope, it seems, will try to put a break on 'the runaway church', set in motion by Pope John's Vatican II Council, and try to restore some of its old stability and certainty.

We might have guessed that the conclave of cardinals who elected him, though forced into some degree of compromise between the curial conservatives and pastoral progressives, were unlikely to run the risk of another John XXIII. They would be looking for another John Paul I – who, though he did not live to produce any encyclical, had made it clear that, for all his pastoral background and famous smile, he was definitely in favour of doctrinal rigour and ecclesiastical discipline. In the second 1978 papal election, the cardinals would be trying to find a man in much the same mould – except with regard, first, to age and health (they had learnt a sharp lesson on that score) and, second, to political and diplomatic acumen (in which Luciani had lived long enough to show himself embarrassingly naïve).

The choice was widened by the fact that, having once taken the unprecedented step of electing a non-curial candidate, they could now take the further step of going for a non-Italian. This wider choice made it possible to keep to the same pattern of conservatism in the areas that really mattered; and the die-hard Italians probably preferred a non-Italian (provided he spoke Italian) to a man who might allow theological and liturgical anarchy, the marriage of priests, and even (horror of horrors!) women priests. The sop to the progressives was that Wojtyla, like his immediate predecessor, was both 'pastoral' and 'collegial' (that is, willing to give the College of Cardinals and the synod of bishops a share in 'infallibility').

The dateline of the encyclical is rather daringly worded 'at the close of the second millennium' – presumably indicating that John Paul II intends his pontificate to last at least 21 years. This prophecy is quite likely to be fulfilled, as the man is not only comparatively young but has always kept himself physically fit.

An innovation in style, indicative of the Pope's native Polish directness and lack of pomp, is the use of the pronoun 'I' instead of the traditional papal 'We'. In spite of this, the overall effect is formal – not so conversational as the encyclicals of Pope Paul VI, who was far less self-confident than John Paul II. The general tone of *Redemptor Hominis* is, in the outspoken *Catholic Herald* editorial description, 'heavily assertive and didactic … tough, confident and headmasterly'. And it is not helped by the poor translation into English.

Although primarily theological, the encyclical touches on a number of ecclesiastical and social themes. The ecclesiastical ones include continuity with the last three pontificates, pluralism in the Church, Christian unity (he says there is no going back, but insists that nothing must be given away), and collegiality. The social ones include human rights and freedom (something about which he feels strongly, having lived under a totalitarian regime), arms sales, poverty, technological progress, and pollution. On most of these social issues many freethinkers would find themselves in full agreement with him, though greatly irritated by the arrogantly patronising assumption that with a little more insight we would all be members of his Church.

His emphatic insistence on the dignity of man and on the need for people to be 'more responsible, more open to others, especially the neediest and the weakest' are things we would gladly endorse, were it not for his dogmatic insistence on their inseparability from faith in God, love of 'the Redeemer of Man', and grace bestowed by God on man through the sacraments of the one true Church. This is the main drift of the encyclical.

The most important thing about the document, however, is the glaring omission of any reference to contraception. It is the first papal encyclical since 1968, when Pope Paul's notorious *Humanae Vitae* forbade Catholics to use any artificial methods of birth control, and it would have been difficult to find a face-saving formula to undo that – but sooner or later it must be done: not only for the sake of human welfare, but also, from the special viewpoint of the Vatican, for the sake of papal authority, since few Catholics now obey this diktat.

Although he is generally described as a 'humanist', Wojtyla has always deferred to the anti-contraception tradition of the Church – especially in his book *Love and Responsibility*, first published (in Polish) in 1960. Since his election to the chair of Peter, he has avoided tackling the issue – but he can hardly hope to get through a reign of possibly quarter-of-a-century without its tackling him.

Though keeping silent so far on the subject of contraception, the Pope has not been slow to make his views known on the related topic of abortion – on which, of course, he takes the predictably inflexible line, stemming from belief in an immortal foetal soul and from the ignorant sentimentality that extends full human rights to the foetus and the embryo, and even the just-fertilised egg. Though there can be no doubt that his joyous love of children (typical of Poles) is sincere, he has exploited the International Year of the Child to promote the cause of extending to the foetus the child's right to life. This has earned him, in Britain, fulsome tributes from two non-Catholic religious bodies – the non-sectarian Society for the Protection of Unborn Children (SPUC) and the Anglican body, the Church Union, which have used the Pope's statements to give impetus to their anti-abortion campaigns and a spurious authority to their propaganda.

The subject of sexual repression brings us to the two other Lenten messages from the papal pen.

The main burden of the lengthy letter to the world's 400,000 Catholic priests is that they must give up hope of any relaxation of the celibacy rule. A lifelong commitment is made by the RC ordinand, at an age when he may not fully grasp the extent of the sacrifice he is making, and is the chief cause of the current rate of high defection among young priests. Some had hoped that the new pontificate would solve the problem of defection by removing its chief cause, but no such luck.

The Pope reiterates the rule of strict celibacy for priests, maintaining that the renunciation of marriage and fatherhood are 'a powerful travail of value beyond calculation' and 'a powerful source of social good', and that 'the priest, by renouncing this fatherhood of married men seeks another fatherhood'.

The other message is addressed to the RC bishops, and is very much shorter – bishops presumably being past the need for the proverbial cold shower. Expressing confidence in his bishops, the Pope urges them to care for their priests with magnanimity and understanding. In other words, authority with a human face, discipline with compassion, laying down the law with a fatherly tone.

Maybe Wojtyla's lack of Western experience has caused him to underestimate the discontent of many of the younger priests in Western countries burdened by sexual repression for which they see no good reason. It could mean a further drop in ordinations, an increase in defections, and a decline in the obedience of priests comparable with that of the laity after the 1968 encyclical on contraception.

[May 1979]

His Grace Hare Krishna Das and Her Logic Miss Barbara Smoker

[Editorial Report by Jim Herrick]

A public debate took place in Conway Hall on 18th May [1979] between a leader of the International Society for Krishna Consciousness and the president of the National Secular Society. Barbara Smoker had been invited by His Grace Hare Krishna Das to publicly defend atheism. The occasion was in some respects bizarre, and in the tradition of nineteenth-century public debates between atheists and Christians. One member of the audience addressed his question to 'His Grace Swami Das and Her Logic Barbara Smoker'.

THE bright lights glared onto the platform. The camera for making a video film was poised, pointing at the protagonists. Swami Das, ceremonially robed and with monkish shaven head, sat opposite Barbara Smoker, resplendent in colourful poncho. (Despite his Eastern garb, Swami Das was a forceful young Dutchman with noticeable accent.) Between them Geoffrey Webster, an occasional contributor to the *Freethinker* and frequent attender at the Temple of the International Society for Krishna Consciousness in Soho, prepared to chair the debate in Conway Hall.

An audience of more than 200, most of whom were Hare Krishna supporters, eagerly prepared to listen to a conclusive demonstration that atheism was logically and scientifically impossible. The key points to be debated, according to the posters proclaiming PUBLIC DEBATE were 'Life does not originate from chemicals', 'God is both scientifically verifiable and logically admissible', and 'Human suffering does not contest the existence of God'.

However, the debate, though energetically pursued from 7 to 10 in the evening, was intellectually disappointing, above all because Swami Das appeared determined to repeat the same arguments endlessly, without recourse to discussion or ability to meet the points Barbara Smoker put to him with great perseverance and patience in an atmosphere of hostility.

In a high-technology environment – whirring cameras, flashing cameras – the protagonists sat before gleaming microphones. The crowds of Hare Krishna supporters enthusiastically cheered and clapped His Grace Das whenever he triumphantly or harshly raised his voice, as though intellectual victory depended upon vocal power. Indeed, there was an unhappily pugilistic air in the hall, hardly conducive to open debate.

The two speakers each opened with a 15-minute outline of their position. First, Hare Krishna Das argued that there was scientific evidence for the existence of God. Since none of the chemical elements themselves possessed a quality of consciousness, there was no way in which they could combine together to create conscious beings without the existence of some other spiritual energy.

He attacked the theory of evolution, which he assumed was essential to the materialist philosophy. His criticisms of evolutionary theory were threefold. Firstly, creation of living cells could not be scientifically explained. Secondly, genetic mutation could not be the mechanism of evolution, since most mutations are regressive and lead to degeneration. (He proudly quoted a little-known mathematician who had, he said, demonstrated the impossibly high odds against favourable mutations occurring on a sufficient scale to produce complex creatures.) Thirdly, the principle of natural selection could not lead to complex organs, such as the eye, something which had even astonished Darwin, as he quoted. The impossibility of evolution in his view proved the existence of a spiritual force in the universe responsible for creating fully developed creatures and acting as a guiding, integrating force.

Barbara Smoker, in presenting her position, countered some of these arguments. She referred to the history of philosophical argument about dualism since Descartes, and accepted that, of course, human consciousness existed.

Consciousness, she explained, was a quality developed from the central nervous system, and the brain was the seat of consciousness. Although consciousness looking at itself could not totally explain itself, nothing was gained by speculating on 'a god of the gaps' to explain what is so far inexplicable.

The fact that living cells had come from energy, which does not possess consciousness, did not destroy the materialist case. There was serious scientific speculation that at an earlier period in the earth's history, when conditions were different, complex amino acids had emerged, which in their turn could develop into DNA chains which replicate themselves (in a way admittedly not yet completely understood).

Mutation, which makes adaptation to the environment possible, was visible in the time-scale of our own lives. Insects, for instance, changed colour in grimy cities, and rabbits had taken to trees in Australia. She said that to quote Darwin's astonishment at the complexity of the eye was absurd, since there was no question of the complete eye evolving suddenly with no previous development. More primitive eyes existed, which could only distinguish light and dark.

Barbara Smoker pointed out that different elements could combine to create qualities which they did not separately possess. When hydrogen and oxygen combine they create a quality of wetness. By the Swami's argument, God was 'the great wet in the sky'. (Hints of humour were not appreciated by the audience.)

Atheists, Barbara Smoker concluded, value the scientific method and its careful examination of facts and evidence.

After a break, the debate turned into a more continuous exchange. The arguments about evolution, probability, consciousness, and scientific method went round and round, with cheers that bore no relation to the circularity of an argument in which positions were continually restated.

Cries from Hare Krishna disciples such as 'Science is religion' did not add to the intellectual level of the debate (although such a catch-phrase indicates clearly how Hare Krishna devotees are impressed by scientific jargon without any desire to undergo the rigours of comprehending scientific theory).

After about an hour the arguments were becoming repetitive and the few secularists requested a more open discussion with questions and contributions from the floor. The Swami firmly refused until the last half hour. Barbara Smoker, in a subsequent letter to him, referred to 'Your reluctance to permit adequate audience participation (even though my supporters were obviously outnumbered by yours)' as an indication that 'you lack sufficient faith in your arguments to allow them to be exposed to a free and equal discussion and debate.'

The Swami's insistence on spending such a disproportionate amount of the three-hour debate on the refutation of evolution and an attempt at 'scientific proof of God' perhaps arose from his determination to continue until his arguments were seen to be conclusive. This point was not, of course, reached.

Later, the problem of the existence of suffering in a world created by an omnipotent, beneficent force was discussed. The ISKCON theory is that suffering is a consequence of behaviour in a former life, those who suffer being punished for previous misbehaviour. Barbara Smoker asked if this meant that someone born with a physical defect, such as a spina bifida baby, was being punished for misdemeanours in an earlier life, and was told 'Yes'. 'Then your God is a big policeman,' she said – a concept about which the audience were rapturously enthusiastic.

The objections to this explanation of suffering were explained by her. There was no way in which identity could be said to survive and pass into another being, so that it could not possibly be the same person who was suffering as the one who had misbehaved. 'And how can moral growth come from punishment for behaviour of which the person has no memory?'

Barbara Smoker said of the Hare Krishna concept of God that if she met him (or it), 'far from worshipping him, I would spit in his eye'. This produced a gasp of horror from the audience.

During the shortish question session at the end of the evening there was an unexpected moment. Asking a hypothetical question, one of the audience said: 'This is a gun here; and if I were to shoot you, why would that matter if there is no meaning to life?' Barbara has told me that she experienced momentary alarm, so unusual was the atmosphere of the evening.

To this piece of play-acting, she pointed out that like all creatures she had a strong instinct for survival. Something which she had amply demonstrated throughout the evening.

[July 1979]

Mother Teresa – Sacred Cow

[Nobel Peace Laureate]

THE Beeb's television documentary, 'Nobel 1979' (shown February 10 [1980]), predictably concentrated on the peace prize laureate, Mother Teresa of Calcutta. And the good lady, equally predictably, used the opportunity of her globally reported speech of acceptance in Oslo to spout anti-abortion propaganda.

While she was denouncing abortion as the greatest evil of our time (worse, apparently, than torture, terrorism, warfare, or the proliferation of nuclear weapons), the camera's eye flitted about the sophisticated, Nordic audience, and not a face among them betrayed any uneasy doubts about this message or the fanaticism with which it was expressed, though statistics indicate that most of those present would in reality disagree with her, and many would themselves have had abortions or would have been involved with abortion. But in Western countries it is simply not done to criticise Mother Teresa. Nowadays you can get away with open criticism of Jesus Christ, but not of Mother Teresa.

In the West, among people of all religions and none, Mother Teresa has become a sacred cow. In India, however – the land of the literal sacred cow and the chief focus of the holy lady's most publicised charitable work – open criticism of Mother Teresa and her activities is certainly heard. Of the various radio and television programmes that have featured her in Britain, the only one that contained any word of criticism was one recorded in Calcutta, where people actually said 'We do not *want* her charity.'

No doubt some of the recipients are pathetically grateful to this paternalistic – or, rather, maternalistic – emissary of alien affluence and an alien god, for the chance to postpone death by a few days or to die in less discomfort; while others resent the capriciousness of her help, too little too late – or at least feel ambivalent about it. Some of them may even perceive that their penury lends purpose to her life; some may be aware that she opposes the only possible long-term solution to their intractable problems – birth control. But it would require a knowledge of modern psychology and of Christian theology to understand the deep masochistic motivation of a woman who, as a lifelong 'bride of Christ', sacrifices herself to a lost cause while eschewing the one chance of making any progress with it; and all for the passionate love and adoration of an all-powerful, invisible, aloof being, who apparently chooses to create this colossal mess faster than she can mop it up, while 'calling' her to dedicate her life to this Sisyphean task.

None of the other controversial issues on which I express an opinion from time to time ever provokes such horrified expostulation as does the mildest criticism of Mother Teresa – and this response comes from people of every creed, and even from atheists. 'But she does so much good!' they all say. Does she really?

If a fraction of the resources she has deployed in Calcutta alone for the purpose of giving some of the dying paupers a little comfort and dignity in their last few hours had been devoted to providing free contraceptive facilities, the amount of human suffering prevented thereby would have been far greater. This, however, would provide no tear-jerking television scenes for the gratification of sentimentalists in the affluent West.

After showing Mother Teresa receiving her Nobel award and making her anti-abortion speech, BBC2 showed a flashback to a visit made by Malcolm Muggeridge to Mother Teresa in Calcutta, when she showed him, and the television camera, that particular day's haul of newborn babies picked out of dustbins by her helpers. Most of these babies, she explained, had been born to desperate adolescent girls, who simply left them in dustbins to die.

It struck me that perhaps some of the adolescent mothers placed their babies tenderly on top of the refuse just before the holy sisters made their known daily round of the bins, rather as desperate mothers in this country a century or more ago used to leave their newborn infants on the doorsteps of orphanages – and, indeed, one hopes this is so. Those who actually do leave their babies to die in dustbins fill one with horror – but so would similar cruelty to a dog or cat or any other animal. They could at least, one feels, snuff out the tiny infant life first. Indeed, the 'crime' of infanticide, carried out instantaneously, would probably be the most rational, humane, and moral solution in these extreme circumstances.

Social reasons alone could hardly qualify as a sufficiently strong argument for infanticide in an affluent country, where adoption is always a feasible alternative; but this is not always the case in poor countries like India – and quick infanticide is surely morally permissible, and even morally preferable when the only likely alternative is slow starvation – though abortion would, of course, be better than humane infanticide; early abortion better than late; and contraception better than abortion. But the pious Mother Teresa is uncompromisingly opposed to all these solutions. The only forms of birth control she would sanction are the uncertain rhythm method and the unrealistic counsel of perpetual abstinence.

She, together with many of her fellow Christians, would argue that the newborn baby, the foetus, the embryo, and perhaps even the zygote, have a 'right to life'. But apart from the medieval doctrine of 'original sin' that puts the 'immortal soul' of the potential human being in need of 'salvation', there is no possible philosophical justification for the alleged right to life in the absence of consciousness, of self-identity, and a desire to continue.

For millions of babies in India, starvation, sooner or later, is the order of the day – and it is beyond human ingenuity to feed them all.

Living as she now does in Calcutta, Mother Teresa sees daily the appalling suffering caused by over-population, yet she refuses to accept the need for population control or the humane preferability of birth control over death control.

This is not to deny her obvious sincerity or her many other positive qualities. No one who saw that BBC film clip with Malcolm Muggeridge and the dustbin babies could fail to respond to the manifest maternal feeling with which she picked up one of these little scraps of human life, and the twinkling delight with which she declared that this one was surely going to live since it had the light of life in its eyes. She is certainly an amazing woman, a warm human being surging with maternal feeling. The normal outlets for this were thwarted by the contemplative religious life which, for the sake of her supernatural lover, was her chosen straitjacket from girlhood to middle age. Only in middle age – a time of life at which most childless women, and many other people, face a crisis of vocation – did she feel the 'call of God' to break out of the enclosed convent life and to found her own active religious order. Her subsequent career, especially its high degree of emotional involvement with the outside world and its public acclaim, must contrast very strangely with her past memories, while compensating to some extent for what she now probably feels were her wasted years.

So Mother Teresa has, besides the minor virtue of sincerity, the major one of warm human feeling and involvement – but even this can be nullified by ignorance, and Mother Teresa's ignorance is frightening. Not only is her mind blocked to reason by orthodox religious superstition, but her long years of convent seclusion inevitably kept her innocent of a wide spectrum of common knowledge and experience. For instance, in the television film she used the give-away, emotive phrase 'the cries of unborn babies' – indicating a completely erroneous idea of the size and nature of a human embryo. If only someone were to show her the little tadpole-like thing that it really is, or even the narrow diameter of the suction tube used for early abortions, she would surely stop talking such fanciful nonsense.

What it comes down to is this: well-meaning people need to be guided by knowledge and reason as well as by feeling. The road to counter-productive action is paved with the best intentions.

The very week that the BBC screened the Oslo ceremony and the film of Mother Teresa fondling that appealing little scrap of newborn humanity, fired with motherly zeal for saving the tenuous little life and its supposed immortal soul, the Indian electorate gave Indira Gandhi a decisive mandate to implement a massive birth-control programme that could, in a few decades, begin to solve India's great problems, while Mother Teresa's sentimental tinkering with them earns her the Nobel Prize. Much as I deplored Mrs Gandhi's excessive repression of civil liberties during her former premiership, I have no doubt which of these two women working in India today is the more deserving of international acclaim for attempting to alleviate the terrible human suffering in that country.

Mrs Gandhi is really doing something to save the Titanic, while Mother Teresa rearranges the deck-chairs.

[February 1980]

Whole Body Transplants

[Reincarnation]

> If it were possible to transplant the cerebral cortex, this would surely raise the whole question of identity. What, then, is meant by the doctrine of reincarnation? This ancient belief has spread in the past few decades from the Orient to Europe and the USA, and has been swallowed in Britain not only by the ignorant and weak-minded, but by such people as a qualified medico and a judge. The BBC (with tongue, it seemed, in and out of cheek) made alleged rebirth the subject of the first programme in a TV documentary on fringe beliefs – here reviewed by the president of the National Secular Society.

ON August 5 [1980], in a television programme entitled 'I Have Seen Yesterday', BBC1 showed an interview with a living English psychiatrist (retired) who recalled being tortured and burned at the stake for heresy in the south of France. Or so he said – and he seemed to believe it. Moreover, many viewers believed it too.

It transpired that the retired psychiatrist, a gentleman with a fine military-looking moustache, had, while still practising his profession, been told by a psychiatric woman patient that she had been his paramour in a previous existence. As an experienced psychiatrist he must have been used to being the romantic focus of women patients' delusions, but instead of seeing the attachment and the rebirth story in this light and proceeding to help the woman to see through it, he apparently accepted her supposed 'memory' as fact. One was left wondering whether carnal knowledge of a patient in a previous existence jeopardised his remaining on the medical register.

And what about the standing of a judge who confesses to similar misconduct with a virgin priestess - even if it did take place some while ago, in ancient Egypt, when he was in the body of a bodyguard to Pharaoh Rameses II? The judge in question is Judge Christmas Humphreys, who, having became a Buddhist as a young man (in this life), unashamedly recalled such indiscretions (from previous lives) for the entertainment of the television audience, though his faith in the doctrine of *karma* (the oriental doctrine of reaping in one life what one supposedly sowed in a former life) is hardly consistent with his readiness to disclose the indiscretions of his former selves.

Were those selves and he supposed to be one and the same person? If not, there is no reincarnation. But if they are, then the judge (who, in his professional career this time round, has sent hundreds of people to prison in the belief that they were responsible for past crimes, even if they had since repented of them) must believe he is responsible for the crimes committed by his supposed former selves. Indeed, that is what *karma* means. Why, then, is he ready to confess to things he did in his alleged former existences which he would never admit to had he done them as, say, a teenager in his present existence?

Apart from this particular philosophical difficulty of responsibility, there is the far more basic objection to the concept of reincarnation, in common with the concepts of heaven and hell and all other forms of personal survival, that a personal identity inevitably refers to a particular body. What gives each of us our unique personality is a combination of the genes we were conceived with, the effects on our physical make-up of life experiences, the memories in our living brains, the hormonal changes in our bodies, our consequent individual likes and dislikes, and the way that we respond to our particular living conditions and social circle. All of this presupposes a continuing living body. When the brain dies, how could the memories that were stored in it survive?

The whole personality can undergo radical change during life, and may be eroded as a result of severe brain damage or senility. When a person is reduced to a 'human vegetable' by brain damage, the identity remains the same only by virtue of the historical continuity of the body. What factor could, even in theory, survive the death and final decay of the body that would retain anything of either individual personality or of historical continuity? In other words, what could survive – whether for rebirth or for resurrection – that would still constitute, in any sense at all, the same person?

Whereas Judge Humphreys insisted in his television interview that once a 'self' had been born as a human being there was no going back to sub-human forms of existence, another Buddhist interviewed in the same programme, the exiled Dalai Lama (a more orthodox Buddhist, uncorrupted by Western arrogance), was equally insistent that, human life being comparatively rare, one would almost certainly be reborn as a member of a lower species; most probably an insect. Naturally enough, Buddhists are squeamish about swatting a mosquito or even stepping accidentally on an ant!

One can understand the seductiveness of a belief in a series of human existences, rather than facing up to the finality of death; but to prefer to be reborn as, say, a worm or a beetle, than to accept death as final, seems to me bizarre in the extreme. And it raises in an even more obvious form the question of identity already discussed: how could a human person (in one century) possibly be one and the same 'person' as a worm or a beetle (in another century)? And when human partners meet again as worms or beetles, do they have human awareness so as to recognise one another? If not, might they not just as well be other 'selves'? Even as wishful thinking, the doctrine makes no sense.

Other interviewees in the programme included pop singer Nick Turner and his Hungarian girl-friend who met in Egypt (in this life), and who explained their feeling of *déjà vu* as a memory of having met there before (in other bodies) at the time of the pharaohs. (Those pharaohs seem to crop up again and again in reincarnation stories.) The pop singer had turned this belief to profitable account by building an act around it – dressing up as an ancient Egyptian mummy and performing his own version of the ancient Egyptian *Book of the Dead*.

Then there was the woman with the upper-class English accent who was convinced she was once King James IV of Scotland. The basis of this belief seemed to be that her rather long, slender fingers resembled those depicted in portraits of the Scottish king. Such fingers were admired at that period, and, in the absence of the camera that cannot lie, court painters were likely to distort the shape of the hand according to the fashion. But even if the lady's hands really were similar in shape to those of a king long dead, it could hardly indicate more than the possibility that she shared some of his genes. Anyway, reincarnation is supposed to be about the 'spirit', not the body – let alone the shape of one of the body's minor extremities. What could be more physical than that? And what about the shape of the rest of the body, which (in view of the sex change) was presumably not the same?

The fact that the supposed former 'self' in this case was a royal personage is significant, for royals and nobles seem to be more numerous among alleged former lives than labourers and milkmaids, let alone worms and beetles.

Another example of this inter-life snobbery that was shown in the programme was the Scots girl, Jean, supposedly in an hypnotic trance, who recalled events in her earlier life as the daughter of a French nobleman. Unfortunately, her French accent sounded very phoney. And so unconvincing was her performance, even as self-delusion (which some of the other televised cases seemed to be), that one wondered whether there was more scepticism behind the film than appeared on the surface and whether this highly suspect sequence was deliberately included so as to throw a little honest doubt on the whole bag of tricks. In any case, it is to be hoped that it did have that effect, at least on some of the viewers. However, my own small-scale haphazard opinion poll, conducted among people I happened to meet in the few days following the television programme, was not very encouraging.

Whilst most of the people I questioned found the performance of the Scots lassie less than convincing, and that of the pop singer more than far-fetched, they felt that they had to respect the 'evidence' given by the psychiatrist and the judge. As one quite intelligent, middle-class, middle-aged man put it to me, 'If these intellectual, educated, high-up people say that they remember these things, well, you've got to believe them, haven't you?'

Although the gospel hero warned his followers against being 'respecters of persons', there seems to be a direct correlation between such respect and religious gullibility. If a doctor or judge – or a theologian or pope – says so, then it must be true.

[September 1980]

Zed's Credo
[Parable in Verse]

A lowly rhesus monkey, I –
born to suffer, born to die;
    bred (my mother said) by man,
    as part of some important plan
designed by human mind on high.
And mine is not to reason why.

My master man, whose name is Ted,
gave me (in likeness) my name, Zed.
    Unnerved by needle? Scared of knife?
    when Ted (to whom I owe my life)
has cared for me and kept me fed?
I'll never fear to hear his tread!

A lonely rhesus monkey, I ...
I miss my sisters, Ex and Wye;
    but master Ted's my company
    when here he walks and talks to me.
Albeit monkeys all must die,
he'll reunite us by-and-by.

Yet, faithlessly, I sense with dread
my time approaching to be bled.
    What is the purpose of 'research'?
    Would man leave monkey in the lurch?
My mighty master, tender Ted ...
he'll surely raise me from the dead.

Else how could mankind justify
denying monkey sight of sky,
  imprisoning in metal mesh,
    withholding warmth of kindred flesh ...?
Ted's just! In Ted I trust for my
reward, when I (to schedule) die.

[May 1981]

[This poem, re-titled 'Monkey's Credo', appears as an appendix to the 1998 edition of my booklet *Humanism*.]

Bearing Witness to Parliament

> The daily evidence to parliamentary Select Committees is published by HMSO. Here the president of the National Secular Society gives the personal story behind some of the evidence on one day this summer.

IF you are ever invited to appear before a Select Committee of the House of Commons to give oral evidence, by all means go – provided you happen to be a cardinal (RC) or an archbishop (C of E) or are dauntless under cross-examination. Unless you come into the first two categories, a little training might be advisable – training, say, under cross-examination on a murder charge. When, on 22 June [1981], I went like a lamb to the inquisitors, I was an untrained novice.

The inquisitors were the MPs comprising the Education, Science and Arts Committee, which had been set up to look into the curricula and examinations in secondary schools. Although there was no mention of religion in its terms of reference, the opportunity of dealing with religion in schools seems to have been recognised at the outset, since the MPs who volunteered to serve on the Committee included at least two religious extremists, who, together with seven other MPs, make up this Select Committee. And the religious aspect of education seems to have become a major theme of its deliberations and of the memoranda sent in. Bodies which submitted memoranda on this theme included the Catholic Education Council, the Religious Education Council of England and Wales (Education Committee), the British Evangelical Council, the Christian Education movement and the Association for Religious Education; a neutral view being represented by the Social Morality Council, and the humanist view by the British Humanist Association and the National Secular Society. We were fortunate in that the Chairman of the Select Committee, Mr Christopher Price, MP, is sympathetic to our viewpoint, and suggested we submit evidence for the sake of balance.

Nobody well acquainted with the BHA and the NSS could have failed to identify their respective memoranda by their style as well as their emphasis – the BHA's abstract concepts and academic language contrasting very much with the down-to-earth style of the NSS. While the BHA emphasised the need to widen RE so as to include naturalistic 'life stances', the NSS simply demanded removal of the present religious bias, with its statutory compulsion and subsidy, nothing necessarily being put in place of it.

The BHA and NSS were also invited to appear before the Select Committee in tandem (one representative from each) to back up their memoranda orally.

Dr Harry Stopes-Roe was chosen as the BHA representative, and I as the NSS representative; and, in order to avoid the possible embarrassment of being at loggerheads before the Committee, we negotiated beforehand to narrow the gap between us. As a result of this negotiation, our respective committees agreed to amplify their memoranda. The BHA, on its side, accepted the need to consider what department of teachers should be responsible for 'life-stance education', since it could hardly be (in their phrase) 'objective, fair and balanced' if left in the hands of the existing RE teachers or teachers trained in the existing RE teacher-training colleges or departments, rooted in Christian theology. The NSS, in its turn, accepted the BHA's concept of 'life-stance education' (though with little enthusiasm for the phrase), not as something that schools should necessarily provide, but in order to prohibit anything narrower than that, whilst assuming that most county schools would drop RE altogether once the compulsory element were removed from the law. Unlike the BHA, the NSS viewed that prospect with equanimity, while conceding the necessity of introducing some replacement legislation to ensure that any schools which did not drop RE would present it as a range of alternative views, including non-religious positions.

The time allotted to our oral evidence was one hour – from 5 to 6 pm on 22 June – the previous hour being allotted to the Catholic Church in the person of Cardinal Basil Hume.

Arriving at the House in time to hear the Cardinal's evidence before giving ours, I was directed to the largest of the committee rooms, where the scene mirrored the large 19th-century painting of a similar committee that hung on one of the walls of carved panelling. Six of the nine members of the Committee took their places on high-backed gold-crested green leather chairs round three sides of the large table, the fourth side being reserved for the witnesses. An outer ring of similar chairs was taken up by two dozen journalists, a few spectators, and members of the BBC with their recording apparatus.

Cardinal Hume took his place at the witnesses' end of the table, flanked by two aides – one a bishop, the other a lay expert in religious education. The chairman thanked them for coming along, and the members of the Committee took turns in questioning him, very gently. It was hardly surprising that Mr Patrick Cormack should be sycophantic and feed him with the right questions, but one hardly expected Mr Stan Thorne, who was at one time a member of the BHA, to begin ingratiatingly 'Like the chairman, I would like to thank you for answering questions this afternoon, particularly as my wife thinks that we should be answering your questions!' However, this excessive politeness was, at least, reassuring for us as we awaited our turn.

The Cardinal justified the need for religious education and for church schools in terms of the malaise and values of the consumer society and of such moral issues as nuclear weapons, disparity of wealth, and race relations. No one asked him why he expected religion to mitigate any of these problems when it had done nothing but exacerbate them throughout history. And so his hour of evidence, with occasional polite interventions by his two aides, wafted by.

As the hands of the clock neared 5 pm, the chairman brought the session to a gentle close, and invited Dr Stopes-Roe and me to take the witnesses' places at the table. Some members of the press left at that point, but a few stayed and the BBC carried on recording. (Part of my evidence was broadcast on Radio 4 the following Sunday.)

The Committee questioned us closely on the membership figures of our respective organisations and of the humanist movement as a whole, suggesting that our small numbers hardly justified our presence there. We insisted that the relevant fact was not our joint paid-up membership but the proportion of the general public that holds opinions in line with ours – but this only brought demands for statistical details that we did not have at our fingertips. (When the Cardinal had made statistical speculations, no such demands were made.)

We were each questioned on points in our memoranda; but Dr Stopes-Roe came off worse than I did, as members of the Committee found no difficulty with the every-day phraseology of the NSS memorandum, whereas they demanded off-the-cuff definitions of some of the academic phrases in the BHA memorandum – and Mr Thorne actually dismissed one such phrase, together with Dr Stopes-Roe's attempted explanation of it, as 'gobbledegook'. When Dr Stopes-Roe turned one question back to the Member who had asked it, he was told sharply that he was there to answer questions, not to ask them – yet when Cardinal Hume had similarly put one of his answers in the form of a question, he had been given a courteous (if noncommittal) answer!

It was a pretty gruelling hour, though we managed to hold our own most of the time. And the fact that we were told we would be expected to write in with substantiation of any statements we had been unable to support with detailed figures, references, and names, was actually to our advantage rather than otherwise.

In the supplementary memorandum which I accordingly submitted on behalf of the NSS, I was able to back up our justification for putting our views to the Committee by quoting the results of the Gallup poll of May 1980 on religious affiliation in England and Wales, which showed that 13 per cent claimed to be RC and 12 per cent non-believers (atheist or agnostic). My comment on this was 'The gap between RCs and non-believers was thus only 1 per cent. Since that was a year ago and the gap has been steadily narrowing for decades, there is probably nothing between us by now. Yet no one asked Cardinal Hume to justify his presence in the Committee room!'

On another point requiring statistical substantiation, I wrote as follows. Referring to Cardinal Hume's reliance on moral issues to justify a need for religion in school and for church schools, I mentioned that the proportion of Roman Catholics in penal institutions is at least twice their representation in the population at large. Though I was under the impression that this was a well-known fact, it caused some derisive laughter. But on checking the statistics, I find that again I erred on the side of caution: RCs comprise 12 to 13 per cent of the population of England and Wales, but 25 to 35 per cent of the inmates of borstals, detention centres, prisons, and hostels for drug addicts, alcoholics, and the like, in England and Wales; and similar ratios pertain in all Western countries.

A book entitled *The Church Now* (published in October 1980 by Gill and Macmillan) contains a chapter by a Catholic priest, Fr Terence Tanner, enquiring why this should be so. He points out that the answer generally given in the past – that RCs are unduly represented among the poorer sections of the community – is no longer valid; moreover, that it is not only in 'working-class' crimes and vices that RCs preponderate, but also in those associated with the middle classes.

The Times of 3 October, 1980, carried a front page comment by its religious affairs correspondent, Clifford Longley (himself RC), under the heading 'The Dilemma over Roman Catholic Delinquents', the first sentence of which reads: 'Roman Catholics are vastly over-represented among drug addicts, alcoholics, compulsive gamblers, prostitutes, night-club strippers and convicted prisoners, for reasons no one seems to know.'

One possible reason – that the seeds are embedded in the religion itself – was suggested by another RC commentator, Hugh Kay, writing in *The Month* of November 1980: 'It goes to the root of the nature and quality of the faith.' It might well be due to the sado-masochistic emphasis in Catholicism on crucifixion, martyrdom, self-abnegation, penance and eternal punishment – especially as, far more than in any other religion, Catholic children are largely segregated in their own denominational schools. In any case, Cardinal Hume's contention that church schools are morally beneficial is hardly borne out by the facts.

Had the Select Committee been as unctuous with us as they were with Cardinal Hume, and as they were two days later with Archbishop Runcie, I would not have been provoked to search out these additional telling facts – which have now not only been circulated among the members of the Committee but published by HM Stationery Office for public consumption and as a permanent historical record. Bigots and hecklers and respecters of persons serve our cause well. Let us give thanks to their God. Amen!

[August 1981]

Catholics and Contraception

[Letter on the Abortion Statistics]

JOHN Watson (July letters) questions the statement that more than 30 per cent of induced abortions in Britain are carried out on Roman Catholics, who comprise about 12 per cent of the population. But research findings published in the *Journal of Bio-Social Science* for July 1972 show that in one particular north London hospital at that time 30 per cent of all abortion patients gave their religion as RC – and presumably some would not have admitted it.

A recent study, also carried out in north London, has produced a figure of just over 30 per cent, but this has yet to be published. Studies in other parts of the country vary from 20 to 40 per cent.

It is true that many Catholic women nowadays disobey the Church's teaching on contraception – but usually only those who are married, while most of the RC abortions are carried out on the young unmarried.

It may seem strange that Catholics who are 'sinning' against their faith by indulging in pre-marital sexual activity should jib at taking precautions against pregnancy, but the first sin can be explained away as uncontrollable impulse, whereas the second would have to be planned in cold blood and might therefore preclude absolution. Besides, why risk damnation in order to avoid something that might never happen? And the Pope's recurrent denunciation of what is 'unnatural' seems almost to condone 'what comes naturally', but not any artificial means of contraception.

John Paul II has not, of course, been in power long enough to bear much responsibility for the present size of the world population. But what of the future?

His *Familiaris Consortio* firmly reiterates the sexually repressive policies of his Church, including the complete prohibition of any birth control other than 'periodic abstinence', and states (without evidence) that the dangers of over-population are being exaggerated.

Even if the earth's resources were shared out more fairly, it would be impossible to feed three times its present population – which, at the current rate of increase, will take only another fifty years to reach.

Because the Pope believes in a life of bliss after death, he thinks it is better to allow 17-million children to be born this year to starve to death after weaning than to prevent their being born at all.

Obviously, those of us who do not share his belief in an after-life cannot condone this pointless human suffering.

[August 1982]

Still Catholics?

[Book Review]

[*Why I am Still a Catholic*, edited by Robert Newell (Collins, £4.95).]

IN this symposium, seven lay people – all of them professional, articulate, and introspectively honest – attempt to give their personal answers to the implied conundrum of the book's title. Being intelligent, thinking people, in the 1980s – 'why', indeed? Speaking, as it were, from a psychiatrist's couch, set against the fast-moving background of the Roman Catholic Church in the British Isles, the seven contributors look back from personal perspectives over the past three decades, with occasional flash-backs to the first decade BC (Before the Council), when the coming volcano was seething just below the surface, and to the decade before that (the 1940s), when the Roman Church had more in common with its 16th-century self than with the present day. The resulting documentary collage is a startling one – more especially to anyone who still has a pre-conciliar image of the RC Church.

The Council referred to was, of course, the Second Vatican Council, inaugurated by Pope John XXIII – who, intending to 'open the windows' to the winds of change, unwittingly set off the volcanic eruption. I myself still react with amazement to books like the one under review, in spite of the fact that my family connections as well as RC publications have enabled me to keep abreast of the revolutionary changes in Catholic liturgy, practice, theology and attitudes.

Any *Freethinker* reader who has taken as exaggeration my observation here, from time to time, that the Catholic Church is now Protestant should read this book. If the 16th-century Protestant Reformation meant, in essence, private judgment, recognition of the individual conscience for self-direction, freedom of discussion, the use of the language of the people, congregational participation, and constant return to the sources of alleged revelation, then the Catholic Church has now gone through that Reformation, and, in the past three decades – mainly, in fact, the past two decades – has not only caught up with four centuries of Protestantism but has even overtaken it, spilling over into 'modern secularism' (to quote one of the seven authors, Bernard Bergonzi).

The degree of assimilation of these changes in the Church has naturally varied greatly, especially among the older generation, not excluding the clergy and the hierarchy; but this variation has only increased the force of the volcano. Now, however, it has taken over, so that only the few counter-revolutionaries led by Monsignor Lefebvre remain true, as they themselves claim, to the real Catholic tradition. The present pope keeps one foot in the past, especially on sexual mores; but, for all his personal popularity, he does not enjoy the unquestioning acceptance by Catholics of everything he says on faith or morals, as his predecessors did until the death of Pius XII. No one feels necessarily bound by John Paul's pronouncements, and some of our seven authors obviously regard him as a country cousin who is apt to be something of an embarrassment.

It has thus become possible for Catholics to be critical not only of the Vatican but of orthodox theology. They now pick and choose, like Anglicans, as to what and how far they believe, and, at the furthest extreme, may attenuate their theology to little more than deism, and their practice to next to nothing, religiously staying away from church for years on end – while (and this is the new thing that is the real theme of this book) continuing to regard themselves as members of the Catholic Church.

Millions of today's Catholics, including all but one or two of the authors of this book, would in my youth have broken away from the Church, and, though never quite disowned by it, would have been dubbed 'lapsed'. That means that they would have been regarded by their co-religionists as having put themselves outside the Church and the means of salvation unless and until divine grace brought them back to the bosom of Holy Mother Church. This required positive penitence and a humble return to the sacraments (particularly Confession), and, according to the prevailing myth, the reunion was frequently deferred for a precarious deathbed repentance.

Nowadays, a hard-and-fast break is far less likely. Many Catholics who are really no longer practising Catholics still regard themselves as members of the Catholic Church. And, though it is fashionable to consider labels of affiliation unimportant in comparison with actual belief and practice, I can well understand the importance with which these seven invest this particular label.

They are under nothing like the inner pressure that I experienced 33 years ago to come to a definite decision as to where they stand in relation to Catholicism – inside it or outside. They feel able to give up as much of its dogma and practice as they choose, whilst still belonging to the clan; so why force the issue? In my day, it could not be avoided. Faced as one was with the apparent immutability and alleged infallibility of the One True Church, with its emphasis on total obedience, there was never the option of just sitting indefinitely on the fence, which has now become quite a comfortable place to remain.

Reading this book, I kept asking myself whether, had I been ten or fifteen years younger, I might never have needed to come down on one side or the other, and whether these authors (most of whom are that much younger) would, if a little older, have been forced as I was to relinquish the label after so much of the substance had evaporated. To some extent, I found myself envying their escape from this trauma. But it was only the superficial envy of the footsore marathon runner for the comfortable spectator: I had completed the course, ordeal though it was, and could not but feel superior to those who had not.

Just as they would probably regard my out-and-out atheism as unnecessarily extreme, so I feel impatient with their vestigial mysticism – but would our ideas have diverged to this extent had our era of decision been the same? Perhaps I would have cut my marathon of philosophical enquiry short of the rational conclusions that shaped my atheistic humanism. I might, for instance, have been content to regard belief in life after death as 'a matter of personal choice', to quote the book's first contributor and editor, Robert Nowell, instead of taking the view that the question of life after death must be, like everything else, a matter of evidence. And I might have accepted the idea of 'absolute good for all men at all times', to quote from Piers Paul Read's chapter.

There is, however, a non-doctrinal difference between us which, though seemingly minor, is really the key to the question posed by the title of the book: the authors are (with one possible exception) impelled by a desire for solidarity with the historical Church, however tyrannical it has been in the past, while I am impelled by a desire to dissociate myself from that historical Church, however humanitarian it has latterly become. Whether this difference is the cause or the effect of completing that marathon I cannot say.

Robert Nowell expresses his desire for solidarity in this way: 'Being a Christian thus means for me somehow accepting and coming to terms with the whole of the Church's history and tradition, including all the disgraceful episodes that have marred the history of institutional Christianity – just as being human means learning to accept and come to terms with the whole of one's life, including all the episodes one wishes had never happened.' A plausible analogy, but a false one: we do not wish to remain children all our lives. Indeed, as the Good Book says, 'I put away the things of a child'. Besides, there are philosophers other than Jesus and historical movements other than Christianity that can arouse feelings of genuine human solidarity, from the whole range of historical perspectives.

Mary Craig, the only woman contributor, recalls almost medieval incidents from her pre-conciliar convent education in Lancashire in the 1940s which paralleled my own in London in the 1930s. For Louis McRedmond, who has similar memories even later in Dublin, 'Pope John arrived not a moment too soon'.

The childhood of Bernard Bergonzi, despite his Italian name, was spent in the same London borough as mine, but he was six years my junior, and those six years could well have been what saved the last thread of his faith from snapping before Vatican II came to the rescue. For him, the greatest strain had been the tension between an authoritarian tradition and his personal liberalism. Although, in pre-conciliar terms, he would now be regarded as 'lapsed', he likens his umbilical attachment to his childhood religion to that of many a non-practising Jew who remains rooted in Judaism.

Clifford Longley, the first Religious Correspondent of *The Times* to profess Roman Catholicism, was, like Robert Nowell but unlike the other five contributors to the book, a convert to Catholicism. But it now sits on him very loosely – to the extent that, alone of the authors, he is now reluctant to adhere to the sticky Catholic label, and he entitles his chapter 'Keeping an Open Mind'.

The last of the seven is James P. Mackay, a professor of theology and a 'laicised priest' ('whatever that contradiction in terms may mean', as the book's editor comments), now not only a married man but a father in the biological sense. His views are ecumenical to the point of his being employed as a theologian in a Protestant university and of his admonishing the Pope to pay heed to the people.

When all the skins of the Catholic onion have been peeled away, and there is nothing tangible left, a strong aroma may nevertheless persist. But for how long?

[December 1982]

God's Peculiar Essence

[Catholic Apologetics]

> God may be dead, but he is still propped up with word-spinning 'proofs' that were shown to be spurious centuries ago. Here the president of the NSS reconstructs a recent verbal skirmish in which she took part.

MY lecturing and debating engagements on behalf of the National Secular Society recently took me north of the border, to address the Edinburgh University Catholic Students Union on secular humanist objections to that faith as part of a series representing various opposing standpoints.

The Catholic chaplaincy at Edinburgh University is run by priests of the Dominican Order (*Ordinis Praedicatorum*, the Order of Preachers), and their purpose in organising this series of talks by devil's advocates was obviously inoculative. One of the priests boasted that it showed how certain they felt of the student's faith, that they were willing to subject it to attack; but another priest confided in me that the greatest danger today was sheer indifference.

They were, I suppose, taking a calculated risk that stimulating the students to rise to the defence of their faith would counteract apathy, and that to pre-empt arguments that might well be met with later would defuse them. I decided it was up to me to give a lethal, rather than an inoculative dose, even at the cost of common politeness. So I did not pull my punches.

Unlike, for instance, the Protestant contributor to the same series, I did not attack the RC church in isolation, but put it in its Christian framework of monotheism and, finally, of religion in general. Not only did I put in question the basic belief in a supernatural creator of the universe in which we find ourselves; I pointed out that since our experience shows it to be a suffering universe (our corner of it, at least), then mental contortion is required to regard its hypothetical creator as a god of love, unless he be incompetent. Furthermore, to worship such a creator, who allegedly had full knowledge of how everything would work out and full power to make it otherwise, is most immoral.

During the ensuing discussion, the somewhat naïve participation of the students was underpinned by more sophisticated (or, at least, more plausibly formulated) arguments by the Dominicans.

One of them played the medieval scholastic, insistently presenting 'proofs' of creation.

'Why', he demanded, 'is there something rather than nothing? When something is the case that need not have been – when something is not self-explanatory – surely it is natural to ask "why", and we are entitled to presume that there must be an answer'.

'Within the world of cause and effect in which we find ourselves, yes – but not concerning the universe as a whole.'

'Why not? The universe need not have been; so I ask, again, why is there anything at all? It is a reasonable question, to which there must be an answer.'

'Not at all', I replied. 'It is not reasonable. What you are asking for is an explanation for everything, as a whole: but what "explanation" means is finding a causal relationship between one event and another; so it is obviously nonsensical to try to explain the whole of existence, when, by definition, there is nothing else for it to relate to.'

'But that is why we are forced to assume that there is a necessary being – God – distinct from and independent of the universe, and in a causal relationship with the universe.'

'Wait a moment!' I objected. 'You are making some unjustified assumptions: first you suppose that the matter/energy that makes up the universe is not self-explanatory, and then you posit a convenient self-explanatory being to explain it. Why assume that the elements of the universe were ever non-existent?'

'Because one can sensibly say of the universe "It exists but it does not *have* to exist"; there must be something else outside it, to explain its existence; and that something else must be such that the possibility of its non-existence is unthinkable as belonging to it.'

'Ah! I see – a reformulation of the discredited ontological argument! Existence does not *belong* to anything or anyone – it is a condition, not a property.'

'Except in the case of God: the whole point is that God's existence is part of his essence; that is what makes God self-explanatory.'

'But even if we assume that there is a God with this peculiar essence, or necessary attribute, of existence, that does not explain why God has this peculiar attribute: it only explains why, if it is so, he then must exist. God would still not be self-explanatory, since having a peculiar essence does not explain why he has that essence.'

'What's your explanation, then?'

'The whole idea of looking for an explanation for something depends on the fact that there are all the other things in the universe among which we may find the explanation. But to assume there is an explanation for the whole universe is to assume that something exists beside the universe – that is, to assume beforehand the very thing you are trying to prove.'

'But you are dodging the question: why there should be something rather than nothing?'

'Just suppose', I said patiently, 'there were nothing. What answer would you expect then as to why there was nothing? There are only two possibilities: something or nothing. Well, as we can see, there is something – the universe in which we find ourselves.'

'But why?', my holy inquisitor persisted, for all the world like a three-year-old. 'Surely that is a natural and legitimate question that deserves an answer?'

'But the "something" is whatever exists, so it would have to include your supposed God if he existed. The answer, if there was one, would therefore have to include an explanation for God's existence – and the only line of argument you have suggested so far is that God must exist in order to explain the existence of everything else! A circular argument if ever there was one.

'If, as you insist, it is reasonable to assume that the universe must have been caused by something or someone, then it can be no less reasonable to assume that that something or someone must also have had a cause, and so on, in infinite regression. It comes down to the old question, "Then who made God?"'

The argument spread out around the hall. I put forward the usual atheistic hypothesis that our world is part of an infinite series of universes, each of which proceeds through the cycle of Big Bang, expansion, disintegration and contraction, its densest form leading to the next Big Bang. No beginning and no end: only continual change.

Not so different, perhaps, after all, from the God idea, except that to drag in a conscious being of purpose is an unnecessary complication, and seems to belittle the majesty of reality by seeking to explain it away with a childish myth – not to mention the psychological and social harm wrought by belief in the all-seeing Big Daddy.

On leaving Edinburgh, I took my leave of the persistent Dominican, and fancied that he seemed just a little less cocksure than at the start of my visit, and possibly regretted my inclusion in the series of inoculations.

A few days later, by sheer coincidence, I was given a pamphlet recently published by the Catholic Truth Society, entitled *Does God Exist?* The author was a Dominican priest, and, although the name of the author was not that of my inquisitor, the arguments were almost word-for-word the same. I can only surmise that at least some members of the intellectual Order of Preachers actually learn the latest reformulation of the old Aquinas arguments by rote. But at least the pamphlet has enabled me to recall the debate, with a reasonable degree of accuracy, for this article.

[January 1983]

Forging the Canons
[Revised Grounds for RC Excommunication]

> In January this year, the Vatican published its new Code of Canon Law, to replace the Code enacted in 1917-18, itself only the second version in the history of Christianity. In this article, the president of the National Secular Society looks briefly at the history of the canons, the changes now made, and their failure to reflect modern, liberal opinion within the Church.

THE much-trumpeted new version of the Code of Canon Law in seven volumes, all in Latin, was signed on 25 January, the 24th anniversary of the announcement by Pope John XXIII that it was to be updated in association with the Second Vatican Council, which he convened at the same time and which finished sitting 20 years ago. There must obviously have been some dragging of feet – particularly, one imagines, those of Pope Paul VI – to account for the 20-year delay in finalising the new Code. And there is now a ten-month interval (until 27 November) before it comes into effect – possibly because it takes that long to plough through it.

Although the Latin version is to remain the sole official text, authorised translations are to be permitted 'for the first time', according to the Catholic press. However, it seems that an English translation of the previous version appeared in America in 1918, though (according to Joseph McCabe) 'the text was almost smothered under a tactful running commentary'. Even so, because of the Code's violent opposition to civil law and the modern spirit, it was apparently decided that 'the less it was obtruded the better for the Catholic propagandist', and it was never published in this country.

McCabe is also interesting on the original *Corpus Juris Canonici,* which codified the rulings (canons) of popes and Councils up to the 13th century. 'This work', he says (in A *Rationalist Encyclopaedia)* 'contained, and still contains, a mass of forgeries, especially about the powers of the Pope, as even Catholic scholars are now forced to admit' – for instance, the 9th-century forgeries used by Nicholas I to boost his own position. McCabe then refers to 'a distinction which Catholic authorities draw between Public and Private Canon Law', and states that the revised (1917-18) Code, which covers the Private Law only, 'does not contain the death sentence on heretics and other monstrosities of Church Law, and the impression is given that they have been abandoned'; but 'the Public Law has several times been reissued, for the training of priests, in the present century.'

McCabe was writing, of course, 35 years ago, and no doubt all this has been quietly dropped by now – the Roman Church is in the habit of dropping embarrassments without fuss, while maintaining its pretence of immutable infallibility.

The fact that the first *Corpus Juris Canonici* held sway for seven centuries and its successor for less than seven decades reflects the increased rate of social change in modern times. Indeed, it would not be surprising if the new [1983] Code were to be superseded in about seven years, especially as it already lags far behind the more progressive sections of RC opinion in many countries.

The titles of the seven volumes have been translated as: *General Norms, The People of God, The Teaching Church, The Sanctifying Church, Temporalities, Church Sanctions,* and *Procedures.*

The two most noteworthy revisions in the first book (which is mainly technical) are both delegations of authority: (a) extending the power of governance to lay people, when so authorised, and (b) giving powers that were formerly vested in Rome to the Episcopal Conference or to individual bishops. For instance, it is now left to the bishops to decide which days shall be holydays of obligation – with the sole exception of Christmas Day, which is to be universally recognised throughout the Church. This exception seems somewhat ironic, remembering that in the first few centuries of Christianity the Church actually penalised any nominal Christian who dared to celebrate the old mid-winter festival!

The second book (as its new title shows) spells out the emphasis of Vatican II on the community and participation of all Church members – even the laity, even women: though it stops short of allowing girls to be altar servers, let alone allowing women to be ordained as priests.

The next two books deal with the prophetic and priestly offices of the Church, while book five is concerned (and how!) with the 'stewardship' of church property and accountability in financial matters – a topic that is all too topical.

The last two books are similar to those of the previous Code, but in the reverse order – possibly to avoid attracting too much attention to the penalties set out in the penultimate volume, though these have been drastically reduced.

The final volume, dealing with ecclesiastical court procedures, simplifies the marriage court procedures as set out in the previous Code, but not to the extent of those actually used in the USA in recent years, which will have to be discontinued after November.

This is just one example of the way in which local bishops have already, for many years past, anticipated the relaxations of the new Code, and even exceeded them. Another example is the practice of cremation: this was strictly forbidden in the 1917 Code, yet has been allowed now in most countries for well over a decade. Cremation is officially permitted under the new Code, though burial is still preferred.

The practical effects of implementing the 1983 Code will therefore be negligible, except for the fact that its publication has drawn public attention to it, and many practising Catholics are aware of these laws for the first time.

Naturally enough, it is the sixth volume, containing the RC penal code, that has received the greatest press coverage. The number of 'crimes' which carry the penalty of automatic excommunication has been drastically reduced – from 37 to a mere six – but to the modern mind that is six too many. Three of them invite special interest: the illicit ordination of a bishop, physical violence to the pope, and (of course) induced abortion.

Inclusion of the illicit ordination of a bishop among the crimes that carry the penalty of automatic excommunication means that the conservative dissidents (adherents to the Tridentine Mass and so on) led by former Archbishop Lefebvre will be unable to have any new priests ordained once Lefebvre dies, so their days seem to be numbered unless Lefebvre (who sees himself as the only bishop true to the faith) is willing to sacrifice himself to the extent of suffering excommunication, papal threats of which have so far not been carried out.

The threat of excommunication is a dire penalty, but only to those who care about it. It is therefore strange that it should be retained for a physical assault on the pope, since anyone likely to want to injure or kill the pope is (unless insane) unlikely to be a practising Catholic anyway. This threat would certainly have been no deterrent to the would-be assassin of May 1981 – a Turk, whose religious background was presumably Muslim. (Incidentally, his trial made no mention of the motive, and there is a persistent rumour that the Russian KGB was behind it.)

Finally, abortion. It is not, perhaps, surprising that this most puritan of popes, who so often rails against abortion, should have insisted on its inclusion in the list of 'crimes' for which excommunication automatically follows, but it is the most appalling single ruling in the whole seven-volume Code – for it must certainly affect many women who, driven by circumstances to seek an abortion, will have a psychological need for absolution and for continued membership of their Church community. And the publication of the new Code, with all the press comment it has received, has brought the penalty to the attention of many Catholics who were unaware of it before. One wonders how many suicides will result from this. It is true that Catholic commentators have tried to hedge it about with contextual qualifications that would, in practice, let most of these women off the hook – but not all of those who have heard of the penalty will have heard of the provisos.

RC spokesmen, quizzed in the media as to a scale of values that demands automatic excommunication for aborting an undeveloped foetus but not for murdering an actual person, with the sole exception of the pope, have explained that there are other (secular) sanctions against murder, but not generally against abortion. However, since the pope is protected from physical violence by the ordinary criminal code like everyone else, yet is given extra protection by canon law, this argument is a rather leaky one.

Double deterrence having been introduced to protect the person of the pope, there can be no valid reason for failing to bring it in also for terrorism. One hesitates to suggest any extension of canonical penal law, but it might well have proved effective against some of the bomb-happy IRA, with whom the certainty of excommunication might carry more weight than the possibility of life imprisonment or even an early death. However, Rome can hardly be expected to alienate a community of such 'good' Catholics as those prepared to murder for their identity in religion.

[March 1983]

What's In A Name?

[Letter on the word 'Humanist']

THE letters (February 1983) on my obituary notice of the word 'humanist' mostly cancelled one another out. But I would just like to say that the capital 'H' proposed by Roy Saich is not always audible, and even in print merely looks a bit old-fashioned.

Like Roy Saich, I have tried challenging self-styled Christian 'humanists' to say whether they put their God first or human beings – but the more sophisticated among them tend to reply that in this life there is no relationship with God except through human relationships and that salvation depends on what one does in this world, not the next. And, irritating though it is that 'our' word should be pinched by members of the opposition, we have to grant that their caring about the poor and the sick and the victims of war and violence, even supposedly for love of God or in hope of heaven, is better than the rich-man-in-his-castle sort of Christianity that plays down human suffering as merely temporal.

In some contexts, of course, where misunderstanding is unlikely to arise, I still use the word 'humanist', without qualification. And even 'secular humanist' or 'non-religious humanist' is by no means foolproof, since neither gives any indication as to rationalist/mystic, collectivist/ personalist, libertarian/authoritarian, or Right/Left-wing secular humanist. I am thinking of ordering a large lapel button proclaiming 'I AM A RATIONALIST, PERSONALIST, LIBERTARIAN LEFT-WING, SECULAR HUMANIST ATHEIST'. The necessarily small lettering might at least result in some Close Encounters of the Forth-right Kind!

Seriously, though, the problem would be solved if only we could bring the word 'freethinker' back into popular usage and understanding, with our own distinctive connotation. But would even that be safe from religious theft? 'It is because I think freely', one imagines the theologian insisting, 'that I know there is a God'.

You can't win against muddled thinking, because the muddled thinker never knows when he is beaten.

[March 1983]

Church Disestablishment
[Letter]

THE National Secular Society welcomes Tony Benn's call last month for disestablishment of the Church of England – a cause with which we have been associated since our foundation by Charles Bradlaugh, MP, in 1866. But we would go further than Mr Benn, who said nothing about disendowment: surely disestablishment and disendowment of the Church must go together.

It would be unjust if the wealth donated (mostly compulsorily) by our ancestors were to remain in the possession of a Church to which only a minority of the population is now committed. Its historical privileges in law, especially its fiscal privileges and its special protection under the blasphemy law, are also an anachronism.

We therefore call for the C of E to give up its establishment, its inherited wealth, and its legal privileges. Those who support its doctrines should support it financially and be subject to the same law as every other system of belief or non-belief.

BS (President, National Secular Society)

[April 1983]

God's Banker's Bubble
[Vatican-Mafia-Masonic Crime Ring]

On 13 June [1983], the inquest re-opens in London into the death last year of Signor Roberto Calvi, known as 'God's banker' because of the close ties the bank he presided over had with the Vatican. Calvi's body was found hanging by the neck from the scaffolding under Blackfriars Bridge, his clothes weighted down with stones. The verdict of the original inquest's jury was suicide; now either 'unlawful killing' or an 'open' verdict seems more likely. Here Barbara Smoker outlines the story as it has emerged so far.

THE *dramatis personae* of this real-life melodrama – clerics, financiers, politicians, gangsters, magistrates – makes a tangled web, too extensive to unravel in the space of this article. But two of the more important characters are: a jailed Sicilian industrialist and financier, Michele Sindona (with Watergate and Vatican connections), and the American-born power behind the papal throne, Paul Casimir Marcinkus, known in the Vatican as 'the gorilla'.

A huge, burly priest, Marcinkus became bodyguard to the late Pope Paul VI, doubling this role with that of the Vatican's chief financier. He was thus both literally and figuratively the power behind the pontiff's throne. He used his intimacy with Pope Paul to gain ever more power, and was made president of the Vatican Bank – *Institute per Opera Religiosi* (Institute of Religious Works) – from which he manipulated the vast international empire of Vatican finance, with bank accounts around the globe, especially in Italy, Switzerland, and South America. He was then made a bishop.

Widespread gossip about financial irregularities – even swindles involving counterfeit bonds – suggested that when Pope Paul died in 1978 Marcinkus would soon be for the chop. A new pontiff, looking at the records, could hardly fail to realise what Marcinkus had been up to. But the prophecy proved wrong. Pope Paul's immediate successor, John Paul I, scarcely had time in his one-month reign to make any changes. The present Pope, however, has had plenty of time to go through the books and shuffle Marcinkus off into early retirement – most likely by promoting him to some prestigious office without responsibility. But no such thing has happened.

Though the Vatican bank (IOR) lost millions, Marcinkus remained in charge; the Pope was shot, but Marcinkus was still his bodyguard. And the Pope not only made him an archbishop, but also mayor of Vatican City – in charge of all its finances and administration, its buildings, its newspaper, its radio station, and its 3,000 employees. Marcinkus was now far more powerful than any cardinal, with the possible exception of the Vatican Secretary of State – and his own cardinal's hat was hovering almost within reach. Not bad for the son of a Lithuanian window-cleaner of Illinois!

Then, however, a year ago, the financial bubble burst, the Vatican bank collapsed, and the central role of Marcinkus in the international financial scandal could no longer be concealed. Though still an archbishop, he has gone to ground in the Vatican, and the imminent cardinal's hat has blown away.

Those of us who, maintaining two cheque-book accounts, have learnt how to play one account off against the other at thin points of the month or the quarter may just imagine what can be done with thousands of bank accounts to play with, many of them offering credit facilities running into millions. The loans went round and round, while actual cash was quietly milked off at various points of the global merry-go-round. But missing millions tend to be missed eventually.

Mafia money, in need of expensive laundering, helped fill the gaps. Forged bond certificates, vouched for by top financiers, served as security. The American printer of the forged certificates was murdered – as were many other people involved. Whenever interest on a loan fell due, more loans were floated to meet it. Barring miracles of messianic proportions, the bubble just had to burst.

Perhaps the players were indeed banking (literally) on a miracle, in the form of investment profits sufficient to offset the gigantic losses that were building up. If so, their prayers went unanswered.

One of the first to get his comeuppance was the Sicilian 'whiz-kid' banker, Michele Sindona. who had first master-minded the whole set-up about 15 years ago. As financial adviser to the Vatican, he had helped Marcinkus revolutionise its affairs by introducing 'front companies' to switch the Church's solid investments into speculative ventures in secret. That was how it all started. But in 1974 the Sindona empire collapsed, with massive debts. Sindona fled to New York, but since 1978 has been a long-term resident of the up-state New York federal penitentiary.

The man chosen in 1974 to inherit Sindona's role as the Vatican's chief lay financial adviser, again working closely with Marcinkus, was the highly respected Italian banker, Roberto Calvi, then in his mid-fifties. From a job as an ordinary bank-clerk, he had risen, through sheer dedication to his work, to be president of Banco Ambrosiano – Italy's largest private bank. Founded in Milan in 1896, the bank was named after the patron saint of Milan, St Ambrose – and its annual balance-sheet always closed with a prayer to safeguard the accounts. Banco Ambrosiano was so closely involved with the Catholic Church, and especially with the Vatican – which had become one of the bank's major shareholders – that Calvi was dubbed 'God's banker'.

During one of the frequent press interviews that Sindona contrived to give in his prison cell, he once said that he had lighted upon Calvi as 'the most internationally minded of all those I came across'.

In 1978, however, shortly before his arrest, Sindona started an astonishing smear campaign against Calvi, apparently in a public attempt at blackmail. Posters appeared in the streets of Milan, giving details of Calvi's personal Swiss bank account – code-named *Ehrenkreuz* (cross of honour) – and demanding his arrest for fraud. But the two men were reconciled, it is said, by the intervention of Lucio Gelli, Grand Master of the P2 masonic lodge, of which both Calvi and Sindona were members – though freemasonry was, until this year, officially proscribed by the Catholic Church. In 1981 the P2 lodge was publicly accused of setting up 'a state within a state'; and the following year its Grand Master – wanted on charges of 'political espionage' – was arrested in Switzerland for using false documents to withdraw a large sum from a Swiss bank: money that had been deposited by an Ambrosiano subsidiary in South America.

Meanwhile, things were not going well for Roberto Calvi. The Bank of Italy began an investigation into the affairs of Banco Ambrosiano; but there was a breathing-space when the judge heading the investigation was gunned down – a Left-wing terrorist group claiming responsibility for the deed – and the senior bank official carrying out inquiries was jailed on the orders of a Rome magistrate, on an entirely trumped-up charge.

The Italian stock exchange then demanded that the Banco Ambrosiano shares be publicly quoted – a move that would entail detailed scrutiny of some very dodgy accounts.

Early in 1981, Calvi began to receive threatening phone calls in Milan from America, demanding that he make good the losses that the caller had sustained at the hands of the jailed Sindona. Calvi, after asking the authorities to tap his telephone, pleaded that he could not be held responsible for Sindona's swindles, but the caller seemed unconvinced:

'You'll have to learn the hard way. If that's the way you want it, that's the way it's going to be. Have a nice Easter.' The caller hung up – and a few days later Calvi's house was burned down.

Next, the Bank of Italy demanded an explanation from Calvi of unspecified foreign loans from Banco Ambrosiano, totalling $1,400-million.

All this Calvi faced with apparent composure. But then he was prosecuted for illegally exporting $20-million, and spent two months in custody awaiting trial. Summoning his wife and daughter to visit him one day in prison, he handed them some documents, on top of which he had written 'This trial is named IOR' (the Vatican bank), and told them to ask Marcinkus and Mennini (Luigi Mennini, IOR's managing director) to remove the secrecy so as to save him from taking the blame. As they got into their waiting car outside the prison, Mennini's son Alex jumped in beside them and tried to grab the documents. 'You must not mention this name' (IOR), he said – 'even in Confession'.

The experience of a prison cell left Calvi a changed man, and when the court found him guilty of the currency offence and sentenced him to four years' imprisonment in addition to a £7-million fine, he was ready to do anything rather than serve the prison sentence. So he appealed against both conviction and sentence – though he knew that, for the appeal to succeed, he must name the recipients of the missing $20-million. He had hitherto steadfastly refused to name names.

Marcinkus, who might have been expected to feel some anxiety at what Calvi would reveal, showed no apparent concern. Calvi's son, Carlo, repeatedly phoned the archbishop at the Vatican to enlist his support, but to no avail. Finally, Marcinkus barked: 'Tell your father not to bother us with bank problems: they are his problems, not ours.'

Problems they certainly were. The Banco Ambrosiano was now teetering on the verge of bankruptcy.

Meanwhile, Calvi – now on bail pending the appeal – had formed a relationship with a shady property dealer and Mafia member named Flavio Carboni, who began to play on Calvi's nerves, warning him against sleeping in his own house or even trusting his own bodyguard.

On 11 June 1982, ten days before Calvi's appeal was due to he heard, Carboni arranged for him to make his getaway from Italy, huddled in the back of a motor-launch owned and operated by a smuggler on the Italian-

Yugoslav run. The smuggler's name was Silvano Vittor. With a hastily doctored passport, Calvi landed on the Yugoslav coast, and a hired car took him over the Austrian border. From there he telephoned his daughter Anna, telling her, in much more buoyant mood, that he was confident he would win through and be able to return soon to his family. The following day, he had a bulging briefcase brought to him by Vittor from Italy – and during the night Vittor saw him methodically burning most of its contents.

The next move was to London, where Calvi decided he would find a hideout. (He knew London, having done business in the City on many occasions.) So he got Vittor to charter an executive jet from Biggin Hill (for £2,650), and together they flew to Gatwick airport, where Calvi's doctored passport aroused no suspicion.

'Ultra-secure' accommodation was found for him in a Chelsea apartment block – but it was not to Calvi's liking. It was a squalid, barely furnished, two-roomed flat, reminiscent of his prison cell; and being virtually confined to the flat had a depressing effect on him. His confidence evaporated, and he became extremely nervous. He refused to share the one bedroom with Vittor, who had to sleep in the sitting-room.

Flavio Carboni now arrived in London, accompanied by a girl-friend and her sister. But no Chelsea dump for them – they booked into the Hilton Hotel. It was suggested that Calvi and Vittor meet Carboni there, but Calvi was frightened of being recognised, so they met in Hyde Park – where the main topic of conversation was the squalor of the Chelsea flat. Carboni promised to look for somewhere equally secure but less dismal. He therefore spent most of the following day on the telephone to estate agents, while Vittor went out with the two girl-friends – leaving Calvi alone in the flat, with only a television set for company. Three times during the day Calvi telephoned his daughter Anna in Switzerland, repeatedly warning her that she could be in danger there and should leave at once for the USA, to join her mother.

Vittor – according to his own account of events – returned to the flat during the evening, but left again at about 11.30 pm to meet Carboni and the two girls. When he came in again at 1 am, he found the flat deserted – though the television was still switched on, the screen blank. No-one, apparently, had seen Calvi leave. Vittor said later that he had waited anxiously all night for Calvi to return – but early the next morning, instead of searching for his charge, he hurriedly left the country. So did Carboni. While Vittor caught a plane at 10.10 am from Heathrow to Austria, Carboni took a strangely circuitous route to Switzerland, via Scotland, from Gatwick.

On arriving in Switzerland, Carboni withdrew no less than $20-million from various Swiss bank accounts – not, presumably, his own.

Meanwhile, at 7.30 am, Calvi's body was found – fully clothed, hanging by the neck at the end of a short length of orange rope (of the sort commonly used on the river), suspended from the scaffolding under Blackfriars Bridge. His pockets were full of stones, and half a brick was stuffed down his trousers. But the published photograph of his body, just cut down from the scaffolding, shows a calm, proud facial expression – strangely beautiful, more handsome than his living portraits. His age was 62.

The police found on the body Calvi's doctored passport, three pairs of spectacles, two watches, and a wallet containing about £7,000 in various currencies and a flight-ticket to Rio de Janeiro. The autopsy revealed that death was due to asphyxiation by hanging – there were no injuries apart from the marks left by the rope, and no indication of drugs apart from a moderate amount of alcohol.

Both Vittor and Carboni made written statements for the London inquest, but neither attended it in person – Vittor because he was now under arrest in Italy, and Carboni for fear of arrest if he were to leave Switzerland. Soon afterwards, Carboni was arrested in Lugano, in connection with the $20-million withdrawals, and was extradited to Italy.

The verdict of the London inquest jury, at the end of a rushed and exhausting 12-hour session, was that Calvi had killed himself. His family, however, refused to accept that verdict – partly because of evidence withheld, it is said, from the jury; partly because of the way the inquest was rushed through, with alleged misdirection from the coroner; and partly because the moral stigma of suicide is too abhorrent for them, as Roman Catholics, to leave unchallenged. (Not to mention the loss of life-assurance benefits.)

Besides, as the family point out, Calvi was a man of unquenchable optimism. And why, if he had intended to kill himself, did he make his way from Chelsea to Blackfriars, four-and-a-half miles distant, to some scaffolding that is almost invisible? The Calvi family believe that he was murdered.

A few hours before Calvi's death, an extraordinary general meeting of shareholders of Banco Ambrosiano was held in Milan to relieve him of his position as its president. (The most 'extraordinary' thing about it is surely the fact that he had, until then, remained in charge of the bank's affairs.) Immediately after the meeting, Calvi's secretary fell to her death from a window in his Milan office. But there is no reason to believe that Calvi ever knew about these happenings.

In November 1982, the Vatican issued a statement saying that it had 'discovered' its bank had 'ownership and thus juridical control' of two front companies – unnamed, but thought to be Manic and United Trading, the formation of which had, according to the documents, been carried out by IOR, which was in regular receipt of statements of their holdings.

On 29 March this year, three judges in the High Court quashed the Calvi inquest verdict and ordered a new inquest to be held. It is down to begin on 13 June – and this time it will certainly take longer than one day.

Meanwhile, in Milan and Luxembourg (where Banco Ambrosiano had an important subsidiary), a regiment of investigators has been trying to uncover Calvi's secrets. The Vatican has clammed up. As a sovereign state, it is able to give Marcinkus protection.

Secrecy is an asset in the world of high finance, especially in Italy, and Calvi was always a secretive man. Some of his secrets have no doubt gone to the grave with him – including, perhaps, the secret of his death.

[June 1983]

[The re-opened inquest failed to rule out suicide. However, almost seventeen years later, the impending Italian trial of three Mafiosi (including Carboni) on conspiracy-to-murder charges entailed exhuming Calvi's corpse for modern forensic tests – and these indicate death by strangulation prior to hanging. A recent film, *God's Bankers*, suggests major complicity on the part of the Vatican.]

Menace of 'Life'

[Infant Euthanasia]

'SEVERELY Handicapped Infants' is a discussion document by Madeleine Sims that considers a number of fundamental problems confronting those most closely involved in a human tragedy. Do parents have the right to choose? Does society have the resources to cope? What should the priorities be? The snooping activities in hospitals of Life and other Christian groups aggravate an already tense and distressing situation.

This eight-page pamphlet, issued by the pressure-group Prospect, comprises an off-print from the current issue of the *New Humanist,* with the addition of a paper cover. It is therefore rather expensive at £1 – especially as the same contents are available, together with other interesting material, for the same price by buying the *New Humanist* itself. On the other hand, this excellent article – which includes a very useful bibliography, the text of the Abortion Act of 1967, and the draft Protection of Disabled Children Bill drawn up by Life in 1981 – is certainly worth the measure of permanence given it by this reprinted format. Another advantage is that distribution by Prospect will put it into the hands of some people who would not have seen it in the *New Humanist.*

Madeleine Sims (an active and able polemicist for secularism, as well as for abortion and euthanasia for severely handicapped foetuses and neonatals) researches the relevant facts with care, and her effectiveness stems from sound argument clearly expressed, never from stridency of assertion.

Here she shows that the scope of the problem, exacerbated first by the indiscriminate application of advances in neonatal techniques and more recently by cuts in the social services, has fortunately been mitigated in the past few years by the readier provision of legal abortion on grounds of foetal abnormality, and also – as the statistics of neonatal survival prove – by a more enlightened medical policy with regard to severely defective infants, in spite of the law and of the menace of Life snoopers.

Although one of these snoopers succeeded in putting Dr Leonard Arthur in the dock for the euthanasia of a handicapped mongol baby whose parents had agreed that that was the best course of action, the jury refused to convict him. As a result, Life turned its attention from the law courts to Parliament, and produced the Protection of Disabled Children Bill. If this became law, it would not only make it an offence to 'withhold any treatment from such a child without which it is known he or she cannot survive'; it would also destroy those sections of the Abortion Act that permit abortion on the grounds that 'there is substantial risk that if the child were born it would suffer from such physical or mental abnormalities as to be severely handicapped'. So far, no MP has been persuaded to introduce such a Bill, though the threat of it will no doubt surface every year at Private Members' ballot time.

It is the organisation Prospect that specifically represents the rational and compassionate opposition to this Bill. Founded by Mrs Peggy Lejeune in 1981, Prospect maintains that 'decisions about severely handicapped babies should be left to parents, guided by the diagnosis and advice of doctors present at the time', and that greater priority should be given to the improvement and availability of pregnancy-screening facilities aimed at preventive abortion. At the same time, Prospect campaigns for the provision of better caring services and community support for parents with severely handicapped children to look after.

The article cites some compelling case histories. It also juxtaposes two news items about the former Director of Social Services for Hammersmith and Fulham, David Plank, who, against the wishes of the parents and doctors, authorised a life-saving operation on a handicapped baby, having it moved from hospital to hospital until he found a surgeon willing to operate. A year later, after a three-year-old had been battered to death by foster parents while in the care of the same Council, Mr Plank resigned his position because there were 47 more children similarly at risk in the borough owing to lack of resources. The baby whose life he had intervened to save would always be totally dependent, thus depleting the resources still further. Apart from such practical considerations, the moral rights of the parents to decide and of the infant to be spared a life of intolerably low quality were allowed by a court to be overridden by an employee of the local borough where the baby happened to be born.

Freethinker readers are urged to get hold of the article, in one format or the other (magazine or pamphlet), and to bring it to the notice of people who may need to be jolted into thinking about the suffering caused by prolonging the lives of foetuses or newborn babies with severe congenital abnormalities – the suffering not only of the handicapped themselves but also of their families, not to mention the additional burden placed on already over-stretched social services.

I am just off to post a copy of this article to my nephew physician, who specialises in neonatals.

[September 1983]

Thin Theology
[Book Review]

[*Why Believe in God?* by Michael Goulder and John Hick (SCM Press, 2.50).]

A DAY-LONG public 'dialogue' that took place last November between two of the seven authors of the Church-shaking revelation *The Myth of God Incarnate* (1977) has been edited and expanded to make this slim paperback volume. The four central chapters of the book comprise two pairs of lectures: the first pair dealing with the question of God's existence and his possible attributes, the second pair the possible actions of such a God in our world.

The first chapter (additional to the 'dialogue' itself) is a potted religious autobiography by Michael Goulder, who reveals that, since the publication of the *Myth*, he has lost the remnants of religious faith to which he was still clinging at that time and, having resigned his clerical orders (after three decades) in 1981, is now an atheist, and takes the atheistic position in the ensuing debate.

What he had come to realise was that the degree to which God's function had been whittled down by advanced theologians such as his co-authors in the *Myth* really left God with nothing to do of any consequence. Since God therefore had no *raison d'être,* Dr Goulder, with commendable honesty, if some reluctance, let him go.

The other protagonist, Bishop John Hick, is now a Professor of Religion in California. Though more advanced in his theology than Goulder at the time of contributing to the *Myth,* Hick has not since changed his theological position. He is as much a theist now as in 1977 – though that is not saying a great deal, in terms of traditional Christianity. In fact, his attenuated theism, unencumbered by any orthodox Christian doctrine apart from that of divine purpose in the moment of creation, is, as Goulder points out, Deism in all but name. In its 18th-century heyday, Deism was associated with Rousseau, Voltaire, and the *philosophes,* followed by Thomas Paine – all regarded in their time as wicked, heretical freethinkers, rather than respectable Christians. To be a self-confessed Deist in those days was to risk persecution and imprisonment at the hands of the pious; now, it seems, it is quite compatible with being a Christian bishop, a theological don, and an author for the SCM Press.

To his Deism, however, Hick tacks on a nebulous belief in some sort of personal survival, that seems to be closer to oriental ideas of reincarnation than to the traditional Christian heaven. His 'reasons' for this belief, as for his belief in divine purpose, are couched in fine academic prose, but really boil down to subjective feelings and wishful thinking. Without these residual beliefs, human lives of deprivation and impoverishment would, he points out, be 'final and unredeemable'. Quite. But the realities of the human situation are not changed by our wishing them to be otherwise.

A third contributor to *The Myth of God Incarnate,* Don Cupitt, though not a participant in the Birmingham debate or a contributor to the present book, is included in the book in the third person, both in Goulder's preliminary chapter and, more importantly, in a final additional chapter by John Hick. Since publication of the *Myth,* Cupitt has, like Goulder, abandoned belief in a God; unlike Goulder's straightforward secular atheism, however, Cupitt's sort of atheism is, to quote Hick, 'a religious atheism, or religious naturalism, which he describes as a form of Christian Buddhism'. In other words, he remains a mystic, falling halfway between Hick and Goulder.

A quarter of a century ago it would have been unthinkable for anyone who had abandoned so much of the traditional Christian doctrine as Hick, let alone Cupitt, to retain the Christian label and continue in the rôle of a leading theologian in the established Church.

It was in the early 1960s that I first came across this brand of demythologised Christianity in the person of John Wren-Lewis, whose new-fangled theology was brought to public notice through Bishop John Robinson's *Honest to God*. At the time it looked as though the bishop, if not Wren-Lewis, was hanging on to church membership more from opportunism than from any genuine residual belief. But now Cupitt has gone even further, and it has become almost commonplace for bishops and theologians to expound a sort of mystic atheism. One wonders how much the simplistic souls in the parishes are aware of what is happening to the creed among the élite.

Hick draws the line at atheism. But, as he admits in his final chapter, 'I do see the Goulder and Cupitt moves as revealing both the difficulties and the dangers of serious and fundamental theological thinking today'. In other words, as freethinkers have always said, freethought is the inevitable result of thinking freely.

Hick's residual faith rests, defensively, on the attribution of psychological phenomena (namely, 'religious experience') to external causation. Goulder, on the other hand, apparently never had the sort of feelings categorised as 'religious experience'. (How unjust it seems of the Christian God to withhold personal revelation of his presence from a man who continues in prayer and good works for half a century, thus abandoning him in the end to reason!)

Hick declares that he always thought Goulder might finish up as an atheist, owing to the combination of his lack of personal religious experience with his literal belief in such traditional but untenable theological concepts as divine intervention in human affairs. His mind is too straightforward in thought to allow him to combine atheism with mysticism. For him, atheism means the end of religion.

Goulder's atheistic journey thus follows a path familiar to most readers of the *Freethinker* – except that few of us have taken so long on the way. We mostly completed the journey by our mid-twenties, whereas it took Goulder, turning over every pebble, till his late fifties to reach the only possible conclusion. But perhaps, like the Prodigal Son, he should be welcomed all the more warmly for that.

To use another metaphor, Goulder slowly peels away the layers of the theological onion, and finds nothing inside. But his painstaking slowness enables him to develop some of the familiar arguments along personal lines with new instances that hold the attention, whereas I sometimes lost patience with the sophistry of the Hick chapters.

Since both authors are university dons, it is not surprising that the tone of their 'dialogue' is rather academic, but it never sinks to the fuzziness of some modern theology. And since they are also long-standing friends and colleagues who know and respect one another, it never sinks to the mere scoring of cheap points. Though intellectual and urbane, the style is generally clear, with no deliberate obfuscation.

Years ago, the SCM Press kept strictly to faith-boosting publications, often presenting simplistic rejoinders to the same anti-theistic arguments that make up this book – not only in the God-is-dead Goulder chapters but in the greater part of the God-is-deaf Hick chapters too. Theology is not what it was.

No longer is it enough for the atheist debater to know he is to take on an Anglican theologian: he (or she) needs to know whether the God that is being defended is a supernatural, personal, paternal God who actually intervenes in the world today; or the eternal self-existent creator that programmed the Big Bang, then stood aside; or no more than a poetic image for human sensibilities and aspirations.

If you would like a glimpse into the current theological academic scene, do read this little book. Its brevity, its readability, and its (with a few Hick lapses) comprehensibility, prompt me to recommend it as a book to be read – though not as a gift to your church-going granny.

[October 1983]

Campaign for 'Atheist Liberation'

[Editorial Report by William McIlroy]

WHEN Barbara Smoker addressed the Annual General Meeting of the National Secular Society on Saturday, 5 November, she remarked that it was exactly 34 years ago to the day and date, and almost the hour, since she finally rejected Christianity in favour of atheism. Miss Smoker, who became NSS President in 1971, told members at Conway Hall, London: 'I would like to take this opportunity to launch a new slogan for the secular humanist movement – "Atheist Liberation".

'Not until the birth of the Women's Liberation movement did most people – women as well as men – even realise that sex-discrimination remained very much a fact of life, despite the female franchise and the Married Women's Property Acts. The introduction of Gay Liberation likewise opened the eyes of the public to the weight of social and legal discrimination that the 1967 Homosexual Act had left untouched. It also gave many gays the courage to "come out" – this, in turn, giving strength to the movement.

'The analogous phrase, "Atheist Liberation", could do the same for our own movement. It would certainly help the media to help us. At the recent commemoration of the 150th anniversary of the birth of our founder, Charles Bradlaugh, I was asked by some of the newspaper reporters what our slogan was. That made me realise the need for one. Trying out "Atheist Liberation" on several people in the past few weeks, I find that it clicks.

'The response to it is never the sterile "What does it mean?", as with Secularism, prompting a boring dictionary answer, but the very same question that Women's Liberation and Gay Liberation have always provoked: "Why do you need it?" And that question is a profitable one, inviting an answer that will concern topical issues rather than dictionary definitions.

'The questioner will probably be astonished to learn that in many areas of life in Britain today one cannot be a first-class citizen without belief – or, at least, no obtrusive disbelief – in an ancient myth. It is generally supposed that religious belief or lack of it is a private matter that, on this side of the Iron Curtain, entails neither penalty nor privilege. But this is far from the truth.'

Barbara Smoker then referred to the wide range of benefits enjoyed by churches and religious institutions. 'First, there are the many monetary perks of religion. A religious organisation has automatic charity status, with its tax exemption and rates concession. A flagrant instance of the injustice this entails is the fact that when the NSS campaigns in favour of Sunday trading and Sunday entertainment it has to do so out of fully taxed income, whereas the Lord's Day Observance Society, on the opposite side of the same issue, enjoys tax exemption.

'Christian chaplains to hospitals, prisons, and the armed forces are paid out of the public purse, while secular humanists who wish to provide an analogous service are not only given no financial help for it but are often not even allowed to do it for nothing.

'The provision of church schools, for which the taxpayer and rate-payer meet 85 per cent of the capital cost and 100 per cent of the running costs, is a wasteful duplication of educational resources as well as denying children access to ideas other than those of the home background, exacerbating the problems of Northern Ireland, and laying the seeds of racial violence in immigrant areas – where non-Christian religious leaders are now demanding the same right to their own schools as Christian denominations enjoy. As for our state schools, the law still requires them to provide religious instruction and a corporate act of daily worship, as though Parliament can guarantee the existence of a god to be worshipped.

'The teaching of contentious subjects as though they were on a level with science or mathematics is grossly uneducational. There is also the inevitable injustice to atheist and agnostic teachers, who must either be hypocritical or jeopardise their career prospects.

'Every radio and television company in this country has its religious broadcasting department, with a special budget for every station or channel, monitored by the Central Religious Advisory Council. There is, of course, no comparable budget of time or money for broadcasting non-religious views – and these therefore largely go by default, apart from a token humanist occasionally participating in a religious programme, with Christian spokesmen invariably accorded the lion's share of time and the last word. Even a minority sect like Roman Catholicism – which now has fewer adherents in Britain than there are people of a secular humanist outlook – has many weekly hours of broadcasting time, both for its religious services and in moral discussion programmes.

'In fact, the persistent idea that morality is associated with religious belief pervades the public consciousness and underlies not only unfairness in the media but school curricula and the survival of many of our archaic laws – such as the common-law offence of Blasphemy, successfully used (against *Gay News*) within the last decade. Law reform to allow freedom of choice in such personal matters as voluntary euthanasia is blocked on religious grounds, thus imposing a god-fearing ordinance on people with no god to fear.

'Atheists are often paid the back-handed compliment, "You really are a good Christian!" Our old enemy, Mrs Whitehouse, prefers to bear false witness, such as her famous alliterative "Disbelief, doubt and dirt". We could retaliate with something like "Faith, fraud and forgery". But it would be more profitable to establish the positive legitimacy of our own position through "Atheist Liberation".'

[November 1983]

Voluntary Euthanasia
[Letter on its Legalisation]

THE letter from E M Karbacz (August) about hypothetical 'abuses' if voluntary euthanasia and assisted suicide were to be legalised is in the realm of horror fantasy.

The law would, of course, stipulate preconditions to safeguard both the voluntary element – i.e. a consistent desire of the patient over a minimum period – and the seriousness and incurability of the illness or disability that was the ground of that desire.

We do not seek a blanket repeal of the clause of the Suicide Act that makes assisting suicide a criminal offence, but would merely make it a good defence to any such charge that the patient had consistently requested euthanasia, apparently for adequate medical reasons, and that the defendant, being motivated primarily by compassion, had acted reasonably. In practice, this would mean that only in cases of doubt would a prosecution be brought, and in the final resort it would be for a jury to determine the facts.

All laws are liable to abuse if the authorities wish to abuse them. (As Miss Karbacz says, the Official Secrets Act is one such example in this country.) But such abuses are not dependent on any law. When the Nazi regime in Germany called the murder of handicapped people 'Euthanasia', this was not an extension of an existing euthanasia law – on the contrary, there had never been any such law, and Hitler was always strongly opposed to voluntary euthanasia.

There is no doubt that euthanasia, at least to the extent of curtailing a terminal illness, is widely practised by doctors in this country – but not on a voluntary basis, since the present law makes doctors frightened to raise the question with their patients.

The law we want is a permissive law – comparable with the laws passed in the 1960s on divorce, homosexuality and abortion. Does Miss Karbacz see any danger of these being made compulsory?

BS (Chairman, Voluntary Euthanasia Society)
[October 1984]

Voluntary Euthanasia Conference
[Editorial Report by William McIlroy]

'THERE is, as questionnaire surveys show, a far greater proportion of Rationalists in the voluntary euthanasia movement than in the general population', Barbara Smoker (chairman of the Voluntary Euthanasia Society and president of the National Secular Society), told the World Federation of Right-to-Die Societies at its fifth biennial conference in Nice, 20-23 September [1984]. 'But there are also, of course, many committed religious believers among its members and supporters', she added.

'However, the opponents of voluntary euthanasia are almost exclusively religious believers. And the arguments they use against voluntary euthanasia are, however rationalised or overlaid with practical problems, based on religious belief; whereas the arguments in favour of voluntary euthanasia are based on common-sense, compassion, and the right to choose for oneself.'

The conference drew an attendance of over 700 from 19 countries. Barbara Smoker was among the listed speakers in two of the three main sessions of the conference: the legal session and the ethics session. The latter included among the speakers the Bishop of Nice (giving the orthodox Catholic objections), a Muslim spokesman (no less hostile), the Chief Rabbi of Nice (slightly less so), and a Protestant pastor and editor of *Evangile et Liberté* (equivocal).

Miss Smoker's arguments in favour of voluntary euthanasia, based on the atheist viewpoint, were enthusiastically received by the majority of conferees. She said that the rational choice of one's own time, place, and manner of death so as to round off one's life appropriately – completing its unique pattern with dignity and good sense, neither prematurely nor belatedly – can be seen as a sort of art form. 'We talk about the Art of Living, so why not the Art of Dying?

'A phrase that Christians, and other religionists, are inclined to use against us is "the sanctity of life". But what exactly does it mean? It has more than one connotation.

'It may imply that life has a supernatural aspect which makes it sacrosanct. But how can this be reconciled with the fact that earthquakes and other natural disasters take such a heavy and indiscriminate toll of human life? And if animals are also regarded as God's creatures, how can the sanctity of life apply when one animal cannot survive without eating another?

'In a different sense, however – the sense that human beings should have humane consideration, compassion and respect for one another – we secular humanists also accept the sanctity of life. And, of course, the very aims of the voluntary euthanasia movement are based on such consideration, compassion and respect. We firmly deny that people should always have to live as long as possible, whatever their condition. Our meaning of "the sanctity of life" cannot be divorced from the quality of life.

'Our religious opponents insist that human lives are a "gift from God"; but is there no right to decline a gift when it is nothing but a burden? God alone, they tell us, is to determine our time of death; humans are not allowed to tamper with God's will. If that were so, then it would surely be wrong to intervene to save life, as well as to hasten death?

'But our case is primarily that what we want is merely permissive. We uphold the right of our opponents to decide against euthanasia for themselves, but not for us. They have no moral right to make laws that impose their views on others, who may not even share the religious beliefs on which those views are based. Believers who uphold the principle of complete freedom of religion often fail to see that, in all logic, this must include freedom *from* religion.

'There is only one person who has the right to decide about euthanasia: in each case the decision must rest with the person most concerned, provided he or she is rational.

'However, no one is morally obliged to carry out active euthanasia for another, or to assist in his or her suicide. Indeed, it would be morally wrong to do so unless the reasons for it were sufficiently serious and apparently incurable. Rationalism recognises that there is an important moral distinction to be made between assisting in a suicide that is reasonable and assisting in a suicide that is not reasonable.

'Christians often talk about a "merciful release" when a distressing terminal illness ends in death: supporters of voluntary euthanasia simply want the merciful release to occur before the suffering has been uselessly prolonged, if that is the patient's wish.

'Everyone nowadays seems to agree that a life-support system may be switched off when the brain is dead – and this has, indeed, become the official definition of death – but I would say that the criterion should be the death of the lobes of the brain that make consciousness possible. Not a contrived definition of death, but the possibility of any worthwhile life. And the main criterion for voluntary euthanasia should not be whether death is imminent anyway, but simply the incurability of an intolerable condition.

'Illogically enough, most religious believers contrive to make a moral distinction between active and passive euthanasia, as does the present law, though no moral distinction is made in any non-theological system of ethics between acts of commission and acts of omission – that is, in this context, between killing and letting die – assuming the same intent and same motive. That there is no such moral distinction is argued irrefutably by leading moral philosophers.

'With regard to infant euthanasia – which, though, of course, outside the brief of this conference, is closely allied to it – the British medical profession encourages its members to let seriously defective neonates die of starvation while sedated, over a period of several days, yet recoils in horror from any suggestion of giving these babies a quick lethal injection. But the idea that withholding sustenance from a baby is any less lethal, or any more moral, than a quicker form of euthanasia is manifestly absurd.

'Pope Pius XII, faced with the facts of rapidly advancing medical technology, declared in 1957 that "extraordinary means" need not be used to keep people alive; but his Church has since extended this in practice to include quite ordinary means, such as the normal administration of antibiotics when an incidental attack of pneumonia happens to offer a "merciful release" from another condition that is incurable. The only discernible ethical distinction between withholding antibiotics (so as not to cure the pneumonia) and actually administering a lethal dose or injection (in the absence of pneumonia) appears to be the implicit principle that you must always give the Almighty a sporting chance!'

The conference, which was held in Nice's prestigious Palais de Congres, attracted media attention in many countries, including Britain. In France, the host country, every important newspaper gave it front-page coverage, *Liberation* devoting four pages to it and *France-soir* the whole of its front page.

The event even made the Vatican paper *L'Osservatore Romano*, which carried a condemnatory article by a leading theologian and quoted the Pope as saying that members of the conference were advocating murder.

The third session of the conference dealt with the medical aspects of the subject, and then came the most celebrated speaker of all, Professor Christiaan Barnard, who was responsible for the degree of media interest. But he was less warmly received than the Dutch medical representative, who put more emphasis on the patient's right to choose. Barnard, while strongly in favour of passive euthanasia and also advocating the legalisation of active euthanasia, thought it was really up to the medical profession to decide on the quality of life in each case. This professional authoritarianism was attacked by many of the participants in the ensuing discussion.

[October 1984]

Eggs are not People

[Embryo Research]

> Public hysteria in the face of new scientific knowledge and techniques has always thrived on ignorance fostered by religious superstition, but never more blatantly and absurdly than in the current furore over embryological experimentation.

TEN per cent of all married couples are infertile – and for many of them it is a distressing disorder. Not only do the techniques of *in vitro* (i.e. test-tube) fertilisation (IVF) enable many infertile couples to have children, but the choice of a normal embryo for implantation in the mother also precludes various congenital defects in the baby and averts risks to the mother's life. Moreover, laboratory observation of spare zygotes, both normal and defective, is opening up whole new avenues of medical research and practice, not only in obstetrics but also in general medicine. (It has, for instance, already produced the rubella vaccine.)

This field of science has been developing, in an atmosphere of open medical and moral discussion, over the past sixteen years, and the clinical treatment of infertility through IVF has become widely available in the past five years. But Mr Enoch Powell – in company with many other public figures, parliamentarians, and church leaders – has apparently only just caught up with it. And unfortunately these busybodies have not acquainted themselves with the most basic biological facts of the situation before leaping to the defence of the poor little human zygote and whipping up a public outcry based on fairy-stories.

The fact is, of course, that the fertilised egg does not, at this stage of development (none has so far been developed artificially beyond fourteen days), have even the most rudimentary nervous system, so cannot possibly have any consciousness, let alone feel any pain or distress. Experiments on the test-tube embryo therefore cause no suffering of any kind. In this respect, embryological experiments are in marked contrast to animal experiments, which undoubtedly cause suffering to vast numbers of laboratory animals each year. Yet few of the people who are so vociferously opposing embryo experimentation also oppose animal vivisection, while many of them are actually demanding more animal experiments as a means of replacing embryo experimentation.

The French geneticist, Professor Lejeune, having thrown in his lot with the religious pro-Life lobby, has actually claimed that all the experiments now being carried out on human embryos could be carried out just as effectively on animals – meaning, of course, not animal embryos, but sentient animals. Speciesism can surely go no further. Even if animal embryos were used, this would involve keeping the mothers in laboratories and operating on them monthly for their eggs, whereas the human eggs used at present are merely by-products of procedures required by the mother. It is as though Nazi concentration-camp doctors were to justify their vile death-dealing experiments on thousands of dark-haired Jewish children by proudly claiming that they had thereby managed to save a hair on the head of a fair-haired 'Aryan' child.

The only genuine basis of moral status is that of sentience – that is, the possession of an inner life. Since an early embryo can have no sentience, it can have no moral status, and there can be no rational objection to investigating it for the benefit of the mother and her family or of humanity in general.

Supporters of Mr Powell's absurdly titled Unborn Children (Protection) Bill who do not oppose legal abortion are obviously confused, since they are opposing the destruction of the earlier and less developed entity and not that of the later, more developed one. On the other hand, those who oppose both are ignoring the fact that investigating fertilised eggs can help to avoid the unwanted, spontaneous abortion of a more developed embryo later.

Religious fanatics confuse the issue by talking about 'the unborn child' and 'little human beings'. The embryo is not a child at all – only a potential child. It is, of course, human, but not a human being – only a potential human being. And to equate a potential human being with an actual human being is sheer superstition.

Certainly, the embryo contains the 'blueprint' for making a complete human being – but so does a fragment of flesh scraped from a grazed knee! Even though the embryo has been 'switched on' to put the blueprint into effect, it is just as remote from the baby it may one day become as a piece of frog-spawn is from a frog, or an acorn from an oak-tree. Yet there are doctors of medicine who, choosing to put their religious ideology before scientific fact, deliberately confuse these very different sorts of entity. One such – Dr Walter Hedgcock – was quoted in 1982 as saying that experimenting on fertilised human eggs was 'like pinning a baby down on a board and doing experiments on it'. The front page of the *Freethinker* for November of that year quoted my reply that this was 'tantamount to saying that boiling a breakfast egg that has been fertilised is like throwing a live chicken into boiling water'.

Opponents of even the moderate Warnock proposals include Lord Denning, who ought to know better – and who hasn't even the excuse of being a Catholic. He has actually declared that, from the moment of conception, a zygote must have the full rights of a human being.

During the first few days after conception, the embryo is no more than an undifferentiated cluster of cells, about the size of a full-stop. Not only is it incapable of feeling anything, it is not even an individual, but could still become twins, triplets, etc.

So much for the idea of an individual soul – which is the basis for the whole irrational outcry. The Catholic who maintains that an immortal soul could be present from the moment of conception has quite a problem to solve: if the zygote becomes twins or triplets or quads, are more souls created as required, or does the one already created divide with the physical cells?!

The number of individuals that the zygote is going to develop into is not finally determined until about the fifteenth day, with the development of the 'primitive streak'. That is why the Warnock Committee recommended a statutory limit of 14 days – a limit which obviously errs on the side of caution, as a sop to the religionists. If only the period for embryo experimentation were extended to 30 days, which is still well before there is any possibility of consciousness, a much wider range of congenital diseases could be diagnosed and averted. And since brain death is rightly accepted as the criterion for organ donation, the reverse criterion of the start of the development of a functional nervous system – i.e. at about 38 days – would be rational for embryo research.

Even at a later stage of development, the embryo is nothing like a human foetus, let alone a human baby. It has far less consciousness than a maggot – and we know how anglers treat maggots, without even the justification that the embryo experiments have of adding to human knowledge and solving problems of infertility, of miscarriages, and of congenital defects.

While the atheist ethical standpoint is consequentialist, and mainly utilitarian, religious believers generally have an absolutist ethical standpoint, based on what they like to call 'natural justice'. And that, essentially, is the difference between the two sides in the IVF argument.

All right-minded people – atheists and religionists alike – agree that there are moral limits to what we can do to a human being, whatever the benefits to humanity may be. But then we have to decide what sorts of entity constitute a human being; and that is where we differ.

Religionists – taking the absolutist line that all human life is sacred and in God's hands – generally see no reason to look into the biological facts, but simply assert 'Life begins at conception'. However, this is not so: life is a continuum. Life is present in the sperm and in the unfertilised egg. Fertilisation is just one stage in the human life cycle – an important stage, certainly, but not even an essential one; for cloning is possible, and the cloning of other mammals is already being carried out.

Some religious opponents of IVF, when they realise that life is thus a continuum, twist the argument to another absolutist one, saying that since there is no stage at which life can be said to begin we must accord it human rights at every stage. But this is patently absurd: in the name of common-sense, we should treat all life as it is, not as it might one day become, nor (to switch to the euthanasia situation) as it once was.

The disquietingly large free vote (238 to 66) in the House of Commons on February 15 [1985] in support of the Powell Bill indicates either an incredible degree of biological ignorance on the part of our legislators, or else their craven response to the Roman Catholic and fundamentalist Protestant lobby. Certainly, several of the 44 Labour MPs who voted for the Bill's second reading represent constituencies with a large RC population or are themselves RC; and Cardinal Hume circularised the whole House beforehand, urging MPs to support the Bill.

The Christian pressure groups, Life (led by Prof. Jack Scarisbrick) and SPUC (led by Mrs Phyllis Bowman), had been busy since November [1984] collecting signatures to a petition against 'embryo abuse'. Bundles of petition sheets, said to contain two-million signatures – if so, the largest petition since the People's Charter 150 years ago – were presented to Parliament during the morning of 15 February by Mr Norman St John-Stevas (himself, of course, RC). He and Mr Selwyn Gummer and the 168 other Conservative MPs who backed the Powell Bill did so in defiance of the wishes of the Prime Minister herself, who is known to favour implementation of the far more reasonable (though still over-cautious) Warnock Committee's Report and who had planned a government-sponsored Bill to this effect.

One of the Catholic Conservative MPs, Sir Hugh Rossi, went so far as to say he would have liked an even tougher Bill than Mr Powell's. Presumably he meant one that would disallow all assisted fertilisation. Tragic though this would be, not only for thousands of infertile couples but for medicine in general, it would at least make more sense than the Powell Bill, as it stands. For that, while allowing IVF, could be interpreted as making it a criminal offence to reject defective embryos. Instead, they would be required to be implanted in the mother, even though the result would be a miscarriage, or a seriously defective foetus (necessitating a later abortion?!), or infection of the mother with a fatal disease. Such protective legislation for the embryo at the expense of foetuses and human beings also ignores the fact that in nature most embryos are rejected – 60 per cent of them, it is calculated, before the mother even realises she is pregnant. If it is 'playing God', as they say, to reject abnormal embryos and choose a normal one for implanting into the mother, then it must be 'playing God' to preserve those that nature itself would reject.

Another requirement under the present Bill is that couples who wish to have children with the aid of IVF (because of some medical bar to conceiving them in the natural way) will have to apply beforehand to the Secretary of State (presumably through an official of the DHSS) for a permit to do so – surely the first instance of statutory government interference with the right of a man and woman to procreate. And, even if granted, the permit will expire after four months, which may be too soon in some cases to complete the treatment. The penalty for failure to comply with this provision will be, for the doctor, an unlimited fine and/or a prison sentence of up to two years.

Rationalists may have underestimated the need to counter the rabid religious propaganda on this issue with the widespread dissemination of factual information. Since no specific organisation seems to have been set up to do this work, perhaps it should be undertaken by the National Secular Society while the Bill is in committee. We need to educate not only the general public in the matter, but parliamentarians and others who will otherwise, out of sheer ignorance, interfere with the rights of individuals, restrict medical treatment, and halt scientific progress. It would also mean a brain drain to the USA, where embryological research will continue.

The week before the Bill was introduced, the RC Archdiocese of Glasgow organised a conference to discuss the Catholic response to the Warnock Report. 'We need to give the embryo legal status to preserve its dignity' was the ludicrous message that Dr John Finnis – Catholic Reader in Law at Oxford University – gave the conference. Even more emotive was the speech delivered by Dr Teresa Iglesias – a Catholic research officer of the RC foundation, the Linacre Centre for the Study of the Ethics of Health Care (London). She declared: 'If Warnock's findings are made law, the embryo, like the nineteenth-century slave, will not be seen as a real human being, but a thing with no soul of its own, to be used in any way for the benefit of humanity'. And she went on to announce, categorically, that 'God became an embryo'.

Another speaker at the Glasgow conference was the director of the Linacre Centre, Mr. Luke Gormally, who, referring to the *Lancet's* description of this 'vociferous minority', cried 'We must make ourselves a vociferous majority!'. Though a layman, he seems to be far more extreme on this and other issues in the realm of medical ethics (such as voluntary euthanasia) than are some of his senior colleagues, such as the Rev Dr John Mahoney, SJ, MA, DD, who is a leading Catholic theologian and spokesman on medical ethics from a more moderate standpoint.

With a superb sense of timing, another conference – the annual conference on medical ethics sponsored jointly by the London Medical Group and the Institute of Medical Ethics – happened to begin the very evening that the Powell Bill was introduced, and included one session on *in vitro* fertilisation. Dr Robert Edwards, the pioneer of this technique, was the medical speaker; Mr Scott Baker, QC, spoke on legal aspects; and Father Mahoney on ethical aspects.

When I first saw the printed programme, I was incensed that the contribution on the moral status of the embryo should be handed over to a Jesuit priest – even though I knew him to be a fairly progressive one – and I wrote to the organisers to this effect. However, I attended that session of the conference, as an observer, and found that Fr Mahoney read a surprisingly rational and balanced paper on this highly topical issue. Catholic MPs could well profit from a course of instruction from him.

He did, nevertheless, end on the inevitable note of unwarranted caution, saying that it is necessary to know more facts before society can come to any moral conclusions in the matter. This is certainly not so, since we know full well what an embryo is at different stages of its development, and its moral status can be based only on its actual characteristics at each stage – not on some metaphysical notion of potential.

Even at five weeks, the embryo is not only extremely rudimentary, it is hardly distinguishable from the embryos of other mammals at a similar stage of development – strong evidence, incidentally, of our close evolutionary links.

It is all too easy to slip into mental confusion when considering an entity that could, in particular circumstances, one day become a human being. Thus, emotive words constantly used in the current debate – 'innocent', 'helpless', and so on – are inappropriate or irrelevant in the context. Can an entity that is incapable of any sort of behaviour be 'innocent' – or guilty? Maggots and blue-bottles – to which such an attribute might be more appropriately applied – are, in this sense, 'innocent'; but few people would argue from this against killing any. As for the word 'helpless', it is totally irrelevant to the embryological debate. Of course an embryo outside a uterus is helpless – but if it is never going to reach a level of development at which it could have any inkling of its situation, what does it matter? Even in the uterus, the embryo is vulnerable to damage from natural infections, such as rubella – and this *does* matter, especially if the damaged foetus is allowed to develop into a child with distressing handicaps.

Finally, as an indication of one's true moral priorities, imagine being able to save one thing only from a burning house, the choice being between an embryo in a test-tube and a newborn baby. Would you need to hesitate before deciding between them? Even if the choice were between a human embryo in a test-tube and a frightened puppy, there could surely, in the name of compassion, be only one moral decision.

[March 1985]

[This article, off-printed as an illustrated pamphlet, was distributed to all MPs, after which Powell's Bill was unexpectedly defeated.]

My Path from Rome

[Autobiographical]

OH, YES – I once had an orthodox creed. I was brought up in a devout Roman Catholic family, and had an old-style convent education – and throughout my childhood and adolescence I was a steadfast believer. That was in the days (before the Second Vatican Council) when the Catholic Church was still Catholic and the Pope was infallible – so I had absolute certitude about God and the universe and my place in it. But in the end – and it took me a very long while – I grew up.

Whenever I mention my Catholic childhood, people tend to assume that the reason I have rejected religion so completely is that an extreme version of it was drummed into me as a child – but it wasn't like that at all. No one needed to drum religion into me: I lapped it up like a thirsty puppy. Of course, I must have been given the taste for it first of all, but I cannot remember as far back as that. What I do remember, though, is that my four younger sisters and one younger brother were coaxed to say, as the first syllables that ever passed their lips, not 'Mama' or 'Dada', but the far more difficult 'Jesus' – so presumably I was equally precocious. Anyway, by the time the good nuns got hold of me, at the age of four, I was hooked on the supernatural.

At home, as in most large families, we were always playing competitive games among ourselves – and Rule Number One, which became standard for any competitive family game, was 'No praying'. This was at the insistence of the others, who thought that praying would give me an unfair advantage.

This indicates that at home I was regarded as the pious one of the family – which is saying a great deal – and the nuns at my first convent school seem to have cast me in the rôle of a future saint. Whenever there was any school entertainment, I was given some religious poem to recite, and once, when they put on a little play in which Jesus appeared, I was given that rôle, without any competition – though, admittedly, my auburn curls may have contributed to the choice.

There was a large sentimental painting on our classroom wall of a guardian angel hovering protectively over a child on the edge of a precipice – and I accepted it quite literally. I never got on a bus or a train without quickly reminding my guardian angel to keep an eye out for danger.

My gullibility embraced not only the supernatural and miraculous, but also the magical. Amazing though it may seem in these days of advanced childhood knowledge, I was actually ten years old by the time I realised that Christmas presents were not really left by an old red-coated gentleman coming down the chimney. When I upbraided my mother for having told me such lies, she protested that Santa Claus did, in a sense, exist – as the personification of generosity and giving. But it was too late to give me a metaphorical explanation. I had accepted the myth literally for too long.

Empathising with younger children on whom the same confidence trick was being imposed, I embarked on a crusade around the neighbourhood, telling all the kids that there was no Santa Claus. This reached the ears of the father of a neighbouring family, who reproved me for spoiling it for the little ones. 'Spoiling it'! I could not understand what he meant. To my mind, they were being made fools of, and I was only saving them from this indignity. I now see this as the beginning of both my loss of faith and of my persistent missionary zeal in proclaiming scientific truth – but it was many years before Jesus went the way of Santa Claus.

On one occasion, when our family, together with a number of aunts, uncles, and cousins, were spending Sunday afternoon at Grandma's, our uncle priest offered a shilling to the best behaved child at the tea-table. When, after a tea-time of unusual restraint, the children were told they could leave the table, I was the only one who remained to say my grace – and that, of course, won me the shilling. The others protested that they too had remembered to say their grace after meals – but quietly, with a less ostentatious sign-of-the-cross. This, however, was apparently not believed. To this day, half a century later, some of my cousins still hold this shilling against me – maintaining that I cunningly planned the whole thing: but it is really not so. I would simply never have thought of eating even a biscuit without saying a grace both before and after.

As my sexual urges developed, I got all my sexual kicks out of contemplating the sufferings of Jesus – the masochism engendered by Christianity, as exemplified in medieval art – but, of course, I would have been horrified had I realised that this had anything to do with feelings associated with parts of the body that one was supposed not to notice. At that time, never having experienced orgasm in any context other than prayer and religious meditation, I interpreted it as one of the 'consolations of religion' – a phrase which I had often come across in the lives of the saints. Indeed, I still think that that is precisely what most of them meant by it. And when those of them who had taken a lifelong vow of chastity wrote in mid-life about 'the dark night of the soul', I think it was really the body they were referring to. Nowadays it is commonplace to say that religious emotions are akin to sexual feelings: but they are not just akin to them – in my experience, they are indistinguishable.

At my secondary school – also a convent – the other pupils laughingly referred to me as 'the saint', though I was fortunate in that my piety did not make me unpopular. Eventually, however, even the nuns told me to spend less time in church and the convent chapel, and more time in study. But they played on my masochism, and were always lending me devotional books and pamphlets about the religious vocation. My favourite book for years was the autobiography of St Therèse of Lisieux, *The Story of a Soul* – which I now regard as utterly sick, and sickening.

By the time I was fourteen, I had no wish to be anything but a nun – not in a teaching order, but in the Carmelite (enclosed) order. I was already saying up half my pocket-money towards my dowry – and I would gladly have entered at 15, as St Therèse did. But my mother said I must wait until the age of 19 to see if I changed my mind. She said the same to one of my sisters who, similar to me in temperament, is nine years younger than I – but whereas the second world war started when I was 16, and I then left school and went out first into the world of work and then into the Women's Royal Naval Service, my sister, in the post-war years, remained at school until the age of 19, and then went straight from one convent as a pupil into another as a novice, with no time between to change her mind. She is still a nun.

In my last year at school I was awarded the religious knowledge medal by the diocesan inspector because, when he unexpectedly departed from the set catechism questions and asked for a proof of Christ's divinity, I was the only pupil ready with an answer. To me it was obvious that God would not otherwise have given Jesus the power to perform miracles, since this would mislead people as to his divine claims. It did not occur to me at the time that it was an unproved assumption that the gospel stories were true. And no one pointed this out.

On other occasions, I would ask the nuns quite probing theological questions – but, of course, my teenage naïvety was no match for their comparatively sophisticated replies, and so, though generally of a questioning turn of mind, I accepted the Catholic creed *in toto*. Indeed, in those days of papal authority it had to be all or nothing; and I remember how amazed I was to hear of a Catholic who had given up practising yet had remained a believer in Christianity. For me, there was never any possibility of a halfway house between the Catholic Church and atheism.

At the same time, I must already have begun to fear a loss of faith, for I remember praying daily that this would never happen to me. It took ten more years to complete the process.

At the age of 19, when, at my naval training camp, I found that there was no provision for Catholics to hear Mass on 1st January (the Feast of the Circumcision) or 6 January (the Epiphany), which were then holy days of obligation, I successfully requested special 6 am 'liberty boats' for that purpose. How my fellow Catholics must have hated me for forcing them to go out on dark, wet mornings, instead of having another two hours in bed!

A year later I was in Ceylon (now Sri Lanka), where I served king and country for the next 21 months. There I not only mixed with non-Catholic Christians, with some of whom I used to discuss moral theology, but I also visited Hindu temples and Buddhist shrines, and so widened my perspective on religion. Consequently, by the time I returned home after the war, I was no longer sure I wanted to become a nun, though I was still a believer. However, my theological doubts now began to build up, and became more and more insistent.

In confession, I was told that I was suffering from intellectual pride. Who was I to pit my puny intellect against the teaching of Holy Mother Church? I saw the force of this argument – especially as there were important Catholic writers I admired, such as G K Chesterton, who, though obviously far more intelligent and learned than I, apparently had no difficulty in accepting doctrines that seemed to me to be irrational and at odds with the world around us. Now, of course, I realise that many people of undoubted mental ability manage to cling to their supernatural beliefs by keeping them, as it were, in different mental compartments from everyday knowledge, not subjecting them to the same sort of scientific scrutiny or rigorous evidence that they would demand for anything else.

As for the accusation of intellectual pride, surely the boot is on the other foot. Atheists don't claim to know *anything* with certainty – it's the believers who know it all.

At school, we were taught that there is no such thing as an atheist – and to some extent I think the nuns were right in this, because they took the word 'atheist' to mean someone who categorically denies the existence of any kind of god. Obviously, it must depend on the definition of the word 'god', which can mean anything from the very human and immoral Old Testament god, Jehovah, to some sort of abstract god, such as Bernard Shaw's Life Force, or even something as indisputable as the whole of existence. The only objection one can make to that last god-concept is to the confusing use of the word 'god' as a synonym for everything.

However, the one function that most gods seem to have in common is to give human existence some ultimate purpose – but, while it is not possible to disprove an ultimate purpose, there is no evidence for it. This is not to say, of course, that there is no purpose in life at all: as well as the collective purposes of human society, we all make our own individual purposes as we go through life. And life does not lose its value simply because it is not going to last for ever.

For most believers, however, the important thing is that death is *not* the end, either for themselves or for their relationship with close friends who have died. Most of us, probably, would find it comforting at times to believe that – but the fact that a belief is comforting obviously does not make it true. And I suppose, in common with other atheists, I just happen to be the sort of person who cannot derive comfort from a belief that lacks supporting evidence.

In fact, all the evidence is *against* personal survival of death. It just doesn't make sense. How could anything that survived the death of the body be the same person?

As for the idea that the universe was deliberately created, which is intended to explain existence, it manifestly fails to do so – for one is still left with the question of God's existence. It is less complicated to suppose that particles of matter and waves of energy have always existed than to suppose they were made out of nothing by a resourceful being that had always existed.

Besides, the idea of deliberate creation raises the moral problem of all the suffering there is in life, for so many people – and also for animals. I am ashamed, in retrospect, that I ever found it possible to worship the supposed creator of over-reproduction, sentient food, disease, and natural disasters. If I still believed in an omnipotent creator, I would have to heap curses on him – or her, or it. But if there is one thing to be said for this creator-god, it is his evident non-existence.

In the late 1940s, however, I was still trying to reconcile belief in his existence with the nature of the world around me – of which I had become more aware. Remembering from school theology lessons that Thomas Aquinas had said it was possible to come to faith through reason, I thought I would give my faith a boost through reason, stimulated by a course of reading. So I read book after book – mainly books written by Catholic apologists, but some by atheist philosophers too. And the more I read the less I could believe.

Finally, one Saturday morning in November 1949, standing by the philosophy shelves of my local public library, I suddenly said to myself, with a tremendous flood of relief, 'I am no longer a Catholic'. And that, for me, meant I was no longer a Christian, or theist of any kind.

After so much mental turmoil, I did not imagine at first that I had really come to the end of it; I expected to go on having doubts – doubts now about my disbelief. But in fact this never happened. I have never for one moment found any reason to suppose that my decision that morning 36 years ago was a mistake.

Cautiously, though, until the mid-1950s, I adopted the label 'agnostic' – only to find this was generally misunderstood as meaning that I was still sitting on the theistic fence: a position I had found so painful, and was so relieved to relinquish in 1949. So I began to declare myself an atheist and a humanist – which suited me far better.

That is not to say that I have not sometimes hankered after my old childhood comforter – but it is no more possible for me to go back to believing in a god and a heaven than it is to go back to the belief that an old red-coated gentleman climbs down chimneys with presents on Christmas Eve.

[January 1986]

The Turin 'Shroud'
[Gullibility of Scientists]

IT would be difficult to find anything less scientific than this BBC Science Unit statement, published in *The Listener* on 3 July: 'To suppose that a medieval European forger would have the knowledge to reproduce ancient Palestinian funerary anointments and the alkaline conditions of a white-washed tomb and post-mortem fever temperature would be to stretch credibility to the limit.' This presupposes some evidence that, assuming the image to be (as is almost certain) a medieval forgery, then the forger must have had this sophisticated knowledge – and there is no such evidence whatsoever.

The so-called 'shroud' bears traces of paint, and it is a matter of historical record that a 13th-century forger of relics confessed to making this particular artefact. At one time it was one of many 'true' shrouds of Jesus brought back from Palestine by crusaders as souvenirs; but, because this particular one was better done than most, it has survived to take in 20th-century wishful-thinkers – including a number of scientists, historians, and others who are prepared to jettison the principles of science and scholarship for the sake of faith, sensation, superstition, and the production of best-sellers.

The introduction of 'post-mortem fever' is a new idea, used as part of an absurd American stunt ('experiment' is too respectable a word) that attempted – and failed – to produce a similar image on a cloth wrapped round a hollow plastic mannikin filled with warm water. This is the only connection that 'post-mortem fever' has with the Turin relic – though 'shroud-fever' seems to have reached epidemic proportions.

[April 1986]

Muslim Schools
[Subsidised Fundamentalism]

THE National Secular Society is appalled by the news that the London Borough of Brent has decided that the Islamia Primary School in Brondesbury Park should be accorded voluntary-aided status.

This fundamentalist Muslim school, run by the Islamic Circle – which, among its many fanatical prohibitions, does not allow any musical instruments within the school walls – is thus likely to become the first (but hardly the last) voluntary-aided Muslim school in Britain.

Establishing separate Muslim schools out of rates and taxes may seem a progressive step, in line with multi-racial education and bilingualism; but in fact it would be a most divisive and irresponsible course of action, which the National Secular Society views with alarm – for Muslim (and Sikh) schools would not only segregate the children of Asian origin from the host population, they would also divide them from one another, importing to this country the religious strife and bitterness that exist on the Indian sub-continent. And they would inevitably exacerbate all the existing prejudice and discrimination against Asians.

Indeed, most responsible Asian community leaders themselves realise the danger of this, and are counselling their followers not to support the demands of a fanatical, short-sighted minority for separate education. Most Muslim parents also realise that state schooling is in the best interests of their children.

It is surely bad enough that we already have in this country Anglican, Roman Catholic, and Jewish schools that segregate children according to their religious background. The divisiveness that this causes – as is seen at its worst in Northern Ireland – would be greatly increased by the addition of denominational schools for immigrant religions, with segregation on the basis of skin colour as well as creed.

The National Secular Society which, since its inception in 1866, has campaigned for the abolition of all church schools, now points to the added danger that their existence poses today: making it impossible, in the name of equity, to refuse Muslims (and Sikhs) the same right to state-subsidised segregated schooling as Christians and Jews – with all the social harm that such a policy is sure to build up for future generations.

Parliament should therefore begin to phase out state subsidies to denominational schools of every kind and to encourage integrated schooling. This would also make economic sense, since not only is the dual system of education notoriously wasteful of resources but at least 85 per cent of the capital cost and 100 per cent of the running costs of church schools are paid for out of the public purse.

We are also opposed to the other Muslim demand, that their traditional faith and practices should be adequately provided for in the state sector. It is not for the school to provide for any religious teaching or practice. Schools are not to be used as part-time mosques – nor, for that matter, as part-time churches, synagogues, or temples. There are enough out-of-school hours for religious instruction and services without trespassing on the time required for legitimate school subjects.

If religion is taught at all in the county schools (as required under the present law, which we wish to see repealed), then certainly Islam should take its place alongside other world religions: provided, of course, that the teaching is objective, and that alternative world views – disbelief (including secular humanism) as well as a range of beliefs – are accorded comparable time and respect.

[May 1986]

Deaths of a King and a Commoner
[Mercy Killing]

> Two family doctors, fifty years apart, helped dying patients to die more quickly, with dignity. The first practitioner was famous for his bedside manner and the patronage of three generations of the royal family; the second, described by his own counsel as 'a man with a very blunt manner', has a National Health practice. Barbara Smoker, former chairman of the Voluntary Euthanasia Society, explains how the two cases came together in a remarkable way at the end of November 1986.

FROM 11 to 29 November [1986], Dr John Carr, a Yorkshire general practitioner, was in the dock at Leeds Crown Court, on a charge of attempted murder. He had, on 1 August, 1985, given a patient, Ronald Mawson, a lethal injection of phenobarbitone. Though the patient had died, the charge was *attempted* murder, since natural causes could not be ruled out. The accused pleaded Not Guilty, on grounds that he had miscalculated the dose in error. But as the evidence piled up, the outlook began to look black for him. Another similar case against him was (in the absence of the jury) mentioned. And the judge was clearly hostile to the prisoner.

Suddenly, on 26 November, as the trial drew to its close, the news broke in the mass media that Francis Watson (author of the book *Dawson of Penn)* had written an article for the December issue *of History Today,* 'The Death of George V', in which he revealed sensational details from the royal physician's extant (but hitherto unpublished) private notebook. At Sandringham, on the evening of Monday, 20 January, 1936, Dawson wrote as follows.

> At about 11 o'clock it was evident that the last stage might endure for many hours, unknown to the Patient but little comporting with that dignity and serenity which he so richly merited and which demanded a brief final scene. Hours of waiting just for the mechanical end when all that is really life has departed only exhausts the onlookers & keeps them so strained that they cannot avail themselves of the solace of thought, communion or prayer. I therefore decided to determine the end and injected (myself) morphia gr.¾ &

shortly afterwards cocaine gr.1 into the distended jugular vein: 'myself' because it was obvious that Sister B. was disturbed by this procedure.

A bulletin was broadcast on the wireless at ten minutes after midnight that the King had died peacefully at 11.55 pm, and the news of his death made the morning papers. That, it transpires, was one of Dawson's motives in hastening the end – 'the first announcement in the morning papers rather than the less appropriate evening journals' – and he had earlier telephoned his wife in London, requesting her to advise *The Times* (the paper that really mattered) to hold up its first edition for an announcement expected (confidently) at about midnight.

The details, withheld for more than fifty years, received considerable press coverage, but most of the papers treated it with a certain flippancy. *The Times,* to whose interest Dawson had given so much weight, now commented: 'Even in those days it was a bit above the odds to be tipped off that the king was about to die by the man who was killing him'.

The *Independent,* surely tongue in cheek, asked in its front-page headline 'Was George V's death treason?', and quoted a Law Society spokesman as saying 'If Queen Mary and the then Prince of Wales did knowingly consent to the King's life being prematurely shortened, they would both have been guilty as accessories to treason and murder.' The *Daily Telegraph* carried a cartoon (by Marc) in which an upper-class lady asks 'But surely, doctor, if it was alright for royalty it's good enough for Mother?' And, in the same issue, a leading article took the strangely British line that any blame should fall not on Dawson or the Queen or the Prince, but on Francis Watson, for having let the cat out of the bag, even though fifty years after the event.

The *Sunday Times* was most openly pro-euthanasia, contrasting George V's expeditious death with the lingering deaths of Churchill and Franco, and commenting 'Let the king, as the last public service of a public life, die with dignity and dispatch' – though, 'to a modern eye', Dawson's consideration of the morning, as opposed to the evening, papers, 'looks bad, carrying a double charge of snobbery and news management'.

Meanwhile, the judge summed up in the Carr case in Leeds, and the jury retired to consider their verdict. They cannot fail to have read the press comments on that other death, and to have been influenced by them in their opinions on the ethics of euthanasia.

Friday evening, the jury were still unable to reach a decision, and the court was, unusually, re-convened for the Saturday. The judge, obviously thinking that their tardiness was due, in all probability, to a single ultra-liberal juror holding up a proper unanimous conviction, told the jury that he would now accept a majority verdict of ten to one (the twelfth juror having dropped out). When it finally came, the verdict was, to everyone's amazement (and most people's delight), Not Guilty.

The judge seemed to regard it as a perverse verdict, since he refused costs to the defence. The media, though more sympathetic, also treated it as a perverse verdict, ignoring the doctor's 'accidental' plea and commenting on the case as one of active euthanasia. Even if it were, there was no evidence that it was explicitly voluntary. Nor was there in the case of George V. But in those pre-war days, patients were rarely told the truth about a poor prognosis, whereas there has been a welcome move in the past few decades towards patient autonomy and informed consent in the matter of treatment. In the final decision, however, the patient, who is the person most concerned, is still, because of the law, generally denied any say as to the manner and timing of his or her own death. Only when voluntary euthanasia is legalised will doctors he able to act openly in their patients' best interests and thus respond to their last wishes.

Coincidentally, just two weeks after the King's death, the Voluntary Euthanasia (Legalisation) Society (founded in 1935) set up a consultative legal council to draft a parliamentary bill to legalise voluntary euthanasia. The resulting Bill was introduced, unsuccessfully, into the House of Lords in November 1936 – and one of the peers who spoke and voted against it was, ironically, Lord Dawson of Penn. In his view, it was for doctors, not patients, to decide on the most advantageous time of death – all things being considered.

And to this day the law remains unchanged.

[January 1987]

Sorry – You've Been Duped
[Book Review]

[*You've Been Duped* by Melvin Harris (Weidenfeld & Nicolson, £9.95)]

SUB-TITLED 'The Truth Behind Classic Mysteries of the Paranormal', this book is well researched and conclusive. It would, if reason prevailed, surely be the last word on the subject – but of course it won't be.

'Cryptamnesia' is shown to be a far more likely explanation for 'past life regressions' than is 'the extravagant notion of reincarnation'.

One paragraph, in a chapter on spiritualists, really sums up the situation.

> Am I being unfair? Hardly! The claims these people make violate all logic and are at loggerheads with everyday experiences. If they are true, then it is up to them to demonstrate that truth. Yet none of these claimants ever submitted themselves to informed and impartial examination. They reserve their antics for believers. And, tragically, believers have a terrible tendency to go on believing, come what may.

Unrelenting, the author pursues the facts behind the fantasies.One of his methods is to show how the early versions of a story become more and more sensational with each telling. Such is the case with the alleged horrors of Amityville (Long Island). Based on little more than a window that (having counterweights that were too heavy) appeared to open of its own accord, the story was built up by an imaginative home-owner into a bestseller and a money-spinning film, the latter being billed as 'more hideously frightening then *The Exorcist* because it actually happened!'

Spiritualist claims – including such phenomena as spirit healing, voice mediums, clairaudience, clairvoyance, the once-popular slate-writing, materialisations, apports, and spirit photographs (of which a number of instructive and amusing examples are reproduced) are all dealt with.

It is clear that spiritualists themselves admit freely that there is both fraud and self-deception in their ranks, yet they cling to belief in a few 'valid' cases – meaning those that have not yet been exposed. And even when a medium is caught out, the claims of validity are still made for him or her on other occasions.

One famous spirit photographer who got away with it during his lifetime was discredited sixty years later, when his alleged spirit photograph of a little girl was found to be a blurred copy of a sentimental Victorian poster.

The most cruel practice of mediums, dowsers and other such charlatans is in connection with missing children. The father of Genette Tate is quoted as saying: 'We discovered that the work of the psychics was not just ludicrous and laughable. It was sinister and evil. Once we got into that web of deceit – and that was what it was – we found it very hard to struggle free. None of it ever led anywhere except to despair and disappointment, misery and confusion.'

A series of sex murders, such as those of Jack the Ripper and the Yorkshire ditto, will always attract these psychic sleuths 'with pendulums and maps, crystal balls, trances and séances and group meditations, to list just some of the strange methods employed', and they are loud in their later claims of success, though they have actually succeeded only in wasting police time and resources. Melvyn Harris takes us through the data.

War, too, breeds psychic phenomena. Like the gospel stories, the story of the ghostly regiments of the Dardanelles campaign in 1915 was, it transpires, not written down for fifty years! The legend of the angels of Mons in 1914 was more contemporary, but Mr Harris shows how it began as a patriotic short story about St George materialising with a large company of archers to help the English soldiers, and how the story was soon being retold as fact by the religious press. In later versions, the bowmen were transformed into shining angels and in that form the story persists to this day.

Nostradamus, alleged apparitions at the exact moment of a violent death, the curse that sank a battleship and the myths surrounding assassinations, are all grist to Mr Harris's meticulous mill. During the first eight months of 1939, it seems, spirit guides galore were busy forecasting that there would be no war against Hitler! Crashed planes invariably give rise to psychic stories of precognition – but in this book, such stories are investigated and exposed for the lies that they are.

I find the style rather too tabloid for my taste, but that might be all to the good if it is to be read by people who really need to read it. Speaking for myself, I must admit that, since I have never placed any credence in any of this nonsense, I find even its exposure somewhat tedious; but the book will certainly be useful for reference the next time someone challenges me to explain one of these 'true' stories.

[March 1987]

Vatican Sex-Instruction Manual

A Vatican *'Instruction'* prepared by the Congregation for the Doctrine of the Faith and issued on 10 March [1987], with the explicit approval of the Pope, has divided the Church in developed countries, has brought distress to many Catholics – especially to childless couples – and has been received outside the Church with some amazement and not a little ribaldry. It is here discussed by the president of the National Secular Society.

THE Church of Rome has surpassed itself. This high-handed pronouncement, which strikes at science, reason and compassion, rivals the gagging of Galileo and the denunciation of Darwin.

It is a measure of its reaction that when the first 'test-tube baby', Louise Brown, was born in 1978, the then Pope, John Paul I (just before his untimely and mysterious death) welcomed her birth and said he had nothing to say against the manner of her conception. Now, under his successor and namesake, the Vatican has found plenty to say against it.

Paradoxically in view of the Church's general unease about the sex act, in this document it effectively rules out any artificial aids to conception that would by-pass the 'conjugal act specific to the love between spouses'. Thus, it not only forbids surrogate motherhood and AID (artificial insemination by donor), but even AIH (artificial insemination by husband), especially in conjunction with *in vitro* fertilisation.

Anticipating this Vatican prohibition of AIH-IVF, a team of doctors in a Catholic medical centre in Ohio had already developed a Heath Robinson modification (first thought up at Monash University, Melbourne) of the *in vitro* fertilisation technique, to satisfy the prophesied strictures of those gynaecological experts, the Vatican cardinals. This modification (known as TOT) is specifically designed to meet the Church's stated objections to the usual IVF method. These objections are two-fold: first, that the sperm is obtained by masturbation; secondly, that fertilisation takes place outside the mother's body.

The first difficulty is overcome by collecting sperm during intercourse, in a specially perforated condom – the perforations allowing a sufficient chance of fertilisation to make the act licit. However, the Catholic geneticist associated with the perforation programme comments 'There's not a large market for them'. (Further comment I will leave to a less puritan pen than mine – that of the editor, in his News and Notes column.)

The second objection proved more resistant, but has been successfully overcome by separating the extracted eggs from the sperm by a bubble of air in a tube, which is then placed into position so that its contents can be blown into the woman's fallopian tube – assuming that she has at least one fallopian tube partly open. Presumably the bubble bursts, and Bob's your baby.

After all that, it is devoutly to be hoped that the Vatican will smile benevolently upon these ludicrous procedures.

In this country, the *Instruction* has been welcomed by Cardinal Basil Hume as 'the official teaching of the Church', though Mgr Vincent Nichols (Secretary to the Catholic Bishops' Conference of England and Wales) has said that the second part of it 'cuts across the natural and proper emotional response to infertility'. And Fr Jack Mahoney, SJ (Professor of Moral Theology at King's College, London), who has consistently taken a comparatively progressive line on embryo research, voluntary euthanasia and other bio-ethical issues, contributed to the *Independent* (11 March) a courageous comment on the document, questioning its whole underlying assumption that the early human embryo must be accorded the status, dignity and natural rights of a human person.

He points out that since it is now known that an early embryo can cleave into genetic twins, which can apparently then even recombine, 'the fundamental question is not, as the Vatican *Instruction* asks, "how could a human individual not be a human person?", but whether the early human embryo can properly be called an individual, in the sense of having arrived at a stage of irrevocable biological development and stability as a necessary prerequisite for further growth'.

Most freethinkers with any grasp of philosophy would, of course, go considerably further than that. We would surely argue that status, dignity, and natural rights belong to entities by virtue of what those entities actually *are,* not by virtue of what they have the potential to become. And what they actually are must include the possibility of their possessing some sort of consciousness before they can have any call on such moral concern.

However, credit must be given to Catholics like Fr Mahoney for at least a modicum of scientific thinking in opposition to the official line of the Vatican – a line that, on family and sexual issues, has been pushed further and further back during the present pontificate.

As for schoolgirl Louise Brown and, by now, the thousands of other perfectly normal 'test-tube' children, Fr Mahoney writes – with a degree of humanity and common-sense that puts his ecclesiastical superiors to shame: 'And a child born of IVF and AIH might well be considered fortunate to be born of a couple who long so much for it that they have gone to such loving lengths to procreate it and therefore to cherish it.'

[April 1987]

Religion in Schools
[The Secularist Case for Abolition]

> The National Secular Society has consistently campaigned against the religious clauses of the 1944 Education Act. It warned that the state financing of church schools would prompt non-Christian religious groups to demand the same privileges, thus increasing the indoctrination and segregation of children. The NSS president's submission to the Department of Education and Science, as follows, gives the Society's views on the Government's proposed changes in the education laws.

WE agree that changes in the education laws are very much needed, and the proposals to give schools greater flexibility with regard to the daily collective worship and to religious instruction (removing the compulsion on state schools, introduced in 1944) are certainly steps in the right direction.

The religious clauses of the 1944 Education Act were contentious even then, and this Society was among those that opposed them at the time, but the social changes that have taken place since then, particularly the decline in Christian adherence (with increases both in non-belief and in non-Christian religions) in this country, has made the 1944 provisions increasingly anomalous and unworkable.

Two of the reasons why non-Christian religious leaders are demanding public funding for their own denominational schools are (a) that it is patently unjust that they should be denied this as long as there are heavily subsidised RC and CofE schools, and (b) that they object to their children being taught their own religion by teachers who do not believe in it. Both these objections would be removed if (a) all denominational schools were to be phased out, and (b) neither religious teaching nor religious worship took place in school hours in the state (i.e. county) schools.

The National Secular Society favours an open, pluralist policy, and opposes segregation on grounds of religion, sex or skin colour. We see denominational schools as socially divisive; as often denying to the children of immigrant families the basic right of contact with children from the wider community and access to ideas at variance with those of their home background; and, of course, as economically wasteful. We would therefore urge Parliament to call a halt to all new applications for voluntary-aided status and to set a date for all existing voluntary-aided schools to become either self-supporting or to be absorbed into the state system.

Unless this is done, the present Muslim, Sikh and Jewish applications for voluntary-aided status for their own schools cannot in equity be opposed. And as soon as one of them is successful, it could open the floodgates to applications from Jehovah's Witnesses, Scientologists, Moonies, Rastafarians, Seventh-day Adventists, and all the rest.

We issued a press-statement in 1986 on the subject of denominational schools, bearing the names of distinguished people who had signed it. And we are gratified to note that Bishop Montefiore has recently come out with a similar statement.

As for religion in county schools, the most comprehensive statement of NSS policy is to be found in the House of Commons publication of Minutes of Evidence, 22 June 1981, to the Education, Science and Arts Committee (cmd no. 110-xii), which includes two long memoranda from the NSS to the Committee as well as my oral evidence on the date given.

In summary: the NSS says that schools should not be used as part-time churches, synagogues, mosques, or temples. There are enough out-of-school hours for religious instruction and services without trespassing on the time required for legitimate school subjects. We would like all religion to be dropped from school assemblies; RE to be cut out altogether; and moral education to be freed from its false association with religion. Facts about religion should, we think, be left to find their natural place in history and sociology lessons; but we agree with the British Humanist Association that, insofar as religious myths and doctrines *are* presented, they should be required to cover a representative range of religious and non-religious views – i.e. to be, in the BHA phrase, 'objective, fair and balanced'.

It is worth noting that in the USA – a country far more Christian than ours – religious teaching and practice in state schools is not only not compulsory, it is actually prohibited.

We are in favour of parental choice as far as this is compatible with local educational policy, with an appropriate ethnic mix, and with the rights of children. But it is important, in our view, that every school should more or less reflect the ethnic proportions in the general population of the catchment area – which would avoid the current situation in Kirklees, where apparently nearly all the Asian children are in one school and nearly all the white children in another, only a mile distant. And, as mentioned above, we do not think that parental choice should be allowed to override the basic right of every child to come into contact with a representative range of religious and cultural ideas. Unless children of different backgrounds mix together, we could be building up for the future the sort of community hostilities which denominational schools have helped to perpetuate in Northern Ireland.

[October 1987]

Apathy, not Attack, is Negativism

[Editorial Report by William McIlroy]

'GIVE me down-to-earth negativism every time', declared Barbara Smoker in her presidential address to the annual general meeting of the National Secular Society at Conway Hall, London, on 14 November [1987]. 'It is undeniable that the negative approach is not invariably unworthy', she said.

Miss Smoker recalled that about 25 years ago she was named as one of the Top Ten Non-Smokers of the Year, obviously for the publicity in her surname. 'The *Daily Mail*, realising that I was opposed not only to tobacco but also to religion and the Establishment, carried a full-page feature article on me, describing me as an utterly negative person, against the defence of this country, against prisons, against Christian values, and even (horror of horrors!) against Christmas. Though I was rather flattered by the article, a number of my friends wrote in to the paper, complaining that it had given an entirely false killjoy image of me.

'The point is surely that the only kind of unremitting negativism is apathy, not attack', she added. 'Everything that is attacked has its obverse, "positive" side. If you are against war, you are for peace; if you are against privilege, you are for equality; if you are against censorship, you are for freedom of speech; if you are against superstition, you are for reason; if you are against humbug, you are for honesty; and if you are against mystical obscurantism, you are for freethought.

'The National Secular Society is often denigrated for not being more "positive" – and this gibe comes not only from its religious opponents, but also from many of its friends in the humanist movement. They presumably mean that instead of wasting our time attacking unreason and injustice we should simply enjoy whatever reason and justice we can find. But that is to fiddle while Rome burns. It is saying "I'm all right, Jack" while others are far from all right.

'People can provide their own positive pleasures in accordance with their own tastes, if only society allows them the space and freedom. It is the essential work of the NSS to clear enough space and remove obstructions to freedom. A gardener may enjoy planting out flowers and produce, but unless he – or someone else on his behalf – has already weeded the ground and is willing to go on weeding around the plants as they grow, the garden will never flourish.'

[December 1987]

The Human Embryo
[Letter on NSS Policy]

S J NICHOLLS (Letters, November) picks a lot of holes in the National Secular Society's submission to the DHSS on proposed legislation on embryo research.

First, he says that our suggestion of the limitation of research to the 35 or 38 days' development stage is no less arbitrary than the Warnock recommendation of 14 days. Any point of time chosen is obviously arbitrary, since development is gradual, but the criterion should be relevant, and we contend that the beginning of the development of a functional nervous system at about five weeks is the most relevant factor in the embryo's gradual acquisition of rights, while the 14-day criterion of an end to the possibility of twinning is, except for those who believe in 'ensoulment', utterly irrelevant. When Mr Nicholls says that consciousness in the embryo 'may well begin early on', he surely cannot really mean before a functional nervous system has even begun to develop?

As for his statement that 'there is no qualitative change in the developing embryo throughout the whole gestation period', this is obviously absurd. Though there are no sudden changes, there are certainly important qualitative changes taking place throughout its gradual development. Is an acorn the same as a mature oak-tree? If so, why do we care so little about the trillions of acorns wasted each year, yet mourn the destruction of mature trees in the recent hurricane?

Mr Nicholls suggests that a newborn baby's intrinsic worth is equal to that of a child of three, but I would firmly deny that. At birth a baby has very limited awareness, has no idea of any future, and has no real stake in life, while a normal three-year-old is a little person, with personal relationships and a concept of life and time – the very things that give human beings full status and rights.

Mr Nicholls derides the comparison between an early embryo and a fragment of flesh from a grazed knee – but in fact they contain the very same reproductive DNA. Only their environment is different. You could produce a new human being from a fragment of flesh if you went through the right cloning processes. 'You might as well compare a twig with a seed', he says; but why not? Doesn't he know you can propagate a new plant from a cutting as well as from a seed?

Finally, Mr Nicholls says that if we want to limit embryo research to the five-week development stage, we are inconsistent unless we campaign against induced abortion beyond that stage. But no one advocates deliberately bringing about a human conception in order to abort it. Abortion is always regarded as the lesser of two evils – the greater evil being to force a woman to continue with an unwanted pregnancy. We rightly demand even more serious grounds for an abortion in the later stages of pregnancy – for instance, that the mother is a schoolgirl, that the pregnancy was the result of incestuous rape, or that the foetus has been diagnosed as defective.

Whereas embryo research is carried out for the sake of human knowledge in general, an abortion is carried out for the sake of the actual mother or of the potential baby. We would never countenance biological experimentation on a human being for the sake of human knowledge in general; only for that person's own welfare.

B S (President, National Secular Society)
[December 1987]

Another Law for Religion
[Unwarranted Exemptions]

AT LAST a responsible columnist, Polly Toynbee, in her *Guardian* article 'The Veil of Tears' (4 February), has dared to risk outraged charges of repression and racism in speaking out honestly on the dangers of fundamentalism, especially among immigrant religions.

Of course we must deplore the imprisonment of anyone anywhere on religious grounds, however fanatical their beliefs and personal practice, but if someone like Melika Salihbegovic is to be granted political asylum in this country, something should be done to deter her from coercing others to follow her lifestyle and impose it on their children.

Many Muslim families resident in this country are already subjecting their children – especially their girls – to an incompatible double culture that often leads to the tragedy of mental illness and even to teenage suicide. Separate Islamic schools aggravate and perpetuate this situation, and now there is a vociferous demand from fundamentalist Muslim leaders that such schools be granted voluntary-aided status. As long as Roman Catholic schools are heavily subsidised in this way, it is not easy to resist the argument that similar public funding cannot, in equity, continue to be denied to Muslim, Sikh, and other religious schools.

Another law that plays into the hands of religious fundamentalists, of every type, is their automatic entitlement to charity status on grounds of religion, so that they are exempted from all direct taxation and (statutorily) from half the local rates. This legal privilege, dating from 1601, is based on the principle that all religion is beneficial – and even the most harmful of the fundamentalist sects and modern fringe cults continue to cash in under this law.

Similarly, places of religious worship are exempted from the general provisions of our planning laws. One consequent piece of vandalism was the destruction in Spitalfields in 1986 of the most complete 18th-century galleried interior in London, in order to convert the building into a mosque. Supporters of Save Britain's Heritage, the Society for the Protection of Ancient Buildings, and other such bodies, were in tears on the pavement outside, but could do nothing against this anomalous religious privilege under the law.

Last October, the Government decided against implementing the recommendations of their own advisory body, the Farm Animal Welfare Council, to put an end to the religious slaughter of animals for meat without pre-stunning. The National Secular Society sent an open letter to the Minister of Agriculture, protesting against the Government's thus giving precedence to the cruel practices of ancient Palestine and 7th-century Arabia over our own comparatively humane slaughter regulations. The Jewish and Muslim communities each deny that their own method of slaughter (which differs one from the other) is cruel – but, significantly, each accuses the other of cruelty!

Not only does Britain allow religious exemption from its general slaughter laws; halal meat is actually on the daily menu of many of our county schools, for the sake of orthodox Muslim pupils – though there could surely be no genuine objection to the daily provision of vegetarian dishes instead.

It is high time that our laws were made universally binding in this country.

[March 1988]

A Spasm of Schism

[The Magic of Apostolic Succession]

> On 30 June, the Church of Rome, confronted by an obstinate old man, Marcel Lefebvre, succumbed to its first major schism since 1902; three weeks later, at the Lambeth Conference, the international Anglican Church, confronted by women priests with episcopal ambitions, was threatened with a similar schism. In both cases, the underlying cause was the magic powers of bishops conferred in the supposed apostolic succession. A bishop may lose his jurisdiction, may even be excommunicated – but since he is a link in the living chain of magic ritual, his sacramental powers can never be taken from him.

THE coincidence of schism striking simultaneously at the Roman Catholic and Anglican churches is matched by the irony of the timing of it – a time of ecumenical fervour when, in response to the common enemy of disbelief, there is a concerted drive to paper over the earlier schisms within Christianity, and even to form an extended religious family with the non-Christian religions of Judaism, Islam, and the various strands of Hinduism. The heady ecumenical vision is of reconciliation of all the major Christian sects and of friendly relations with all the major world religions. But it is the new disputes within each sect that tend to prove the most intransigent.

Indeed, ecumenism itself is a basic cause of both disputes. In the RC fold, it gave rise a quarter of a century ago to the historic Second Vatican Council, the far-reaching ecumenical reforms of which were bound to upset traditionalists within the Church.

As for the Anglican communion, even the elasticity that is its main characteristic has been stretched to breaking point by its attempts to meet with Rome on the one hand and the various evangelicals on the other. One obdurate issue of contention has been that of women priests, on which a truce has been maintained for some years by allowing them in some national churches and postponing the evil day in others. By now, however, there are thousands of Anglican women priests in the USA, some of whom were ordained as long ago as men who are beginning to be considered as candidates for episcopal promotion – and in a society opposed to sex discrimination, the day of women bishops can be postponed no longer. But could a mere woman receive episcopal powers in the apostolic succession? In the eyes of those who think so, a female bishop would be empowered to ordain priests, and if those priests were recognised as valid priests in some parts of the Anglican communion and not others, that could only mean schism.

However, it is the RC schismatic upheaval that has caused the most stir. Just as the previous schism of the Old Catholics, spreading from Germany to a number of other countries from 1870 to 1902, resulted from their rejection of the First Vatican Council – particularly its definition of papal infallibility – so the present schism results from the rejection, by the French Archbishop Marcel Lefebvre and his supporters, of the Second Vatican Council's ecumenical reforms: for religious liberty, participation by the people in liturgical rites, and the revised Mass in the vernacular.

It is said that on the very day the Council ended (8 December, 1965), Lefebvre declared to some friends with whom he was sitting in a café near St. Peter's that he would never accept the conclusions of the Council in which he had been a participant.

The rejection of papal infallibility by the Old Catholics made it comparatively easy for them to defy the Vatican, but the fact that Lefebvre has always been a stickler for papal authority adds a paradoxical element to his rebellion.

However, eighteen years have now passed since he first openly raised the banner of revolt in 1970, founding the Priestly Fraternity of St Pius X (dedicated to the pope who was the scourge of modernism in the years 1908 and 1909) and opening his first seminary in Switzerland for future priests – eighteen years during which he has hardened his position as the professed upholder of the one true faith and of Catholic tradition, and has come to regard the present pope as one of the 'anti-popes' of history, whose names have subsequently been expunged from the official list of popes. At the same time, Lefebvre's claims for himself and his new bishops have hitherto been carefully limited to the pastoral power of Order (*pastestas ordinis*), not extended to the power of Jurisdiction, which would set them up as a separate sect, like the Orthodox and Protestant Churches.

Seen in this light, his revolt does not amount to schism – though the official Vatican daily paper, *L'Osservatore Romano* (in a front-page, black-bordered article), declared the consecration of the new bishops to be a schismatic act.

Since it takes a bishop in the apostolic succession to pass that succession on to new priests and bishops, the Old Catholics were faced a hundred years ago with pastoral extinction within one generation – but then an heretical Dutch bishop offered them the laying on of his hands to ordain not only new priests but, more importantly, new bishops who could in turn ordain new priests and bishops. Consequently, there are still today some 2·4 million members of the Old Catholic communion.

Lefebvre's consecration of four new bishops of his own choosing on 30 June [1988] was, according to BBC news bulletins, 'the last straw' that broke the Vatican's lengthy negotiations with him and thus caused the dreaded schism. But the use of a phrase like 'the last straw' shows the ignorance of the BBC – though it is not surprising that they should fail to grasp the significance of the new bishops, since even the Catholic press has skated around it. The possibility of creating his own bishops was the ace that Lefebvre had held in his hand for almost two decades, using it as a bargaining-counter to gain concessions and avoid excommunication. But he finally decided to play the ace, because, far from being a 'straw', it was crucial to the historical survival of his breakaway traditionalist group.

In eighteen years the group had proved to be viable – now boasting five seminaries and countless schools and churches, as well as the support of around one per cent of all Catholics – but hitherto, its supply of new priests had, apart from the uncertain continuation of an influx of dissident priests from Rome, depended on the ordination powers of only two aging bishops in the apostolic succession. The succession had to be secured.

In attempting to prevent the creation of new Lefebvrist bishops, with all the magic powers bestowed on the original twelve apostles, the Pope had, humiliatingly, and often secretly, given way to Lefebvre on point after point during the past few years, including a return to the Tridentine mass for those who want it. The Pope even offered in the end to appoint a younger bishop himself to the Society of Pius X, and the date of this proposed appointment had been agreed : 15 August, which marks the end of the great Marian year of pilgrimages, dedicated to papal supremacy within Christian unity, and which was to have been the day of the prodigal son's return to the bosom of Holy Mother Church. The agreement also incorporated the setting up of a Roman commission of liaison, comprising two of Lefebvre's members and three Vatican nominees, to help run the Society and give traditionalists more say in Church decisions.

Suddenly, however, Lefebvre decided that for traditionalists to be in a minority on the commission was not good enough, and to be allowed only one extra bishop – and that one with a suspect allegiance to the Pope (since his own four candidates had been turned down by the Sacred Congregation's prefect, Cardinal Ratzinger) – would not ensure the survival of the Lefebvrists until Rome saw the error of its ways and recognised the traditionalists as the repository of the one true faith. So, breaking the agreement he had already signed on 4 May, he defiantly wrote to the Pope on 2 June that on 9 June he would be consecrating his own four new bishops – unlawful bishops, but valid in their divine orders. The Pope replied on 9 June:

> 'I ardently invite you to return in full obedience to the Vicar of Christ. I not only invite, I ask you in the name of Christ. To this request and this invitation I add my daily prayers to Mary, Mother of Christ. Do not allow this year, dedicated in a particular way to the Mother of God, to strike another blow to her heart.'

But Lefebvre went ahead with his plans, and is now officially outside the Church – an octogenarian *enfant terrible* who has rocked the chair of St Peter.

The Vatican has responded by warning priests and laity not to 'adhere to the schism of Mgr Lefebvre, since they would incur *ipso facto* the grave penalty of excommunication'. Some will doubtless be frightened into renouncing support of Lefebvre's fraternity, but this will probably mean no more than a shake-out of his weaker supporters. The schism prevails.

[August 1988]

The Fraud of Turin

[Carbon-dating Tests on the 'Shroud']

When, at the end of August [1988], the news was leaked that the 'Shroud' of Turin had been scientifically proved to be less than seven hundred years old, many of its devotees refused to accept this verdict unless and until it was actually announced by the Vatican. The control fragments had, they said, been confused with the true ones; besides, there are still mysteries in it, they said, for no medieval forger could possibly have been clever enough to achieve such an accurate image; then, the carbon content of the atoms would, they said, naturally have been affected by a burst of radiation caused by a resurrection from the dead; alternatively, they said, God might have wrought a miracle thirteen centuries later; and in any case, they said, what really matters is the emotional effect that the mysterious image of a suffering man has on those who see it.

FROM the outset, the 'Shroud' industry had little to gain and everything to lose by having a scientific date put on the relic. Had it transpired that the flax from which the linen was made had grown during the Roman occupation of Palestine, it would not have proved that the relic was genuine, for doubters could still postulate a medieval forger who was sufficiently perfectionist to obtain an ancient piece of cloth; while the more likely finding, that the flax had grown many centuries after the alleged lifetime of Jesus, would inevitably weaken the shroud theory, even if some persistent believers managed to find ingenious ways round the scientific evidence.

However, the late deposed King Umberto II of Italy, who had owned the alleged shroud, was in favour of its being carbon-dated – which suggests that he believed in its authenticity. But the cathedral authorities in Turin, who were its *de facto* guardians, apparently had less faith in it, for they refused to allow such tests to be carried out, even when the improving techniques reduced to quite small fragments the pieces of cloth that would need to be destroyed in the process. Their reluctance was rational enough, as the relic was the cathedral's greatest material asset, bringing in a considerable revenue from gullible pilgrims. Umberto, however, outwitted the Archbishop of Turin by bequeathing the relic to the Pope, whom he understood to be in favour of carbon-dating – and whose wishes the Archbishop could not override as easily as those of a mere deposed king.

John Paul II thus became the owner of the Turin relic on Umberto's death (on 18 March, 1983), and last year [1987] gave his consent for a series of C-14 (carbon-dating) tests to be carried out on the relic. As their timing was, we were told, intended to be a celebration of the tenth anniversary of the Pope's accession, it seems that he genuinely believed the tests might produce a 'good' result.

The announcement of the carbon-dating verdict was originally to have been made on Good Friday this year, but negotiations with Turin caused delays, after which the number of separate tests was cut down from seven to three, and one of the two methods that were to have been used was cut out entirely. Eventually, however, the Vatican chose three laboratories – in Oxford, Zurich, and Arizona – to do the tests, which were to be carried out in the early summer, the findings being passed to the British Museum for identification and co-ordination.

Until that stage, they were supposed to be 'blind' tests, the samples being identified only by secret numbers; but since the unusual weave of the twill linen of the Turin relic was well known from the literature, it would be easy enough for the technicians to pick it out, or at least to eliminate some of the other samples. So the three laboratories were additionally placed under pledges of secrecy.

The Zurich and Arizona tests were completed in July, the results being made known to a few trusted believers only – though some of those few (including David Sox, on 'Sunday' on BBC Radio 4) began trying, all too obviously, to prepare the faithful for a disappointing result. Meanwhile, the Oxford technicians had lagged behind schedule, explaining that they had other jobs to do first – this one obviously not being regarded as anything special. Then, on completing its tests, Oxford apparently leaked its result to the Catholic Professor Richard Luckett in Cambridge, who, it seems, leaked it to the London *Evening Standard* – though Oxford's Professor Hall later denied both the leak itself and the century that was said to have been leaked.

The *Evening Standard* naturally made the most of its scoop on 26 August, devoting not only a main front-page slot to the story but also finding space for a comment on it in its Diary and for a feature article by Luckett. The national and overseas papers were left to follow on with the news the next day, some even citing the London *Standard* as their source. Three weeks later, the *Sunday Times* devoted almost a full page to the story as though the findings were unexpected.

The timing of the leak was acutely embarrassing for the Pope, as he was to pay an official visit to Turin the following week. Indeed, it was no doubt with this visit in mind that he had arranged that the results would then be known to him but not generally known – thus enabling him to make a sensational announcement himself there and then in the event of a 'good' result, but otherwise to hold it back until his visit was over.

Turin's intermediary in contact with the testing laboratories, Professor Luigi Gonella, did what he could to retrieve the situation by hastily announcing that one of the three laboratories had received no genuine sample at all – and suggesting that that laboratory was the Oxford one. It was not a very credible ruse, but at least it would postpone an admission of the truth until after the Turin papal visit.

Four weeks later, Gonella admits to being 'disappointed'. He said: 'It is like having a portrait in your attic that turns out not to be of your grandfather – but you don't love him the less.' On the day of the leak, 26 August, the Diary feature in the *Standard* quoted the immediate wriggling reaction of RC Group-Captain Leonard Cheshire, as follows.

> If you accept the idea of the Resurrection, you are already in the realms of something which science cannot understand. It is on the frontier of time and eternity. How do the scientists know that the Resurrection did not induce a change in the Shroud, imparting it with a false age?

The following morning, the *Daily Mail* published a full article by him under the banner heading 'Why I still believe in the Turin Shroud'. One of the reasons given is that the anatomical details of the image are so 'exact that no 14th-century artist could have got them right'. In fact, however, the professional makers of Christian relics at that time were so experienced and meticulous in the art that it is hardly surprising if the maker of this relic was clever enough to mystify pundits of the 20th century wanting to be mystified.

Cheshire also relates how, in the year 944, the ancient Mandylion of Edessa (bearing an image of the face of Jesus) is taken to Constantinople, where the cloth is unfolded: the image is not just a face, it is a whole body. This scenario first appeared in 1978, in *The Turin Shroud* by the historian Ian Wilson – put forward there not as historical fact, founded on evidence, but merely as a possibility, thought up by Wilson himself. Now, ten years later, this unlikely speculation has become history!

Finally, Cheshire writes: 'It will *always* remain a matter of personal opinion whether to believe in the Shroud or not. I, personally, find my belief in it unshaken, and helpful.' To a rationalist, of course, it would be a matter of evidence, not opinion, and being 'helpful' does not make something true.

Professor Richard Luckett, in his article in the *Evening Standard,* takes a slightly more sophisticated line than the Group-Captain, pointing out that the formal position of the Catholic Church has always been that the relic 'is a "representation", an object that might well prompt profitable prayer and meditation but is not the true shroud of Our Lord' – adding that, despite the medieval date, 'it still remains an extremely mysterious, if not a mystical, object', and that here we do in fact have the real image of a man who was tortured and crucified. In other, plainer, words, it is a clever fake – as freethinkers have never doubted.

It is true that, for the first five hundred years of the relic's six-hundred-year existence, the Church authorities recognised it as a forgery; but they have been only too ready in the present century to go along with the popular surge of acceptance of the relic. As early as 1389, the French bishop in whose diocese the 'shroud' had been discovered denounced it as a fake, and later he reported to Pope Clement VII that the artist had since confessed to having made it and to trying to pass it off as the genuine article. Shroud enthusiasts have always known this – which makes their recent faith in the authenticity of the relic all the more perverse and difficult to understand.

It is significant, however, that whereas, historically, such credulity would have been limited almost entirely to Catholics, in the past few decades it has been Protestants who seem to have been the more easily gulled by miraculous relics and 'paranormal powers' – perhaps because of the invocation of science, ironically enough, on behalf of these 'signs and wonders'. Uri Geller, spiritualist mediums, popular writers like von Däniken – all make a good living by using gullible scientists to uphold their sensational claims, on spurious scientific evidence, while Catholics (inoculated against alien superstitions) tend to be under-represented among those taken in by them.

It was actually the progress during the late nineteenth century in the science of photography that, by disclosing the Turin relic's startling negative image, first led to the revival of popular belief in the shroud, upheld by the argument that no medieval forger would have bothered with the negative image since he could not have foreseen the invention of photography that would reveal it. In the past few years, exponents of a whole range of scientific expertise, employing every possible piece of technological hardware, have got in on the act and vied with one another in the sensationalism of their findings and interpretations.

In the 1970s, one 'expert' not only managed to discern the imprint of a coin supposedly placed over one of the shroud-man's eyes but even identified the emperor depicted on it – needless to say, one who reigned early in the first century. When no paint could be detected on the cloth, that proved it was not made by human hands; then, when traces of paint were found, that must have been used later, simply to touch up the image. This is the sort of conclusion to be expected when researchers are self-selected for their readiness to believe in miracles.

The fashion for any particular alleged relic of Christ comes and goes. Less than fifty years ago, the 'Holy Coat of Treves' (allegedly 'the seamless garment' for which the Roman soldiers cast lots at the Crucifixion) was far better known and more widely accepted than the 'Shroud of Turin', which, indeed, was still described unequivocally at that time in the *Catholic Encyclopaedia* as a forgery – but nowadays one hardly ever hears of the seamless coat outside Trier, where it is still preserved in the cathedral.

The 'Holy Coat' entry in *Harmsworth's Universal Encyclopaedia* of 1920 - 22 (which, incidentally, has no entry on the Turin Shroud at all) states that an 1891 photograph of the 'Coat' had revealed a negative impression of the supposed face of Jesus – probably a technique developed by medieval relic manufacturers so as to lend a mysterious aspect to such sacred images. Yet in his book *The Evidence of the*

Shroud (1986), Ian Wilson stated that the famous negative image revealed by an 1898 photograph of the Turin relic is unique. He went to great lengths in his researches to 'prove' the authenticity of the Turin relic, yet either knew nothing about a similar image on the relic in Trier or else chose to ignore it.

Many statements made in the past few years by academics, including scientists, about the Turin relic have been amazingly credulous. One American statistician actually asserted that the odds on the 'man of the shroud' not being Jesus are 'one chance in 82,944,000'. How he reached this precise figure is not revealed, but in any case it is beside the point. The suggestion has never been put forward, except as an Aunt Sally to he knocked down, that the image might be that of another man – a man who not only looked just like the medieval concept of Jesus but who showed signs of having likewise suffered scourging, crowning with thorns, nails through the wrists and feet, and a sword through the side. There has always been a consensus that the image on the cloth is that of the gospel hero; the only disagreement has been how the image got there.

By the time this article appears in mid-October, the Vatican will have announced the findings of the carbon-dating laboratories – hiding its disappointment by stressing that the Church had never proclaimed the shroud to be more than a devotional 'representation' of the passion of Christ. At the same time, many of those like Leonard Cheshire who have fervently believed it to be the genuine shroud of their 'saviour', miraculously impregnated with his image and miraculously preserved over two millennia, will continue to do so. After all, what is mere science when confronted with faith? Indeed, science is the traditional enemy.

Believers are glad to invoke scientific facts to back up their beliefs; but if the facts let them down, it is the mark of the true believer to jettison the facts, not the faith.

[October 1988]

Celestial Private Patient Plans
[Miracle Cures]

Throughout history, miracle cures have been big business. The patient needs only to be touched by Jesus – or merely to touch the hem of his garment; to visit a special shrine; to be prayed for by someone (whether 'in the body or out of the body') who has a special relationship with the almighty; to wear a miraculous medal or a holy relic or a piece of cloth that has touched a holy relic; to bathe in a miraculous spring; to be touched by the hands of a faith-healer in touch with the life force (or merely to go on his absent healing list); to take medicaments that have been diluted to nothing but water: the variety of prescriptions is endless, and so is human credulity.

THE traditional definition of miracles as 'breaches of natural law' has caused many of the more educated Christians to abandon faith in them. The pantheist philosopher Spinoza, who, more than three centuries ago, identified 'natural law' with the divine will, therefore declared miracles to be *a priori* impossible. Yet even today, many Christians who otherwise appear to be both intelligent and honest somehow contrive to cling to a belief in miracles.

A century after Spinoza, the rationalist philosopher David Hume pointed out that belief in miracles would entail a rejection of our statistical knowledge of the uniform laws of nature and of the very principle of cause and effect, which underlies all rational human behaviour.

In the present century, that modernist churchman Dean Inge declared that 'Miracle is the bastard child of faith and reason' – but that was more than half-a-century ago; since then, many Christian theologians and prelates seem to have slipped back to medieval beliefs, and, in an age of science, alleged miracles still proliferate.

These thoughts are prompted by two news items in the Catholic newspaper *The Universe* about babies diagnosed as having terminal cancer. The first item took up most of their front page on September 25, under the banner heading 'Lourdes cancer baby's "miracle cure" amazes doctors'. The cure to which it refers certainly seems to have been unexpected – but doctors are not infallible, and there are unexpected remissions in many patients who have not been to Lourdes or been prayed for. Moreover, on reading the text one finds that besides being taken to Lourdes the child had also undergone a course of chemotherapy.

The very next week, there was in the same paper (but much smaller, on an inside page) a moving story of the courageous last hours of a three-year-old who died from cancer in Great Ormond Street Hospital. Though he, too, had no doubt been prayed for by his Catholic parents, there is no mention of his having been taken to Lourdes. But if it is supposed that that fact accounts for his not having been cured as the other child was, not only would believers be faced with the objections of Spinoza, Hume and Inge; they would also be faced with the problem of their god being the sort of cruel, capricious, irrational god that would choose between two small children on such an absurd criterion. How can such a god possibly be envisaged, let alone worshipped, by believers in Lourdes and other triggers of divine miracle?

The physical condition of the first of the two babies may have been considered good enough to stand up to the journey and that of the second one not. In any case, neither child could have made the decision for himself. Besides, the number of patients who die in Lourdes or on the way there is very high every year – a fact that is no longer kept as secret as it used to be – and not surprisingly in view of the communal bath. It is also not unknown for patients to go there with one malady and come back with something worse. Moreover, it costs a considerable sum to take a patient overseas and across Europe. Does the Christian god (or his Lourdes mediatrix, the mother of one-third of him) take patients' bank balances into account when allocating cures?

However, the theological problems raised by divine miracles go deeper than that. If, after deciding to end a patient's life, the putative deity were to change that decision as a result of prayer or a pilgrimage to a miraculous shrine, that would surely contradict the doctrines of divine omniscience, pre-knowledge and absolute wisdom – which are also generally accepted by those who believe in Lourdes and other such sources of supposed miracle cures. How can they possibly go on believing in a god with such contradictory attributes? Only by a readiness to believe simultaneously in things that are mutually exclusive.

Like the first of the two cancer patients featured in *The Universe*, one of my own sisters – who is a nun and a cancer patient with secondaries – was taken to Lourdes this summer. She went by plane, with a wheelchair, accompanied by two of her fellow nuns and a nurse – and I am glad to report that since her return her X-rays show diminished tumours, she has been able to walk up a flight of stairs for the first time in many months, and she looks and feels much better. No doubt most of the members of her order put this down to the pilgrimage. As it happens, however, before she went to Lourdes she was already three-quarters way through a course of chemotherapy to which she was responding well. Indeed, her plans to visit Lourdes had been made provisional upon her condition improving sufficiently for her to undertake the journey.

I am glad she enjoyed the experience, and am willing to admit that the stimulating change of scene may have helped to some extent to boost her return to health which the chemotherapy had already set in train – and which now, I am glad to say, looks very promising. In spite of her being a professional believer, however, I suspect (and hope) that if she had been forced to choose between the chemotherapy and the pilgrimage she would sensibly have opted for the former.

Allied to miracle cures are some forms of nature cure. Herbal medicine often has a sound medical basis derived from statistical evidence, sometimes over many centuries, even though science may not yet have analysed the active ingredient or discovered the way it works. But this cannot be true, for instance, of homeopathic remedies in which the purported active ingredients have been diluted to less than one molecule per patient: i.e. nothing. Such prescriptions will certainly enjoy a proportion of successes – possibly, indeed, higher than spontaneous cure alone, because of the well-known placebo effect of making the patient more optimistic – but that is all. And if they dissuade the patient from undergoing more scientific treatment, they can, of course, impede alleviation or cure. Reliance on homeopathy could well have been the cause of death of the comedian Peter Sellers, who had refused a bypass operation (which has a high success rate) in favour of homeopathic treatment.

Many kinds of faith-healers have likewise dissuaded patients from accepting orthodox medical treatment, sometimes with fatal results. Of those patients, some would no doubt have died even with orthodox medical treatment or surgery, but others would not.

Among the most histrionic and the most successful (financially, if not medically) of the faith-healers are still those who perform their 'miracles' in the name of Jesus – especially the American confidence tricksters known as televangelists. So far we in Britain have been spared their tricks on TV, but with the imminent introduction of Thatcherite 'choice' via satellite, only the off button on the set will stand between these religious criminals and vulnerable viewers in this country too.

The spectacularly gory 'psychic surgery', performed mainly in the Philippines and televised over here some years ago, has conned many a Western patient who ought to have known better – proving not only very lucrative for its practitioners but sometimes, through neglect of more scientific treatment, fatal to its victims. It simply relies for its effects on the conjuror's expertise in production and sleight of hand, using animal gut and blood supplied by the local butcher – and the rationalist conjuror James Randi, who has duplicated these effects on American TV with an honest explanation, showed a video of this performance at a recent dinner in London at which I was present. Though rather gory to watch immediately after eating, it was well worth a little queasiness, both for its entertainment value and its instructiveness; and it is to be hoped that Randi's message will percolate to those patients contemplating a trip to the Philippines when they would be more likely to benefit from a visit to hospital.

However, perhaps the greatest harm done to humanity by belief in miracles is simply the general effect of the denial of reason and the power this gives to ruthless charlatans.

[November 1988]

The 'Shroud' in Shreds

[Conclusive Dates]

Six months after it was known that the 'Shroud' of Turin had been proved, by C14 dating, to be only about seven hundred years old, the actual facts and figures have been released, putting the lost nail in the Shroud's coffin – but that is, of course, no guarantee that its devotees will not continue to believe in it and try to explain away the scientifically irrefutable findings.

WE had received from the British Museum Society a plain typed leaflet bearing a print of the familiar Jesus head from the so-called Shroud of Turin, advertising a lecture entitled 'The Turin Shroud: A Lesson in Self-Persuasion', to be given on 15 February by Oxford's Professor E T Hall, who had carried out one of the three carbon-dating tests on miniscule portions of the relic last summer. Since no one seemed to have seen any other publicity for the lecture and there was a £5 admission charge for it, as well as the fact that the full scientific details were to appear the following day in the journal *Nature*, a large audience did not seem likely. However, I decided to blow a fiver on it myself, as, having taken a close interest in the pretentious piece of cloth for so many years, I felt like being in at the kill.

To my amazement, more than a thousand people thronged the largest lecture hall at the Institute of Education – and, judging by the reactions to well-known facts and by the questions afterwards, few of them were experts in the subject. The secret of attracting a large audience for such events is obviously to build up a membership through a public institution.

Professor Hall said he had been agnostic about the Turin relic but would really have liked the age of the flax from which it was made to have turned out at about 2,000 years. Since the man in charge of the test at one of the other two laboratories was a committed Catholic, who was very disappointed at the result, this adds credibility to the findings – which in any case, without any collaboration, were remarkably (and, from our standpoint, satisfactorily) close.

The Arizona laboratory came out with an age of 646 (plus or minus 31) years; the Zurich laboratory with 676 (plus or minus 24) years; and Oxford with 750 (plus or minus 30) years. This means that the material dates from the thirteenth or fourteenth century AD – somewhat late for shrouding the holy corpse. And, since the first authenticated mention of the relic is in 1359, the scientific dating of it is exactly what we expected. Of those who wished to ask questions after the lecture, one of the handful called upon was Ian Wilson, author of two best-sellers on the relic, using the popular technique of contriving to blind the average reader with a scientific smokescreen. He is adept at lending a spurious air of academic respectability to religious sensationalism by discounting much of the alleged evidence he puts forward but keeping enough of it in reserve for a concluding question-mark at the end of each chapter. Far from wearing sackcloth and ashes or offering to refund money paid for copies of his misleading books on the Turin relic, Mr Wilson's postscript to Professor Hall's lecture smilingly put the speaker right on a peripheral historical date.

When he saw me going over to him afterwards to say 'I told you so' he quickly disappeared – no doubt hurrying home to work on yet another book advocating mind-bending superstition to please the heart of his bank manager. Indeed, while the carbon-dating of the Turin relic was awaited, he had prudently turned his attention to 'after-death experiences', on which he published a book a year ago, using the same well-tried technique of mystification.

Our work of de-mystification is therefore equally unending – but without best-seller status.

[March 1989]

New Sex Teasers for the Church

[Current Contentions]

> Internal Christian disputes on matters of sex, sexuality and sexism seem to be proliferating. Or have they just come out into the open? There are also repercussions with regard to Church authority and the pursuit of Christian unity. Here the president of the National Secular Society surveys recent events, with a discernible twinkle in her typewriter.

SEX and sexuality have always loomed large in the problems that beset Mother Church – from the neurotic hang-ups of Saint Paul, through the sexual scandals of the medieval papal court and of supposed celibate clergy and monastics, through the Anglican schism triggered by Henry's lust for Anne Boleyn, to the insidious rebellion of millions of Catholic women since *Humanae Vitae* (1968) against the Vatican's continued ban on contraception. In every century there was some new aspect to the war between sex and the Church, but the time-span has now shrunk to that of the daily press. The advent of feminism, gay rights and (horror of horrors!) sex-change operations, has brought problems thick and fast to most Christian denominations; but above all to Rome.

Most far-reaching is the setback to ecumenism posed by the appointment in February this year of the first woman bishop (the black American woman, Barbara Harris) in the Anglican communion; for a bishop has the apostolic power to ordain new priests.

Until the consecration of this first woman bishop was announced, a truce had been maintained for some years within the Lambeth Conference by allowing the ordination and ministry of women priests in some national churches and postponing the evil day in others. While it was undoubtedly an awkward situation that, while the Church of England does not itself recognise women priests, it heads the multi-national Anglican communion that includes several countries which do recognise them, the Conference was nevertheless able to cope with it. Now, however, there is a woman bishop – who, any day now, may actually ordain new priests, including male priests. Short of the archbishops somehow having the passports of all Anglican priests confiscated, this means that the purity of the male line can no longer be guaranteed by simply barring women from priestly functions within this or any other country. Anyway, even the fantasy of passport control becomes ineffective with the latest news, as we go to press – that the Church of Ireland (which is, of course, part of the Anglican communion) has voted to allow women priests to be ordained for the Irish ministry. That brings the curse of Eve closer to home.

If the priests (male or female) ordained by a female bishop were to be recognised as valid priests in some parts of the Anglican communion and not others, it could only mean schism within this Christian schism. That is the main problem raised by the appointment of the first Anglican woman bishop – and not just because of the rifts it is causing within the Anglican communion itself: it has also stymied the long-hoped-for reunion with Rome.

It is one thing for the Vatican to consider changing its infallible mind on the validity of four centuries of schismatic ordination in the Anglican Church, and quite another to expect it to recognise the validity of a female priesthood or that of any priest ordained by a female bishop. How, it is asked, could a mere female possibly inherit the powers received by the all-male band of apostles from the male Christ, and then pass them on into the future? The introduction of even one female into the apostolic succession nullifies the chain of male priestly powers conferred by JC himself.

In response to the common enemy of disbelief, there had been a concerted effort in the Roman and Anglican Churches during the past quarter of a century to bridge the rift occasioned by the divorce of an amorous monarch in 1533. The visit of Archbishop Ramsey to Pope Paul VI in 1966 marked the first major step towards the proposed annulment of the four-centuries-old schism, with amazing concessions from each side, on a Jack Spratt basis: Rome agreeing to differ on points of theological doctrine but not on authority, while the Anglican community was willing to grant ultimate jurisdiction to the Pope (a return to 'the universal primacy of the Bishop of Rome') in exchange for autonomy in matters of theology.

The way now seemed open to the great final reconciliation of priestly orders – as long as the Protestant priests were, of course, male. And there was no suggestion at that time that the Anglican ordination of women, let alone female episcopal powers, would soon demand recognition.

Now Robert Runcie is faced with an impossible task: preserving the tenuous union of the Lambeth Conference while, at the same time, pursuing reunion with Rome. Characteristically, he is trying to have his cake and eat it. He has actually come up with the idea of requiring any ordination by a woman bishop to be backed by a male bishop laying his hands, as it were, on top of hers; but, not surprisingly, this suggestion is seen by feminists as an insult to women, and has caused a furore among the American (and other) opponents of sex discrimination with regard to episcopal powers.

Following in Ramsey's 1966 footsteps, Runcie is to visit the Vatican in September [1989] in an attempt to resolve this dilemma. Between those two summit meetings, there was a visit by the Pope to Canterbury in 1982, likewise part of the 'quest for unity'. But its fruition looks very much less hopeful since the episcopal consecration of Barbara Harris.

Much as the Pope would welcome the Anglicans back into the One True fold, he is sure to strike a hard bargain, as is indicated by a letter he wrote to Dr Runcie six months ago (that has only just been made public) in which he declares that the ordination of women 'has created a new and perplexing situation', and, referring to a the 1982 mandate to 'study all that hinders the mutual recognition of the ministries of our Communions', states that 'the ordination of women to the priesthood in some provinces of the Anglican Communion, together with the recognition of the right of individual provinces to proceed with the ordination of women to the episcopacy, appears to pre-empt this study and effectively block the path to the mutual recognition of ministries'.

Anglican traditionalists, both clergy and laity, having lost hope now in the progress of official unity, have been defecting to Rome in considerable numbers. One of them, the Revd William Oddie, explains that 'the attraction to most Anglo-Catholics is that the Roman Church still has a theology of doctrinal authority'; adding 'I feel that many people may come over to the Catholic Church'. The Revd Keith Haydon, leader of a group of Oxford Anglo-Catholic theologians and clerics whose recent letter to *The Times* expressed solidarity with the Pope on the issue of women priests, comments: 'Many are getting closer to Rome by the week now that it seems full, visible unity has become a fantasy'. And the Revd Robert Gould, another prominent Anglican traditionalist, is quoted as saying, 'It may well be the case that more Anglicans will join the Catholics now that unity discussions look doomed'.

On their side, Catholics are pointing to the dramatic consequences of democracy in an ecclesiastical structure with too great a willingness to allow different regions of a Church to go their own sweet way; and those who have been tempted to gloat over the Anglicans for their lack of any magisterium to hold the line have been counselled by a leader in the *Catholic Herald* to 'consider what could happen to their own Church without a man as sure of his views as the current Pope at its centre'.

Sure of his views he may be, but he no longer exercises the sort of authority over the hearts and minds of members of his Church that was accorded to popes as a matter of course before Vatican II. In most cases, those who disobey him (mainly, in the Western world, by using contraception) contrive to salve their consciences and remain within the Church. Anyway, individuals who kick over the traces, whether by unrepented sinful behaviour or by doctrinal heresy, can always be accommodated. Indeed, heresy (which means 'choice') can actually be looked upon as an aspect of freewill. Collective erosion of the papal unifying authority is far more serious. The Church of Rome has always seen schism – a collective denial of Jurisdiction – as worse than heresy, which is limited to the pastoral power of Order.

The papal way of dealing with incipient schism – as in the recent case of the recalcitrant Lefebvre – is to isolate it as far as possible by excommunicating the principals and issuing a grave warning to supporting priests and laity that those who persist in the error of their ways could likewise incur the 'grave penalty of excommunication'. Though this threat may no longer inspire among many Catholics quite the terror it once did, it can still be largely effective – while, of course, it is not open to Cantuar at all.

On the other hand, when, last summer, Lefebvre went ahead and consecrated his own four new bishops, there was no way that the Pope could deny them the magical powers of the apostolic succession. Unlawful as they are, their divine orders must be valid. It is a disadvantage of belief in magic that once the power has been supernaturally conferred, it has to work – no matter for whom. Hence, for instance, Black Masses.

What, then, about the priest who has changed sex and is now a woman? 'Once a priest, always a priest': that is an immutable principle, necessary to safeguard a gullible laity against the fear of non-transubstantiation, ineffective absolution, and other void sacraments. But women, of course, can never be priests. There is, however, one highly publicised instance of a transsexual priest, now known as Sister Paola: a classical case of the irresistible force and the immovable object. It is, surely, the stuff that papal nightmares are made of; but when the Pope wakes up the nightmare doesn't go away. His one consolation is that, so far, sex changes among the clergy remain rare.

More recent press reports concern a related, but comparatively minor, matter for decision in the papal in-tray: the case of a young Spanish woman who, having been baptised as a boy now wants her baptismal certificate changed retrospectively so that she can be married in white. Come back Solomon!

Also in the news is a report on pornography from the Pontifical Council for Social Communications, saying that the root cause of the spread of pornography is a 'persuasive moral permissiveness' and that the media have 'tragically succumbed to the temptation of exploiting human weakness'.

Another aspect of that permissiveness is the number of priests who come to regret the vow of celibacy that they took in their youth. During the pontificate of Paul VI (1963-78), their requests to leave the priesthood were received sympathetically, and many were able to give up their priestly vocations (though not, of course, their priestly powers) to marry, whilst remaining in the Church. The present Pope, however, has put a stop to this laxity, and it is now much more difficult for a priest to leave the priesthood without being excommunicated.

Homosexual priests also have their difficulties. On the other hand, in many religious orders – behind monastic walls – gay monks and nuns have never had it so good. All homosexual Christians, however, are subject to attempts by their churches to make them feel guilty about their own nature – even more guilty, that is, than the average Christian miserable sinner – and the more conscientious they are the more they suffer. But as more and more gays 'come out of the closet', and more of the specialist mutual support groups are set up (such as, for instance, Quest – the society for Catholic gays in this country), the psychological oppression of Christian homosexuals is minimised.

Controversy over divorce goes back, of course, to Henry VIII; but there is an ever-widening gap on the issue between contemporary culture and the Church's view that marriage is indissoluble. Vatican officials, and the Pope himself, have complained that RC diocesan tribunals in the USA, for instance, are granting too many annulments on psychological grounds.

Among other interesting religious news items in the past few months has been the eruption into the open of the increasing rumblings of discontent among progressive Catholic theologians. In January, a game old octogenarian, the German Redemptory priest, Bernard Haering, who insists that the encyclical *Humanae Vitae* admits of exceptions to the ban on contraception, and in any case is not eternally infallible, spoke out in favour of a 'worldwide birth-control inquiry to consider the real feelings of Catholics', and openly castigated Mgr Carlo Caffarra (the theologian closest to the Pope) who had likened contraception to murder.

A week later came the Declaration of Cologne, signed by 163 North European (German, Austrian, Dutch and Swiss) theologians, since supported by about 200 more. It was a scathing attack on Vatican centralisation trends and intransigence on social issues, especially the Pope's hard-line anti-contraception policy, which, it said, 'mortifies the conscience of husbands and wives'. Declaring that 'the dignity of their consciences consists not only of obedience but above all of responsibility', the document demanded a modification of the total ban on contraception and a more speedy implementation of the collegiate and other reforms proposed by Vatican Council II. Countering this treacherous uprising, the Prefect of the Congregation for the Doctrine of the Faith, Cardinal Ratzinger, tried to downgrade the standing of the Council by saying that, being really only pastoral, it lacked the doctrinal weight of earlier councils with their infallible pronouncements. This has brought a protest, in the form of a three-page 'open letter', from, most unexpectedly, 63 of Italy's leading theologians – including the president of Italian theologians and the president of Italy's moral theologians. Raising similar objections (though in far more moderate terms) to the Declaration of Cologne, they claim that theologians should have a right to freedom of research, even in the field of ethics, 'with no spirit of intolerance'. Tit for tat, there has been an immediate response from the old guard of the Italian Episcopal Conference – a stern rebuke, in the very spirit of intolerance that proves the theologians' case.

Ironically, none of this rebellion of the Left threatens to become schismatic, as the right-wing rebellion of Lefebvre (whose views are, in many ways, closer to the Pope's) proved to be last year, when Lefebvre consecrated his own bishops in the apostolic succession. That magical laying-on of hands again.

As long as these internal Christian disputes stop short of persecution and religious wars, it is all good fun for atheists. And, more importantly – assuming the good book is right – 'if a house be divided against itself, that house cannot stand'.

[June 1989]

Islamic Terrorism

[Editorial Report by William McIlroy]

FRESH from her painful personal encounter with a recent Muslim demonstration in London, Barbara Smoker chose 'Melting-Pot or Multi-Culture?' as the title of her Sunday lecture to South Place Ethical Society on 2 July.

The president of the National Secular Society said she was as concerned as anybody about the right of minority groups to pursue their own chosen lifestyle. But she was also concerned about the rights of minorities within those minority groups, particularly their women and children.

'If families come to settle in this country, surely they should be willing for their children to become part of it', she said.

'By demanding their own religious schools, and the public funding of those schools, they are continuing to prevent their children from assimilating with the host community.

'While upholding the right of immigrant groups to foster elements of their own cultural background in their adoptive country – and, indeed, seeing this as a positive contribution to the varied general culture – I do not think this communal right should override the rights of individuals within those groups. Particularly affected are the members of those groups born since immigration, and, especially in patriarchal groups, their women. After all, the individual is not only the smallest, but also often the most oppressed, of all minorities.'

Barbara Smoker said we must safeguard the fabric of our own culture.

'The nation's laws and the hard-won rights of its population as a whole should not be waived too readily in favour of the newcomers, generally in the name of religion.

'When Ayatollah Khomeini issued the notorious death sentence on Salman Rushdie, a British citizen of Muslim origin living in Britain, our government was slow and half-hearted in its condemnation of it, and members of the Labour Party joined in the apologetic regrets for the hurt feelings of Muslims. So did spokesmen for all the major religions; the Archbishop of Canterbury urging the extension of blasphemy protection to Islam and other religions, rather than renounce it for his own.'

Referring to the large Muslim demonstration organised [on May 27, 1989] to demand the extension of the blasphemy law to Islam, Barbara Smoker said that while disagreeing with the demand, she upheld their right to demonstrate peaceably in support of it.

'However, not only was the Muslim demonstration far from peaceable; the blasphemy issue was largely lost in violent incitement to murder', she added.

'Those guilty of this incitement to murder were not apparently told that this was prohibited on the demonstration, nor were any arrests made on a charge of incitement. Even those demonstrators arrested later for physical violence against the police were released without charge. And none of the Muslim spokesmen who have used television programmes to call for murder have been prosecuted for this offence.

'Having thus flouted, with impunity, British laws and customs and sensibilities, Muslims have proceeded to further acts of violence, such as arson, and have continued their monstrous demands for the banning of *The Satanic Verses* and death to the author.

'Many other Muslims in this country are appalled and ashamed by all this. They realise that nothing is more likely to cause real racist hostility against their whole community. But their voices are hardly heard above those of the religious leaders and the rabble behind them.'

Miss Smoker claimed it is unlikely that any of this would have happened had not Muslim religious leaders got away with earlier demands for exemption from various laws in the name of religion.

'For instance', she declared, 'our slaughter laws, which demand the pre-stunning of animals killed for meat, are waived in favour of both Jewish and Muslim religious methods of slaughter, which forbid pre-stunning. Each of these religions denies that their particular method is cruel, but agrees that the other one is... If the law is unnecessary to ensure that animal slaughter is as humane as possible, then it should be repealed. If it is reasonable, then it should apply to all.

'I have become quite accustomed, over the past few years, to the charge of being "racist" whenever I have opposed the provision of halal and kosher meat, the waiving of conservation and planning laws for the building of mosques, the demands for publicly funded schools for Muslim and orthodox Jewish girls, and other such special provisions. The same charge was repeated when I was instrumental in allowing the anti-Zionist play *Perdition* to be put on at Conway Hall last year after it had been denied access to theatres all over the country.

'In vain have I protested that it is hardly racist to oppose policies that are put forward by fundamentalist co-religionists who are not always of the same race and that are opposed by some other people who are of the same race...

'Soon, Muslim religious leaders in this country may well demand, in the name of religious freedom, that they be allowed to follow the Koran in the matter of judicial penalties — to chop off the hands of any members of their community caught stealing and to stone to death any of their women caught in adultery. What would be the "progressive" response to that?'

[July 1989]

Ghetto Schools in Britain?

[Muslim Demands]

> Our perennial campaign for the abolition of church schools has escalated in urgency and importance over the decades – but never so rapidly as it has in the past eight months, as a consequence of the Rushdie affair, which has brought to the fore the demand of Muslims for their own state-subsidised schools, on a par with those of Christians. As this up-to-date survey reports, the Muslim (and other religious) schools controversy is now approaching crisis level in major political parties – especially in the Labour Party, which it has split down the middle, torn between one principle and another and between principle and electoral expediency.

THE long-simmering demand by fundamentalist Muslims living in Britain for the public funding of their own religious schools, in line with those of the Anglicans and Catholics (and a handful of Methodist and Jewish schools), has been fuelled first by the reactionary religious clauses of the Education Reform Act, 1988, with its new emphasis on Christian teaching and worship, and then by the late Ayatollah Khomeini's death sentence on Salman Rushdie.

The simmer has consequently come to the boil, and some of the more responsible newspapers – notably *The Times* and *Independent* – have woken up to the social harm that acceding to such demands would entail. The policy of the *Guardian*, on the other hand, seems to be divided – their editorials and articles coming down finally on the side of separate schools, while the letters editor appears to favour the secularist arguments. Letters on the subject went on appearing in the *Guardian* day after day, from 22 July to 4 August, almost all of them on the secularist side.

The main argument supporting the demand for Muslim (and other non-Christian) schools is one of parity with Christians: as long as Christian sects are allowed their own state-aided schools, non-Christian religions should, on grounds of equity, be given the same privilege. This argument is certainly difficult to brush aside unless one is campaigning at the same time (as the NSS and the *Freethinker* have always done) for the existing church schools to be phased out – but, even so, most of the applicant schools are (and are likely to be) far more discriminatory and socially divisive than the existing voluntary-aided schools.

This parity argument is closely paralleled by that used in support of the extension of the blasphemy law to non-Christian religions – and in both cases it is basically the argument that two (or more) wrongs somehow make a right.

The Archbishop of Canterbury and other leading members of the major Christian churches have given open support to both of these Muslim demands – for the extension of the protection of the blasphemy law to Islam (and other religions) and for Islamic (and other religious) schools to be given the public funding associated with voluntary-aided status; presumably preferring this to the logical alternative of losing these privileges for themselves. However, in his usual manner of attempting to have it both ways, Dr Runcie also preached (on 16 July) against religious bigotry and fundamentalism in general.

The Conservative Party has tended to warn Muslims against extremism – for instance, on 4 July, Mr John Patten (the Minister of State at the Home Office responsible for race relations) said that the Government felt it would be unwise to extend the blasphemy law to Islam ('To rule otherwise would be to chip away at the fundamental freedom on which our democracy is built'), and two weeks later he wrote a letter to the Advisory Council on Race Relations concerning the need for the Muslim community to integrate with the rest of society, warning that 'one cannot be British on one's own exclusive terms, or on a selective basis'. The second leader in the *Independent* of 20 July commented: 'If Britain's more extreme Muslims ignore John Patten's advice and continue to adopt hard-line positions, they are likely to turn educated, as well popular, sentiment against them.'

[September 1989]

Six Of One...

[Letter on religious leaders]

KENNETH DOUGHTY (Letters, January) criticises the 'negative attitude' of my presidential address to the National Secular Society in which I asserted that certain religious leaders are typical of their followers. If Ayatollah Khomeini did not represent the average Muslim, why have millions of Muslims world-wide supported his sentence of death on Salman Rushdie, with no fewer than 20,000 demonstrating violently in London on 27 May 1989?

If Marcinkus, and the Pope who protects and promotes him, do not really represent Roman Catholicism, how is it that Peter's Pence still pour into the coffers of the Vatican?

If the affluent televangelists do not represent the Protestants of the United States, how is it that their gullible viewers have made them millionaires?

Those millions of believers who support the 'lunatic fringe' of each of the major religions are surely more lunatic than the religious leaders who ponce off them!

[February 1990]

Women Against Fundamentalism
[Meeting]

It is just a year since a group of (mainly Asian) women, in response to the Rushdie affair, set up the pressure group Women Against Fundamentalism. On 23 March this year, in commemoration of International Women's Day, they organised a public (but women-only) meeting in central London on 'Women's Struggle Against Religious Fundamentalism Across the World'. It was attended by some two hundred women, including the president of the National Secular Society, who writes this report.

THE platform, this Friday evening, comprised eight very articulate speakers, all women, representing East and West, Black and White, several far-flung parts of the globe, and various social issues.

The first speaker, representing Iran, spoke on Islamic fundamentalism in that country, from its revival under Khomeini in February 1979. Within a few weeks, all women judges in Iran were dismissed, as Khomeini asserted that women were incapable of making judicial decisions. He made abortion a capital offence, both for the woman and her doctor – the woman to be either stoned to death or thrown from a height – and a law was passed forcing women to cover themselves in public from head to toe. Any woman walking about without such covering runs the risk of being attacked with acid.

In Britain, it is important to find ways of enabling women and men of Asian origin to establish their identity other than through organised fundamentalist religion.

A well-known woman from a Hindu background spoke on the rise of Hindu fundamentalism in India. Having just returned from a visit to India, she said she found the political situation there depressing, confusing, and frightening. Originally founded as a secular state, India is now ruled by a coalition of the right-wing Hindu and Muslim parties, based on religious sentiment and the principle that all religious traditions must be preserved. What sort of secularism is that?

A speaker from Bangladesh said that her country, though 85 per cent Islamic, remained ethnically Hindu, and had seceded from Pakistan in 1971 in the name of secularism, but the present right-wing government, supported by Iranian money, was unfortunately espousing the idea of Islam being made the state religion. Progressive women's organisations, realising that this constitutional change would mean the oppression of women, are opposing it and the Mullahs, but the illiterate masses are unaware of the implications.

A member of the Jewish organisation, Women in Black, spoke on Jewish fundamentalism, women and Zionism. She said that women are victims of the alliance between religion and the state, and that the dissolution of that alliance is a prerequisite of liberty. In every country Jews are supposedly united by their religion; in reality, Jewish fundamentalism is basically political and divisive. The Zionist movement claims to be socialist, and in theory upholds the equality of women; but is ready to sacrifice it to political expediency. The feminist movement in Israel has always been the main route for women opposing Zionism. It is a strong movement, though small: many Israeli women, looking for national identity, are attracted to Jewish fundamentalism and like to claim that they keep to the Orthodox rules more than the men.

A West African representative of the organisation Forward spoke about the amalgam in West Africa of two patriarchies, with the worst features of each, where fundamentalist Islam is superimposed on the traditional tribal religions. Christian Pentecostalism and other fundamentalist movements, mainly from the USA, are also gaining ground. Many West African women, suffering hardship in everyday life, rush into the fundamentalist sects for the sake of welfare handouts, but are then controlled by the Church, which, forbidding contraception and abortion, uses the myth of Adam's rib to foster the idea that women were created to serve men.

The next contributor, speaking on science, religious fundamentalism and the New Right, made the point that while the fast-growing cult of quasi-scientific socio-biology makes an ally of anti-feminist fundamentalism and the New Right, this development is opposed by many feminist scientists: true science is the real ally of women's liberation.

A spokeswoman from the Soviet Union said that though the Revolution had promised equality for women, this promise had been betrayed for seven decades. Economic demands were denounced, and the shamefully high infant mortality rates are only now beginning to be seriously discussed. Besides, the attitude of men towards women has never changed in the Soviet Union. When, for instance, women were told they could become tractor drivers, they were given only the oldest rusty tractors to drive. It is impossible for women to liberate themselves in a climate of general political oppression; but with the advent of *perestroika* women are now beginning to take leading social roles in the Soviet Union – though many simply want to rest at the moment, following years of bearing the double burden of work inside and outside the home. The Orthodox Church still insists that women should emulate the Madonna. In the refugee camps in Azerbaijan, young Muslim men are forming fundamentalist gangs which bully women who do not follow the strict Muslim rules of dress – though (contrary to Gorbechev's propaganda) in those regions struggling for their ethnic liberation there is also a freer strand of Islam.

A particularly horrifying instance of Muslim male chauvinism coupled with fundamentalist Islamic injustice is the case of a young Pakistani woman, Rabia Janjua, who was also present at the meeting. She has two children (one aged four years, the other five months), both of whom were born in Britain, but she is now faced with deportation to Pakistan, where she will either face death by stoning or 30 lashes followed by ten years' imprisonment. Her crime, in Muslim eyes, is that seven years ago, aged 20, she was raped. Since this meant she was unable to return to her family, she married the rapist, who, as a British subject, brought her to this country five years ago. But he deliberately obtained only a visitor's visa for her, instead of bringing her in officially as his wife. He often assaulted her, and, while in hospital (for a second time), she admitted that her serious injuries had been caused by him. By way of reprisal, he informed the immigration authorities that she was an illegal immigrant, whereupon the Home Office took her into custody and prepared to deport her. Pressure from MPs, the press, and women's organisations, has now resulted in a stay of deportation, but she is still liable for detention and deportation at any time.

By chance, only a few hours before the meeting – not thinking I would see her there – I had written a letter in the name of the National Secular Society to the Home Secretary, asking him to reconsider his decision to deport her.

She bravely agreed to tell the audience her story (in Urdu, which was translated into English), though she was obviously shy and said she felt ashamed to reveal her sufferings in public. It seems that the British immigration laws can be waived for a political refugee, but not for a refugee from the injustices of fundamentalist religion.

A representative of the National Abortion Campaign spoke of attempts to put the legislative clock back in Britain and the United States.

During audience participation in the second half of the meeting, I objected (not for the first time) to men being refused admittance – and was surprised to receive a lot of support, though not from the executive.

Although I am in favour of there being women-only pressure groups (as, increasingly, there are on many issues), my view is that public meetings held on public issues should be open to members of both sexes. The standard of speeches at this particular meeting was so high that I would have liked them to be heard by sympathetic (and even less sympathetic) men. They need not be allowed to speak, but it would surely do them good to listen – and learn. Anyway, a similar meeting restricted to men would definitely be denounced as sexist, and I maintain that sauce for the gander should be sauce for the goose.

[April 1990]

Answers to Prayer?

[Letter]

IN HIS letter on prayer (December), S J Nicholls says he has no doubt that 'an infinite personal God' hears and answers prayer 'according to his own will'. Big deal!

I am sometimes the target of begging in the street from Moonies and other religious beggars, beseeching me to donate to their unspecified 'charity', and I answer their prayers according to my own will – in other words, as Mr. Nicholls' god apparently does most of the time, with an emphatic 'Certainly not!' But unlike the divine potentate, I expect no thanks for my answer.

Mr Nicholls adds that, if he and his fellow believers are right in their belief and we are wrong, 'then what'? The implication of this question is, I suppose, that then we will reap our just deserts for unbelief in this life – an eternity of 'weeping and gnashing of teeth'. But if there really were a god who prepared an eternity of torment for *any* of his creatures, I hope I would have the moral courage to curse him rather than worship him, and, if this world of suffering were deliberately created by him, I hope I would have the unselfishness to curse him for the sufferings endured by so many of his putative creatures, rather than thank him for my own relative good fortune.

[January 1991]

God 'n' Chips No Substitute for Care

[Jamie Bulger's Murderers]

THOUGH thousands of children throughout the world are murdered daily in wars, and millions in the Third World die of neglect and starvation, it is difficult not to feel more deeply about the murder of a child on our own doorstep – and the mass media play on this emotive reaction.

The horrific details that came out in the James Bulger murder trial made me close my eyes and ears. But the pathos of the two diminutive accused was almost equally unbearable.

They were only just old enough to be tried under English criminal law; in Germany they would have had to be four years older, in Scandinavia five years older, and in Spain six years older. Only in Scotland is the age of criminal responsibility even lower than in England and Wales.

Throughout the long, inhuman, nine-month delay before the case came to trial, they were deliberately denied post-trauma counselling, lest it prejudice their Not Guilty pleas. Now, before even leaving primary school, these two little boys have begun serving life sentences.

And how appalling it was that, as soon as the verdict was announced, adults gathered outside the court to shout demands for the children to be hanged. But scarcely less sickening has been the bleating of churchmen, politicians and media pundits, in the aftermath of the trial, about Evil and Original Sin and the need to impart to children so-called spiritual values.

After enduring this claptrap on Radio 4's 'Moral Maze' the morning after the verdict, I stopped listening to all such chatter programmes. But Government ministers joined in the hubbub, and one of them, Criminal Justice Minister David Maclean, was quoted on the news as saying that churchmen should stop talking about social issues like housing and start talking about teaching children the difference between right and wrong. My reaction was that politicians should stop talking about right and wrong and start talking about social issues like housing. (Anyway, was Maclean implying that, while humanists can be trusted to know that children need moral training, Christians need to be told?).

It was a novel experience for me to find myself disagreeing with a criticism of the Church. However, I do feel that the Church must accept some responsibility for the murder of the Bulger baby, since the school that the two little murderers attended – even though sporadically – is a Church of England school. And that is a significant fact; for in church schools moral education is generally replaced by religious education, with bible stories about a punitive tribal god and, central to Christianity, the cruel death of an innocent person to appease God's sense of justice. The children are then expected to join in collective worship of this same sadistic god.

The most important school lesson should be moral discussion, with the aim of fostering the children's fellow-feeling for other human beings and animals, using incidents throughout school life to inculcate kind behaviour and eradicate unkind behaviour. But when children in church schools are unkind to one another, instead of being confronted with the Golden Rule question 'You wouldn't like it yourself, would you?', they are often told that God is angry with them and will punish them – just like the cruel adults in many of their young lives.

Unfortunately, the recent education laws and the present Roman Catholic Secretary of State for Education are aiming to subject children at ordinary state schools also to this damaging pattern of Christian teaching. Other countries in the Western world rarely allow religious teaching and practice in their state schools, let alone make them compulsory.

Let us take religion out of school, and bring in moral education – based on human empathy.

At the same time, we must look outside school for many of the causes of the murder. Convicts Robbie and John were deprived children. True, they were not actually starving, as similarly neglected children would be in the Third World: they had plenty of chips to eat, if nothing else. But they were certainly starved of adult concern, and no doubt felt deep, uncomprehending jealousy of an obviously cared-for toddler.

The Government must take a share of the blame for the care-starvation that they suffered. Just as it is implicit government policy for people to live in cardboard boxes because it would be costly to house or hospitalise them, so is it implicit government policy to leave children in appalling home situations since alternative solutions would be too expensive for the taxpayer.

[December 1993]

Quite Contrary
[Letter on Mrs Whitehouse]

IF, as Mrs Whitehouse claims ('Last Word', March), her campaigns have always been against gratuitous violence, not against sex, I assume that we have all misunderstood her motives in the famous criminal case instigated by her against *Gay News* for publishing a poem by James Kirkup.

Hitherto we had supposed that her objections were to the centurion's thinking (yes, only thinking) about Jesus in a sexual way, to the explicit sexual language used, and to the fact, moreover, that the sex fantasy was a gay one. We had also suspected that, because of her hatred for the gay community, Mrs Whitehouse aimed to bankrupt *Gay News* with legal costs.

Now, however, we realise that it was only the violent aspect of the poem to which she objected: that is, its dwelling on the cruelty of a crucifixion.

[April 1994]

DIY Virgin Birth Irks Christians
[Lesbian Mother's Choice]

THE tabloid press made a big story out of the birth of a 6-lb. baby girl, Ellesse, on January 17 to a young woman, Natalie Wilson, who has never copulated with a man.

The *Sun* newspaper, for which it was an 'exclusive' on January 18, not only sensationalised the story with a double spread, but also lifted its editorial hands in judgmental horror at a lesbian couple having a baby – especially as Natalie and Denise were on invalidity benefits at the time. That made them 'scroungers' who had no right to have a baby at the taxpayers' expense – though they have both worked for years as geriatric carers, and will go back to work as soon as they can. Would married heterosexuals be castigated for having children while jobless through sickness?

181

The *Daily Mail* compensated for being a day late with the story by publishing an interview with the couple on the 19th, and was thus more sympathetic. Radio and TV coverage followed over the next few days. Not surprisingly, most of the shocked comment came from the religious lobby – though it concentrated on such non-religious criticism as the unemployment aspect and the likelihood of the baby's growing up to be a lesbian. (Even if that were true – which is by no means certain – so what?) Having officiated at about fifty lesbian commitment ceremonies, I knew that it is not nearly so unusual as the media seemed to think for lesbians to have children, though most of them have had them through copulation, either in a former marriage or with an accommodating male friend, and a few have resorted to artificial insemination with donated deep-frozen semen. Natalie and her partner, Denise, had considered the latter method, but the cost of it and the failure rate were both too high, so they decided to do it themselves. A 19-year-old gay male friend moved into their home so that, at the crucial time each month, he could provide fresh semen, with which Denise was to impregnate Natalie, using a syringe.

This DIY method seemed to me unusually ingenious, but I have since met another lesbian couple who had successfully used the same method, and I have been told of many others. Instead of a medical syringe, however, several of them have used a culinary gadget – to wit, a turkey baster!

I was invited to Birmingham by Central Television on January 20, to present a secularist viewpoint on the lesbian birth for their *Weekend Central*. I always like this programme because it goes out live, which means I cannot be censored. My chief opponents on this occasion were an evangelical Protestant MP, Harry Greenaway, and a Catholic spokesperson, Lynette Burroughs (who is almost a clone of her sister, Victoria Gillick). I decided to have some fun.

Mr Greenaway's opening diatribe was mainly concerned with the procedure being 'unnatural' (though, of course, it *is* natural to wear clothes and cook food) and against the divine will, to which he is apparently privy. Asked to respond to him, I remarked: 'I find it puzzling that Christians should be so hostile to the idea of a virgin mother'.

The reaction from the studio audience was a mixture of laughter and consternation, while Mr Greenaway accused me of 'blasphemy'. I went on to make the point that if every baby were as precious to its parents as Ellesse, we would have a more healthy society.

A fundamentalist clergyman who spoke against me from the audience came up after the programme to upbraid me once more for 'blasphemy'. I asked him why a virgin birth is supposed to be good in Christian mythology but bad in reality. He insisted that the lesbian mother was not a virgin in the same sense, and that anyway the Christian nativity story was not myth but reality – whereupon I asked him if he also believed in Father Christmas.

[February 1995]

A Matter of Life and Death

[Papal Bio-ethics Encyclical]

A MEETING of the College of Cardinals in 1991 requested the Pope to formalise the Church's teaching on bio-ethics, particularly in light of developments in embryo research. The result, after an inexplicable four years in the writing (for there is really little new in the document, apart from some unusually colourful phraseology), is *Evangelium Vitae* ('The Gospel of Life' - or Diatribe Against Good Sense), which was published on March 30 [1995].

This, John Paul II's eleventh encyclical, is described by *Newsweek*, with tacit approval, as the 'signature statement' of his reign. Its main message is denunciation of those who uphold the right to contraception, as well as legal abortion, voluntary euthanasia, and the medical use of foetal tissue and embryos.

It is obvious that the Pope has no insight as to the principle behind the right to life. All rights must depend on consciousness – and, indeed, on the actual level of consciousness. The reason that human beings – and animals, too – deserve our moral consideration is that they are capable of experiencing pain and pleasure, misery and happiness; they have a sense of personal identity; and they can recognise other conscious beings with plans and purposes similar to their own. None of this is applicable to newly fertilised ova. It is true that it could apply to them later if they were allowed to develop; but morality depends on actuality, not potential.

Although the Pope does not claim infallibility for the content of the encyclical, in practice it is held to be binding on the world's one billion Roman Catholics, and it also seeks to influence the rest of the world. Cardinal Basil Hume insists that 'no Roman Catholic is free to dissent at all'. This is implicit in the encyclical's key declaration by the Pope, as follows.

> Therefore, by the authority which Christ conferred on Peter and his successors and in communion with the Bishops of the Roman Catholic Church, I confirm that the direct and voluntary killing of a human being is always gravely immoral.

Though chiefly concerned with the Church's teaching on abortion and euthanasia, the encyclical also denounces artificial birth control and *in vitro* fertilisation. Only on the issues of war and capital punishment does it soften the stand that the Church has traditionally taken; but whereas the Pope states that the death penalty could be morally legitimate 'in extreme circumstances', there is no such let-out for abortion: 'Direct abortion, that is abortion willed as an end or as a means, always constitutes a grave moral disorder.' This indicates retention of the Church's traditional distinction between killing the 'innocent' or the 'guilty'. Since a newly fertilised egg cannot be guilty of anything apart from original sin, it manifestly has a greater right to life than a mature person convicted of a capital crime. However, the Pope's innovative disapproval in general of the death penalty will probably necessitate a change in the recently revised Catechism.

In the past – as John Paul admits, and sees as a paradox – it has been mostly those on the side of legal abortion and euthanasia who have opposed war and the death penalty; his conversion to expressing disapproval of warfare and capital punishment enables him to set himself up as global defender of the 'culture of life'. However, there is a medieval ring to his metaphor of a battle between the primal forces of life and death.

The evening following publication of the encyclical, I was paired with the editor of the *Catholic Herald* to discuss it on the 'London News/ Talk' radio programme. Neither of us had actually read it – but that hardly mattered, since it clearly reiterated every reactionary statement that John Paul had previously made on the practices of contraception, abortion, IVF, embryo experimentation and euthanasia.

On April 2, Radio 4's 'Sunday' got Cardinal Winning to speak on behalf of the encyclical, and a young Catholic woman named Claudia to oppose him. She began in a rather diffident, respectful way; then the Cardinal made the mistake of addressing her in the patronising manner in which cardinals have always been wont to speak to members of the laity – especially young people of little public status, and especially women. Claudia was provoked to respond with the same patronising phraseology, and this gave her the confidence to voice her views uncompromisingly. In fact, she wiped the floor with His Eminence, and, I am sure, had half the listening public cheering her on.

This has been the subject of continuing correspondence on 'Sunday', with a surprising preponderance of support for the young woman; though one correspondent did upbraid the BBC for not having chosen a more mature person to reply to the Cardinal. But who could be a more appropriate commentator on the Church's attacks on contraception and abortion than a young woman of child-bearing age? I would merely ask her why she is still in the Church. Before long, indeed, she may let it go – though there is something to be said, perhaps, for staying inside a totalitarian institution while disobeying it and fighting it from within.

In fact, nothing has so weakened papal authority over the past 27 years as the widespread flouting by married Catholic couples (at least in developed countries) of the ban on all artificial birth control, as confirmed in Paul VI's encyclical, *Humanae Vitae*. The long delay before that encyclical was published had led the Catholic laity to expect a lifting of the ban on (specifically) the non-mechanical method of the Pill, and many of them had jumped the gun – only to be told in 1968 that they now had to give up the practice to which they had become accustomed. This was seen as a counsel of perfection, and it became commonplace for married Church members to disobey the ban, with many progressive priests conniving at their disobedience. And once you disobey a Pope in one matter, you can no longer regard him as infallible. It is then but a small step to pick and choose among his edicts in general. This was the climate in which the present Pope took office; and, though not for want of trying, he has failed conspicuously to regain the lost authority.

However, the loss of authority he has suffered is, in a strange way, poetic justice: not only, throughout his sixteen-and-a-half-year reign, has he quoted approvingly from *Humanae Vitae* in his speeches and encyclicals, 'apostolic exhortations', and other messages to his Church, but also – as I have only just discovered (from reviews of Tad Szulc's recent biography) – much of that 1968 document had actually been drafted by him.

Three decades ago, when Paul VI was wracked with indecision about sanctioning the Pill, he invited leading prelates from different countries to advise him on it, so as to avoid a conservative backlash. Karol Wojtyla, Archbishop of Cracow, claimed to be a celibate expert on human sexuality, having already established an institute devoted to sexual ethics and written a book on sexuality – including physiological details of orgasm! So he was ready with copious reactionary advice to the Vatican. This was necessarily in writing, since the Polish government of the day restricted foreign travel; but for that very reason the text was all the more easily accessible to Pope Paul for direct plagiarism in his agonised encyclical, of which he always seemed rather ashamed.

In the papal election of October 1978, Karol's uncompromising stand on sexual matters, the rôle of women, and 'family values', may well have given him the vital votes of die-hard members of the College of Cardinals, while his left-of-centre reputation in the economic sphere would have made him acceptable to the more progressive cardinals. Only Poland could produce such a conjunction in one man.

During the papal visit to London in 1982, I wrote John Paul a letter pointing out that in this country more than a third of abortion operations are, disproportionately, carried out on Catholic women, who are reluctant to take contraceptive precautions – since that would indicate an unforgivable prior readiness to 'sin' rather than mere human frailty. Needless to say, I never received a reply, and have no means of knowing whether he ever read my letter; but in the new encyclical he specifically denies that the prohibition of contraceptive facilities leads to more abortion. Indeed, he sees the two as 'fruits of the same tree', or, to vary the metaphor, 'a seamless garment'. Fruit-trees or shirts, he denounces them as 'a veritable culture of death'.

To women who have already had recourse to abortion he says, with cruel paternalistic 'compassion', that God will respond with mercy to their humble and honest repentance, and then 'you will come to understand that nothing is definitely lost and you will also be able to ask forgiveness of your child, who is now living in the Lord'. What could be more calculated to create feelings of guilt? (On second thoughts, it would have been worse a few decades ago, when mothers were told that the soul of the unborn foetus was in Limbo, not Heaven; and worse still a few centuries before that, when it would have been consigned to Hell for all eternity.)

The whole gamut of Catholic bio-ethics, from embryology to euthanasia, turns on the doctrine of an immortal soul. At one time, theologians laid down a particular week in the pregnancy when the soul entered the foetus (a few weeks later for female foetuses than for males!), but since modern theologians admit they have no knowledge of the actual timing, to be on the safe side it has been assumed that 'ensoulment' takes place at the moment of fertilisation of the human ovum – and most Catholics, including the Pope, now seem to regard this as fact. It is expressed in the favourite statement of all 'pro-lifers', repeated yet again in this encyclical: 'Life begins at conception'.

That is of course a biological nonsense: there is no beginning for an individual life. Both the spermatozoon and the unfertilised egg are living entities. When the two come together, that is an important stage in the life cycle, but no more than that. Another favourite pro-life phrase is 'The embryo is human'. Of course it is human – it isn't a non-human embryo, such as that of a chicken – but that is not to say that it is a human being, any more that a human finger-nail is a human being.

It is impossible to point to a particular moment when a human being develops, since development is a gradual process. By analogy, at what moment does a boy become a man? Nobody really believes that it suddenly happens, say, on his 18th birthday, except for arbitrary legal purposes. However, this is not to say that a small boy should be given the same responsibilities as a mature man; only that such gradual change requires flexibility.

However, even the dictum 'Life begins at conception' fails to explain the Catholic prohibition on artificial means of birth control. That seems to hinge on the anti-sex attitude that sexual pleasure can be justified only if it entails a chance of conception, thus enabling God to bring another soul into being. All other sexual activity is 'dirty', presumably because the reproductive organs are so close to organs of excretion – a puzzling error made by the Creator!

On basic principles, it might be supposed that the technology of artificial insemination, which has already produced many thousands of 'test-tube' babies that would otherwise never have existed, would meet with the Pope's approval; for this is surely 'pro-life' if anything is. However, it, too, is 'morally wrong' in his eyes, for three reasons: first, because it is 'unnatural' – it's a wonder that the Church allows the faithful an unnatural laxative or aspirin; secondly, because the semen is generally obtained by masturbation – another dirty unpaid-for pleasure; and thirdly, because the practice of producing half-a-dozen ova at one time entails the destruction of those that prove to be surplus – or, worse, their preservation for medical research. IVF is therefore acceptable only when the semen used is that of the husband and has been obtained during coitus with his wife – for which a condom is allowable, provided it has been specially perforated! More important, no extra eggs may be fertilised so as to save the mother from repeated operations, as all fertilised ova must be implanted, even if known to be defective, and even if resulting in life-threatening multiple births.

At the other extreme of the individual life, the Pope strongly denounces voluntary euthanasia, though repeating the principle that pain-killing drugs may be used, even when they will shorten human life, provided the intention is to relieve pain, not to cause death. (This principle of motive becomes more casuistry in practice, but that is the Church all over.)The encyclical also reiterates Pius XII's 1957 declaration that 'extraordinary' or 'aggressive' treatments to prolong life need not be accepted, but does not give detailed examples – while medical practice has changed greatly since 1957 and some treatments that were seen as extraordinary then have become quite ordinary.

Though there are a few mitigant things in the encyclical, it is an authoritarian attempt to perpetuate the most injurious doctrines of the most harmful of all historical institutions; and it is sad that it has been received so sycophantically by the non-Catholic media.

The serious papers in this country, apart from the *Independent* (with its bold headline 'Standing firm in his time warp'), treated it with far too much respect. Perhaps the best of the other dailies was the *Daily Telegraph*, with a balanced article by Clifford Longley and a leader which was sound on contraception and abortion, though reactionary on euthanasia.

Even the American international journal *Newsweek* chose a fan of the Pope's (Kenneth L Woodward) to write on the encyclical: 'In the "Gospel of Life" John Paul II has sealed his papacy with a comprehensive and persistent vision', and '...the issues the "Gospel of Life" addresses are too volatile, too political – too personal and pressing – to be ignored'. For the sake of humanity, the encyclical *must* be 'ignored' – with the disdain it deserves.

[May 1995]

How Free is Freewill?
[Letter]

SEVERAL readers' letters in recent issues of the *Freethinker* indicate a lingering belief in the theological doctrine of 'freewill'. This is seen not only in the series of letters opposing Leslie James's article on that subject, but also in the series on the proposed restoration of capital punishment – opponents as well as supporters of the death penalty basing their comments on the question of guilt or innocence. But this distinction can have no place in rational argument, since conscious behaviour is determined by a combination of nature and nurture.

If the question of guilt is taken simply to mean whether or not an accused person carries out a criminal act, then that is a matter of (sometimes) ascertainable fact, which will underlie both the penal element of deterrence and assessment of the likelihood of future offences, so that the public may be adequately protected; but it has little to do with the notion of justice. Indeed, few judicial systems impose punishment (as distinct from restraint) on those who are clearly mentally deranged – but that is surely a matter of degree. We do not choose our subconscious compulsions. 'But he should have used more strength of will', people say – apparently not taking into account the fact that strength of will is as much the outcome of nature and nurture as anything else.

When using the term 'freewill', it is all too common to switch imperceptibly from the rationally acceptable meaning that in the absence of external coercion one has the feeling that one is free to make personal choices to the theological meaning that unconscious neuronal activity culminating in conscious decisions is under the control of a personal monitor (the soul – the essential self) and that the person is therefore blameworthy or praiseworthy. Hence hell and heaven.

In practice, there is something to be said for generally responding to conduct as though conscious acts that are free in the first sense are also free in the second. But that does not make them so.

[September 1995]

'All Shook Up' Over the Resurrection
[University Debate]

As Christians celebrate the death and resurrection of their Saviour and pagans joyfully mark the festival of Eostre – the Saxon goddess of the East, the Dawn, and the Spring – the *Freethinker* presents the text of Barbara Smoker's contribution to the Cambridge Union Society's recent debate on the motion that 'This house believes that Jesus Christ rose from the dead and the tomb was empty'. Miss Smoker and Daniel O'Hara opposed the motion. They lost the vote; who lost the argument is another question ....

ONCE upon a time, a boy child was born in humble circumstances, and in poverty he grew to be a man. But his charisma was such that the multitude acclaimed him, hailing him as the King. Having suffered greatly, he died in torment, while still in his prime, and was buried. Whereupon stories began to spread of people having seen him since his death and burial, as though alive, and speaking with him; then hundreds more eye-witnesses added their like testimony. Death seemed to have no dominion over him, and many came to believe that he had indeed risen from the grave. And his name was called ... Elvis Presley, the King.

I am sure that no one in this academic audience is among those simple Elvis believers, but it is apparent from contributions to the debate we have already heard that a number of you believe the same unlikely story about the man named Jesus; though in fact the alleged resurrection of Jesus is even less likely to be true than that of Elvis – for at least there is no doubt that Elvis did live, and we know his biographical dates, which would make him only about 60 years old today, whereas not only is it impossible for a human being to survive nearly 2,000 years but there is no satisfactory evidence that Jesus ever lived at all.

Even Christian theologians admit that the references made to him in commentaries of the time are obviously later interpolations. So – though the preceding speakers this evening, on both sides of the argument, have assumed we are talking about an historical character – Jesus may well have been fictitious, or possibly a composite of a number of actual itinerant first-century faith-healers and preachers, such as are still found in India under the name 'godmen' and in the United States under the name 'televangelists'.

However, the resurrection of Jesus, we are told, is a miracle, and a miracle has been defined as 'a breach of the natural law'. Now, the 17th-century pantheist philosopher Spinoza identified the divine will with natural law, and therefore felt he had to declare miracles to be an impossibility. Dean Inge – known in my childhood as 'the gloomy Dean' – was a liberal modernist Anglican cleric who, in 1930, wrote: 'Miracle is a bastard child of faith and reason'. And, more recently, the former Bishop of Durham, David Jenkins, was honest enough to deny the literal truth of the Resurrection, as well as the Virgin Birth and other alleged miracles.

In fact, countless honest Christians in the present century, trying to reconcile their theology with scientific knowledge, have been forced to give up many of the former articles of faith altogether, or else explain them away so that the story-line survives but its miraculous element is abandoned.

When we are told that Elvis Presley or Jesus Christ is still alive, is it more likely, in terms of common-sense, that the statement is true, or that those who proclaim it are liars – or, at least, gullibly mistaken? As for those who believe it at second- or third-hand, or some decades or centuries after the supposed witnesses, they are themselves all-too-willing victims of the original liars, and perpetuate the lie for later generations to swallow.

David Hume, arguably the most acute thinker of the 18th century, wrote that believing in miracles is 'a determination to believe what is most contrary to custom and experience'. He also wrote: 'The knavery and folly of men are such common phenomena that I should rather believe that the most extraordinary events arise from their concurrence than to admit to so signal a violation of the laws of nature.'

Today, with no fear of being tortured to death for heresy, we can express the same view in more simple, direct words. To a rationalist, accepting *anything* as a literal fact is a matter of probability based on the available evidence. And what could be more improbable than the story of someone rising from the death – not by resuscitation within a few minutes, while the brain is still oxygenated, but days later, when *rigor mortis* will have set in?

When the forebrain of a victim of illness or accident is so severely damaged as to register no brain-waves on an encephalogram, it is generally recognised that the brain can no longer process thought or even a dream, and the person can no longer experience desire or understanding or any other feature of consciousness. How much more certain is it when the body that houses that brain is irretrievably dead, and the brain itself succumbs to the process of decay!

Consciousness depends on the functioning of a living brain – or possibly, in decades to come, on the functioning of a very sophisticated computer. But the computer will always need some sort of hardware, which is analogous to the brain, as its output is analogous to consciousness. How on earth could any form of consciousness survive the disintegration of the physical brain? And the absence of consciousness when the brain is dead means there is no possibility of spirits existing – whether ghosts, gods, angels, devils, or the alleged 'spirit guides' supposedly in contact with mediums. Equally, there can be no future life, whether in Heaven or Hell or through reincarnation, haunting, or resurrection from the dead.

An atheist friend of mine who was brought up in a devout evangelical family tells me that at the age of about six he became obsessed with the idea of death and the resurrection, having seen funeral processions pass the house on their way to the cemetery, and being familiar already with the gospel stories. So one day he decided to put his teddy-bear in a tomb, for which he used a cardboard box, placing it upside-down in the garden with Teddy under it and a large stone blocking the opening that he had cut in one end of the box. The next morning, he ran down the garden to the 'tomb' – and to his amazement found that the stone had been rolled back and Teddy was gone. No doubt one of his parents had found it and rescued the toy from the damp earth. To the little boy, however, it was a miracle, and he raised his childish eyes to the sky in religious fervour. But he is now a mature man, so has put aside such childish notions, together with Santa Claus and goblins – as anyone who actually reaches maturity must.

There are no miracles for teddy-bears, or for Elvis Presley, and certainly not for the alleged Jesus. So I ask you all to show your maturity by voting against the superstitious motion before the House.

[April 1996]

When Life is Intolerable
[Murderer's Bid for Rational Suicide]

THE NEWS that the Home Secretary had confirmed the earlier decision that Myra Hindley should be kept in prison for the rest of her natural life was immediately followed by news of a request by her partner in crime, Ian Brady, for voluntary euthanasia; and one wondered if he was jumping on the Hindley bandwagon. It transpired however, that he had been making the same request repeatedly for the whole of the eleven years he had been in the high-security hospital, Rampton – for, unlike Hindley, he was certified insane and removed from an ordinary prison.

When my brother was doing his national service in the army, he was friendly with a fellow conscript who, having murdered an officer and been committed to Broadmoor, later wrote to my brother saying how much better life was in there than in the army. However, whereas my brother returned to civilian life a couple of years later, his erstwhile friend the murderer is presumably still detained. As with the concept of

Hell, or with the actuality of an incurable illness or disability, the worst aspect of such a fate is its permanence – the deprivation of any hope of light at the end of the tunnel. And it precludes any pretence that the purpose of punishment is rehabilitation.

Brady's situation is no doubt exacerbated by the aversion of his fellow inmates for him – since those who have merely murdered adults generally look down on child-murderers. So Brady's wish for euthanasia is sane enough, however insane he may be in other respects.

I was asked on February 11 to take on Judge Pickles in a late-night BBC radio discussion and phone-in on this news item. The retired circuit judge – a nephew of the radio entertainer Wilfred Pickles – has long carried on the family entertainment tradition, and is well known for his unpredictability.

On the present occasion, he was at least predictable in his insistence on the illegality of voluntary euthanasia in this country; and of course I agreed with him on that, making the point that until voluntary euthanasia is legalised for the terminally ill it is hardly likely to be made available for Ian Brady. But Pickles went on to assert that it was not only illegal but also, without exception, immoral – as, he said, was suicide; whereas I argued that they could be compassionate and rationally requested, and therefore moral.

My opponent then did a characteristic U-turn by saying that if Brady, like Fred West, were to take his own life no one would shed any tears over that. So there are apparently exceptions to the immorality of suicide after all.

However, it did not seem to occur to Judge Pickles that even unsupervised people do not always find it easy to end their own lives – there have been doctors of medicine who, taking what they believed to be a lethal dose of a drug, have succeeded only in damaging their brains or livers – and it might be even more difficult for an inmate of Rampton to take his own life than for a prisoner on remand. Pickles mentioned the almost foolproof method of a hose-pipe fixed to the exhaust-pipe of a car – but is Brady likely to have access to a car, a suitable hose-pipe, and the lengthy seclusion necessary to carry out this operation?

On the wider question of voluntary euthanasia for terminal illness or (in my view, even more important) for an incurable severe disability which the patient finds intolerable, Pickles was adamant that this must never be legalised: and we argued over that.

The listeners who then phoned in seemed almost entirely motivated by vindictive feelings towards Brady; but, strangely enough, came down on opposite sides of the argument: one saying that Brady deserves to be incarcerated for life, however long that may be, while another said he deserves to die as soon as possible. While vindictive feelings are understandable enough in the light of the terrible crimes he committed, they hardly make a good foundation for penology, let alone for treatment of the insane. It is essential that our feelings in such matters be controlled by reason.

An eminent exponent of the desirability of killing the criminally insane was Bernard Shaw. He was opposed to the whole concept of punishment, but saw the need for protecting the public against incurable criminals. When, at the turn of the century, he was asked to write a preface to a Fabian pamphlet on imprisonment, he wrote that while he regarded capital punishment as abhorrent, a quick death would be far better, from everybody's standpoint, than lifelong incarceration. However, the Quaker author of the pamphlet refused to accept the preface if it were to advocate the killing of convicted criminals. Shaw then agreed to rewrite this paragraph, so as to assert that lengthy prison sentences might be imposed, as long as there were enough Quakers willing to act as jailers!

In his play *Saint Joan*, Shaw makes Joan retract her confession when she realises that she is to be imprisoned for life: she prefers the fire. In one of his last plays, *The Simpleton of the Unexpected Isles*, Shaw depicts the mysterious disappearance, suddenly and painlessly, of those who do not pull their weight in the social boat. And in his book *Everybody's Political What's What*, written in his late eighties, Shaw writes: '... there are people like Ibsen's Peer Gynt, who funk doing anything irrevocable, and will commit the horrible atrocity of imprisoning a human creature for life rather than mercifully kill him anaesthetically, and, if possible, without his knowing it'.

Only the final phrase is repugnant to me. In the name of a basic human right, not only should the alternative of death be dependent, over a reasonable period of time, upon the free choice of the prisoner himself; there is also a general evil in killing people without warning – for once the practice became known, everyone at risk would live in perpetual fear of imminent extinction. Shaw himself was aware of this, yet he actually suggested extending the risk from criminal psychopaths to the idle rich – thinking it 'would produce a sense of social responsibility'! I can only assume that he was playing the octogenarian *enfant terrible*.

Coincidentally, the very day of this radio discussion of mine, the *Nursing Standard* carried an article by the pro-lifer Peggy Norris in which – intent on proving that, if voluntary euthanasia were legalised, 'the slide to involuntary killing will occur' – she quoted several sentences from an article I wrote in 1991 for the journal of the Voluntary Euthanasia Society. However, she put three little innocuous looking dots in the middle of the quotation, to replace two entire sentences that happened to be essential to the context. Fortunately, I was able to unearth the original, and have now written to the journal asking for the omitted sentences to be published. They were as follows.

> The two most important criteria are surely the intolerable nature of the condition and its incurability – the proper question being whether an intolerable condition is apparently incurable, not whether it is terminal. As for the voluntary element, this is, of course, fundamental in the case of adult patients who are capable of communication, but in many other cases it cannot apply.

If I believed in lifelong imprisonment, I might reserve it for those who quote others' words out of context!

[March 1997]

The Heaven's Gate Spaceship
[Suicidal Cult]

'JUST checking you are still alive,' I said, phoning an American friend when the news broke of the 39 ritual suicides in California at the time of the Hale-Bopp comet reaching its closest point to Earth. This old friend of mine had informed me twenty years ago that he was one of 10,000 (or was it 100,000?: I forget) enlightened people destined to be collected by a huge extraterrestrial spacecraft for immortality elsewhere in the cosmos – and he really believed it. I might mention he is a member of Mensa, a university graduate, and a computer engineer.

Yes, he was still alive – apparently his time had not yet come. Again, I asked him, as I had done twenty years earlier, what evidence he had for the existence of the jumbo spacecraft for which he has a boarding-pass, and his reply was that I myself believed in the force of gravity, though no one had ever been able to explain it. To the inflation of my telephone bill, I countered that, whether or not gravity could be explained in the abstract, it could certainly be demonstrated, while the predicted UFO had to be taken completely on trust – and a scientist should be able to see the difference. But science is no match for wishful thinking.

The 39 suicides – 21 women and 18 men – were likewise intelligent, educated people. Most of us find it difficult to understand how they could have swallowed the spacecraft story with such utter conviction that they were willing to kill themselves in readiness for it, many of them having submitted to castration first.

When you come to think of it, however, why should that be any more surprising than the faith of millions of equally intelligent, educated people in the similar (though more traditional) story of Christian salvation, resurrection and immortality? Yet press commentators have mostly been blind to the parallels, and the religious ones blindest of all.

If anything, to postulate an inter-galactic spaceship for the journey to 'the evolutionary level above humans' is a tad less absurd than believing in the individual flight of disembodied spirits to 'the other side'. In both cases Heaven, of one kind or another, is the final destination – though for the putrefying bodies found in a palatial rented hilltop mansion in the Californian millionaire suburb of Rancho Santa Fe, the actual destination proved to be the San Diego morgue.

The Heaven's Gate guru was Marshall Herff Applewhite, or 'King Do', who died with 38 of his followers. It was his hypnotic intensity and gentle but passionate way of speaking – the hallmark of orthodox Christian televangelists too – that seduced many in western USA to join his group. Some had been members for more than two decades.

Like traditional Christian monks and nuns, they were supposed to be completely celibate, they dressed all in black, they cropped their hair, and they called each other 'Brother' and 'Sister'. Their rigorously ascetic lifestyle, though in a plush setting, would put medieval monks to shame – though these latter-day monks did have the pleasure, at restricted hours, of watching videos of selected old episodes of *Star Trek* and *The X Files*, with their fictitious apocalyptic scenarios.

Applewhite himself, the 66-year-old son of a Presbyterian minister, had left theological college to take up music and opera-singing, but in his late thirties had been sacked as a music professor because of a homosexual scandal. He then became a voluntary patient in a psychiatric hospital where, in 1972, he was put in the care of a woman nurse, Bonnie Nettles – an astrology and flying-saucers freak, who was clearly even more crazy than her patient. Persuading him to be castrated for the sake of androgynous immortality, she convinced him that he was a new messiah sent to Earth by extraterrestrial beings to fulfil a divine prophecy – leading earthlings to an inter-galactic spacecraft for transit to a distant utopian planet. After Bonnie's death from cancer in the 1980s, King Do lived on under her posthumous influence, pursuing her fantasies to their grisly conclusion.

Since 1994, he had been using the latest digital technology to recruit more followers – naming his internet website 'Higher Source', changing the name of the group from HIM (Human Individual Metamorphosis) to Heaven's Gate, and moving his headquarters from New Mexico to a succession of rented houses in California.

Fulfilment of his destiny became urgent when Applewhite learned he had a terminal heart-condition – a fact which he did not see fit to share with his keyboarding followers. Had he done so, they might well have cut loose from his timetable of death. But he told them that planet Earth was about to be recycled and their only hope of survival was to pass through death at the right time to be beamed up by an inter-galactic UFO, piloted by the late Ms Bonnie Nettles, for their journey back 'home' – like ET – to their native planet. In the words of a Christian spiritual song, the spacecraft was 'comin' for to carry me home'.

The predicted approach of an unusually bright comet, first discovered by American astronomers Alan Hale and Thomas Bopp in 1995, gave rise to the idea that the awaited flying saucer was travelling earthward in the comet's slipstream. And the cultists' expectation of it seemed to materialise in March 1997, as the comet came close enough to Earth to be seen with binoculars, and then, tail and all, with the naked eye – 'the marker we've been waiting for'. So their time had really come.

If only they had seen the last issue of the CSICOP magazine *Skeptical Inquirer*, containing an article by Hale about his comet, it might have given them pause for rational thought, for in it the astronomer recounted similar cases of 'comet madness' in relation to other bright comets over the centuries, and predicted even greater madness this time – partly because of the coincidence of the comet's appearing so soon before the end of the second millennium.

Photographs taken in November 1996 of the alleged spacecraft in the wake of the comet were, Hale discovered, actually of a 'red giant' star that had appeared in that part of the sky at the time. To stem the flood of inquiries that he and other astronomers began receiving, he put the real explanation on the Internet – only to receive a large amount of vicious hate mail from UFO buffs, accusing him of being involved in a federal 'conspiracy' to hide information about the comet and its attendant spaceship. So perhaps King Do's disciples were too fixated after all on their own mythical theory to be saved from mass suicide by a more scientific explanation.

A comment in *The Times* notes similarities between the spheres of computer fanatics and religious cultists – 'both of them requiring a mental rigour to the point often of excluding common-sense'.

The doctrines of the Heaven's Gate group – who claimed to be 'inter-galactic angels' – are akin to those of the Church of Scientology, which teaches that humans were brought to Earth by an inter-galactic warlord, Xenu.

Unlike the many other cultic mass deaths in recent years – in Guyana, Mexico, Waco, Vietnam and Solar Temple sites in various countries – the one in Rancho Santa Fe apparently entailed no forced suicides or murder. The victims all went voluntarily, even leaving euphoric video messages, two by two, as animated suicide notes. 'It's not a big deal,' said one; 'We couldn't be happier,' smiled another.

Applewhite is described as having a very gentle personality, a non-violent ethos, and a lovely speaking and singing voice; but he was not too saintly to milk his recruits of their assets while isolating them from their families and friends outside the cult, in line with most fanatical sects, whether New Age or old-time religion. They were also set to work on designing commercial Internet websites to swell the Heaven's Gate coffers.

King Do's final broadcast, in his musical intonation, was this message to his resident followers: 'Light is coming to this planet. An opportunity is offered to humans. Those ready can graduate from this garden. You must leave behind loved ones, security, possessions. This is known as the harvest.' It was also known as 'shedding our containers' and 'transcending'.

Because the phenobarbital-alcohol-plastic-bag method of 'harvest' or 'transcending' used in Rancho Santa Fe – in shifts, over a period of three days – is the chief method of 'self-deliverance' recommended by the Right-to-Die movement in the USA, many commentators have put the blame for it on that movement: but euthanasia literature sanctions rational suicide only, for those with an intolerable and incurable illness or disability; while cult mass suicides are far from rational.

Ironically, a recently added section to their website was headed 'Our Position Against Suicide'. Declaring their opposition to suicide, which they did not equate with 'the spacecraft to take us home', it emphasised the importance of looking after our bodies, called 'containers'.

The Heaven's Gate website was cross-linked to a plethora of others, mostly with religious themes – today's equivalent of the Book of Revelation. In Britain, the Cult Information Network has urged parents to supervise children who may be surfing the Internet.

The number of mind-controlling cults is said to be about 2,500 in the USA, 800 in Canada and 500 in Britain. But that is a mere fraction of the number of sects of Christianity and Islam, which belong to the same genre – to a greater or lesser extent sacrificing present life, in the world we know, for a nebulous future life.

In the words of a contributor to the *Independent on Sunday*, writing from the USA: 'If you consider that 222-million Americans, or 87% of the population, believe they will go to Heaven; that 125-million believe in the existence of UFOs; and that 200,000 believe that they have been abducted by aliens – then the decision by 39 people to hitch a ride to eternity on a passing spaceship does not seem as strange as all that.'

[May 1997]

Postscript

SINCE writing my article on the mass ritual suicide in California, I have learned that another American, Charles Spiegel, who is leader of the Unarius Academy of Science, has announced that sadly the Heaven's Gate group got it all wrong. A number of inter-galactic spaceships will indeed be landing on Earth – to be precise, on the estate he himself has purchased for them near San Diego – but their arrival is not due until the year 2001.

[June 1997]

The Patient's Choice
[Auto-Euthanasia]

COMPUTER-AIDED euthanasia, devised by compassionate doctors of medicine with the requisite technological skills, has been the subject of recent simultaneous news reports from opposite sides of the globe – the USA and Australia – and in both countries the religious lobby, spearheaded by hard-line Catholics, has rushed to stamp it out.

In both countries, as in Britain and most parts of the Western world, suicide is legal but assisted suicide is not – which means that incurable patients are often forced to kill themselves prematurely, before losing the physical strength to do so unaided. Moreover, deprived of monitoring by a doctor or anyone else to see that they manage it successfully, many of them regain consciousness – sometimes with added complications caused by the suicide attempt.

Most religious believers contrive to make a moral distinction between active and passive euthanasia; that is, between killing and letting die. However, though completely discredited in secular moral philosophy, this spurious distinction – assuming the same intent and same motive – is by no means confined to religious teaching: in almost every country, it underpins the current secular law on expediting death, for laws tend to be based on theological criteria rather than common-sense.

A number of compassionate doctors – wishing to do the best for their patient and, ultimately, seeing their best as helping him/her to cut short the process of dying when it is prolonged and painful – have jeopardised their careers, and even risked murder prosecutions, for the sake of a patient. Most doctors, however, contrive to keep on the right side of the law by making use of the blurred area between passive and active euthanasia – particularly by administering increasing doses of painkillers as required, even though they have reached a lethal dose. This procedure, which is now almost universally followed, was developed by the hospice movement which, founded on a combination of care and religion, has made use of religious casuistry to insist that it is morally and legally defensible to give a patient a lethal dose provided the motive is palliative care, not euthanasia. Though hospices generally oppose the legalisation of voluntary euthanasia as such, at least they seem to be carrying it out in practice.

However, theirs is not an ideal solution, for it does not address any distressing incurable symptoms other than pain. Besides, there are some types of pain (for example, thalamic pain) which cannot be controlled except by rendering the patient comatose; and if one is permanently comatose, one might as well be dead. Anyway, such patients are usually subjected to the horror of regaining consciousness between doses of anaesthetic.

Although the churches have traditionally regarded suffering as a valuable means of acquiring grace, even religious opponents of euthanasia and suicide often talk about a 'merciful release' when a distressing illness ends in death. Supporters of voluntary euthanasia simply want the merciful release to occur before the suffering has been uselessly prolonged. But, except in the case of infants, there is only one person who has the moral right to decide on euthanasia: the decision must always rest with the person most concerned – the euthanasia candidate – provided he or she is adult and rational. It is thus akin to suicide.

On April 22 [1997], Channel Four screened a documentary, sensationally titled *Witness: An Appointment With Doctor Death*, about a retired pathologist from Michigan, Dr Jack Kevorkian. Targeted by pro-life demonstrators and hounded by police, he claims to have got round the law by creating the 'Mercitron' or 'self-execution machine' –

a computer-driven intravenous syringe operated by the euthanasia candidate himself. Though 46 of his patients had already used it, several juries have refused to convict him.

The relatives of one of the 46 were distressed because, they said, she had taken several minutes to die instead of the few seconds promised; but that is surely a direct result of the doctor's having to leave the whole operation to the patient herself instead of being allowed to intervene when required. And a coroner who conducted post-mortem examinations on 39 of Dr Kevorkian's 46 computer suicides claimed that three of them showed no anatomical evidence of terminal disease – but that, too, is hardly surprising in the enforced climate of secrecy, which means that no second medical opinion can be sought.

The legalisation of voluntary euthanasia, which Kevorkian advocates and most members of the public (even Catholics) want, is to be considered by the US Supreme Court this summer.

Australia's Northern Territory was in the news last year when it passed the world's first 'right-to-die' law – which was to last only eight months. In that period, several terminally ill patients who satisfied its strict guidelines were legally allowed the induced death they had requested. But a coalition of 'pro-lifers', led by (literally) die-hard Catholics, had already called a high-powered meeting (co-chaired by representatives of Australia's three major parties), at which the campaign 'Euthanasia No' was formed.

In March, Euthanasia No managed to force a Private Member's Bill through the Australian Federal Senate (by 38 votes to 35), preventing the Territories from passing their own laws on Voluntary Euthanasia.

Last year, Dr Philip Nitschke, a physician in Darwin (capital of the Northern Territory), developed, and used for a number of patients, a DIY euthanasia machine similar to Kevorkian's in the USA. On May 14 this year he disclosed that he had now, in view of the change in the Australian law, invented a 'coma machine', designed to keep the dying unconscious. Its computer-programmed sensor detects emerging consciousness and controls the flow of drugs through an intravenous drip.

Dr Nitschke is quoted in the *Guardian* of May 15 as commenting: 'It is considered to be good medical practice to allow a person to die over two days, and yet if you increase the infusion rate and they die over two hours it is considered to be murder.' This sums up the absurdity of the law, based on the split hairs of religious superstition.

A more common example of the same split hairs is the accepted practice of leaving pneumonia untreated if a dying patient happens to contract it – though there is no discernible ethical distinction between withholding antibiotics (so as not to cure the pneumonia) and actually administering a lethal dose or injection (in the absence of pneumonia) – except, perhaps, the implicit principle that you must always give the Almighty a sporting chance of a miraculous cure! Ironically enough, it is usually expressed in the words of the humanist poet Arthur Hugh Clough – 'Thou shalt not kill; but needst not strive/Officiously to keep alive' – though, of course, Clough intended this satirically, as the context makes clear.

Religious opponents of euthanasia often insist that God alone is to determine our time of death; humans are not allowed to tamper with God's will. If that were so, would it not be wrong to intervene to save life, as well as to hasten death? But human life is, they tell us, a 'gift from God'. Even if we were to accept that as true, is there no right to decline a gift when it is nothing but a burden?

Besides, the case for legalising voluntary euthanasia is that the required change in the law would be merely permissive. We uphold the right of our opponents to decide against active (or even passive) euthanasia for themselves, but not for us: they have no moral right to make laws that impose their views on others, who may not even share the religious beliefs on which those views are based.

Believers who uphold the principle of complete freedom of religion often fail to see that, in all logic, this must include freedom *from* religion.

[June 1997]

How to be a Virgin Mother

[Joint Obituary of Princess Diana and Mother Teresa]

IT WAS a drama of coincidence – the deaths within the same week of Diana, Princess of Wales (36) and Mother Teresa of Calcutta (87). The one a glamorous privileged English woman in her prime, the other a wrinkled Albanian nun, they nevertheless had a great deal in common.

They both allowed superstition to rule their lives – in the one case a mishmash of ancient and modern folklore, in the other a rigid acceptance of institutionalised dogma. Both were hailed as charismatic; both had an insatiable appetite for worldwide adulation; both manipulated the media. And they were both in the laying-on-of-hands healing business – the nun pressing heads and praying (instead of providing medical treatment), the Princess touching and hugging (alongside the medical treatment provided by others).

While Diana was a sort of pagan goddess, Mother Teresa was a more traditional saint: but both were in the Virgin Mother mould. Diana's attested virginity was the main criterion for the arranged marriage she went through in 1981, and, although subsequently twice a mother, she still looked virginal; while the octogenarian Bride of Christ, though literally ever a virgin, undoubtedly had a strong maternal instinct for all babies – even for foetuses. However, she always asserted that, unlike the Princess, she was motivated not by love and compassion for her fellow humans but by love for Christ – an aloof, omnipotent being who, she believed, 'called' her to dedicate her life to the impossible task of relieving suffering that he could presumably have prevented, had he so willed.

Even before she died, there were popular demands for MT's canonisation, and she said nothing to discourage them. Indeed, she boasted that St Peter would have no difficulty in recognising her when she reached the Pearly Gates. In the first few days after her death, the Vatican was besieged with demands to curtail the usual lengthy investigatory procedures before beatifying her in readiness for speedy canonisation, and may well do so.

As for the Princess's brand of superstition, she and Dodi Fayed had travelled 250 miles by helicopter only eighteen days before their fatal car accident to consult an expensive clairvoyant – the self-styled 'priestess' of spiritualism, Rita Rogers – presumably about the future of their relationship. Though we cannot be sure what Ms Rogers told them, she certainly seems to have neglected to warn them about nocturnal car journeys!

It seems most likely that she assured them of a long and happy life together. That might account for Dodi's inviting Diana to select an unofficial engagement ring. She chose a magnificent £133,000 diamond ring (diamonds being a girl's best friend), of which Dodi took delivery early that fatal Saturday evening and no doubt tried on Di's manicured finger before they left for their Last Supper at the Paris Ritz.

Such a prediction might also have contributed to a feeling of unassailable security which would make it unnecessary to take such mundane precautions as fastening seat-belts and avoiding excessive speeds in a tunnel – not to mention an apparently drunken driver.

The media and the public rushed to blame the persistent free-lance photographers for the tragic accident, then the chauffeur for drinking (though he was supposed to be off-duty), and, in the background, the royal family, especially Diana's former husband. Even conspiracy to murder was postulated. But Dodi and Diana must bear some personal responsibility for their manifest irresponsibility – in which they were emboldened, perhaps, by their heady courtship, by the clairvoyant's positive predictions, and (who knows?) by the wine at dinner – possibly combined with Di's usual prescribed Prozac.

The paparazzi certainly seem to have behaved intolerably, but it would have been far more intolerable for Diana had they ever ceased wanting to photograph her altogether. Besides, if she and her playboy lover wished to avoid cameras on this particular occasion, why not simply use blinds in the back windows of the car; why not ask for police protection; why not even order a Ritz takeaway in the first place, rather than turn the public highway into a suicidal speed track?

Presumably innocent of the sin of drinking alcohol, Dodi was given a traditional Muslim funeral. Then, on the eve of Diana's funeral, every mosque in this country included her, too, in its Friday prayers – though in most of the worshippers' homelands she would probably have been stoned to death as a self-confessed adulteress. It was all part of the mass hypocrisy, hysterical adulation, and excessive public mourning that engulfed the country.

Some of the tributes to the Princess described her, amazingly, as 'intelligent'. That made me smile – and would have made her smile too, for she was well aware that she was all heart ('Queen of Hearts') and little brain (O-levels: nil). At the same time, she had perceptive intuition, genuine concern, and impish wit, as well as the cunning to win people over to her side.

It was Diana's volatile, emotional, irrational nature that made her 'this impossible girl' (as the Queen is said to have called her) and that so endeared her to the British and worldwide public. Most little girls learn to get their own way by flirting; and Diana flirted shamelessly and effectively, with the whole world. But her one-to-one relationships were punctuated by bitter quarrels – even with most of her staff.

Had her relationship with Dodi not been so tragically cut short, it might have lasted a year or two – long enough, at least, for her to acquire a new father-in-law able to install the couple in a recently restored villa in the Bois de Boulogne, extravagantly designed half-a-century ago for the British abdicatee-in-exile. In fact, they toured it just a few hours before the car crash. It seems that Diana (like Jackie Onassis), having tasted the aphrodisiac of public grandeur, now craved the aphrodisiac of pampering private wealth and personal worship.

However, in spite of everything, I must admit I rather took to the Princess myself – smitten, as most people were, by her lovely expressive eyes and her undoubted empathy with those who suffered. And she did, after all, succeed in rescuing AIDS and leprosy victims from untouchability and in raising public awareness of the victims of anti-personnel landmines.

As it happened, I was called upon to defend her in a television programme *(Stand and Deliver)* earlier this year, against an attack by a brittle young media woman who blamed Diana for single-handedly bringing down the monarchy. I pointed out that if the monarchy had indeed been brought down, the royals must take a share of the blame. Anyway, the Princess was herself a monarchist, and clearly wished her elder son to become king. Yet in death she was seen as a quasi-republican; she almost turned the nation to republicanism within days, and forced the Queen herself to eat humble-pie.

To my mind, Diana's campaign against anti-personnel land-mines expunged all her self-centered silliness, and it is to be hoped that her legacy will include a complete international ban on them.

There is no such extenuating legacy from the life of Agnes Gonxha Bojaxhiu, better known as Mother Teresa.

She actually declared, in one of the poorest and most densely populated cities in the world, 'Have all the babies, and I will look after them!' How arrogant can you get? And she admitted, without shame, that saving the lives of severely defective newborn babies was primarily a propaganda exercise against contraception, abortion, and euthanasia.

Many Indians saw her as a 'disaster' for Calcutta. Social justice was simply not in her vocabulary. Not only did she use her considerable political influence to obstruct the availability of contraception and abortion, she also wasted huge sums of money from the West that might have gone to those trying to deal honestly with the underlying problem of over-population and to provide India with modern hospitals.

The obituarist in the *Calcutta Telegraph* forthrightly accused her of using the dying poor as 'stepping-stones in a relentless ascent to sainthood'.

Her self-righteous submission to poverty and suffering, in accordance with medieval Catholicism, was likewise forced upon her clients, though the majority were not even Christians. One of them, told by her that he was privileged to be caressed by Jesus on the cross, replied 'I wish he'd stop caressing me!' – and she repeated this as an amusing quip.

Hers was a grandiose form of sado-masochism. Putting on an act of humility, she hobnobbed with the world's most powerful and wealthy people, including its most corrupt dictators, and maintained a special hot-line to the Creator himself.

A considerable proportion of the donations she attracted came from very dubious sources (Papa and Baby Doc Duvalier and Robert Maxwell are examples), and were given with very dubious motives. Even when told it was stolen money, she refused to give any of it up.

Soon after Malcolm Muggeridge had put her on the world stage, casting her as a 'living saint' in his sickeningly titled TV film (1969) and book (1971), *Something Beautiful for God,* she chose to spend a large donation, presumably intended to relieve poverty, on a gold ciborium for a new convent chapel, to glorify her cruel god; and St Mugg perversely applauded the choice. At the same time, he castigated me (in a Sunday paper) for having dared to dub her a 'sacred cow'.

In 1979 she was awarded the Nobel Peace Prize. Ten years later she arranged a meeting with the Princess of Wales, shrewdly recognising in her a twin soul.

The funeral journey for each of them was by state gun-carriage, in London and Calcutta. Diana was buried with the rosary given her by Mother Teresa – though she would not have known how to use it. Some assert that the two women are now together in Heaven, beaming their spiritual gifts to Earth. Others see Dodi as Di's more likely soul-mate in the after-life.

I too think Diana will live on – but as an undying legendary icon of immaculate womanly beauty, like Helen of Troy. And the little island in the Althorp Park lake will become a place of lasting popular pilgrimage.

Had true precognition been possible, Diana might well have regarded death as not too high a price to pay for the adoration of her that has ensued; especially if the alternative were to be survival with disfigurement. Furthermore, she has avoided both the trauma of another broken marriage and the physiological ravages of time and of Prozac.

Blessed art thou among women!

[October 1997]

'Psychics' and the Princess

[The Duping of Di]

IN MY article last month, 'How to be a Virgin Mother', I mentioned that, less than three weeks before their fatal car crash, Diana and Dodi had visited a clairvoyant spiritualist, Rita Rogers, to consult her, it seems, about the future of their relationship. Only after writing this did I learn that she was one of several 'psychics' – astrologers, and so on – that they visited over a short period, and none of them apparently warned the star-crossed lovers about imminent road dangers.

It has also been brought to my notice that when their visit to Ms Rogers came to light (through some children spotting the landing of the helicopter), the *Daily Mail* cashed in on the story by commissioning two professional psychics to report on the future of the great romance. One of them, Jim Chivers, asserted: 'The wedding will take place in about a year's time, and I think they'll be very happy.' The other, Craig Hamilton-Parker, disagreed: 'The relationship will fizzle out soon after Christmas' was his prediction, and he continued in some detail, as follows.

> It will be Diana who walks away from it, but Dodi won't give a damn when she does. The feeling will be mutual. In the meantime, though, they'll have some fun. I can see them going on a skiing holiday together.'

Well, perhaps there are ski slopes on 'the Other Side'.

Two weeks after the tragic event, *Psychic News* revealed that the accident had actually been predicted by a number of psychics, who had since informed the paper of the fact.

It seems unfortunate that none of them bothered to reveal their predictions in time to alert the people most concerned. In any case, however, I wonder if any infallible prediction could logically (rationally does not come into it, of course) have the effect of nullifying itself!

[November 1997]

Politically Correct Torture
[Female Genital Mutilation]

THE subjection of small girls to female circumcision, or female genital mutilation (FGM), is a common practice, especially in Africa, affecting two-million girl children each year.

There are various degrees of FGM, ranging from 'Sunna' – excision of the prepuce, with or without excision of part or all of the clitoris – to 'infibulation', which additionally involves narrowing of the vaginal opening. Carried out without anaesthetic, it is extremely painful; it has dire consequences with regard to the girls' future health and happiness; and sometimes it causes death.

The underlying motive for it is to ensure that girls remain virgins until marriage, and then, supposedly, to enhance their husbands' enjoyment of the sex act while curtailing their own. It is therefore patriarchal in its origins, but the people most adamant in advocating it are, strangely enough, often the women, especially the girls' grandmothers, who were victims of the practice themselves. One is reminded, in our own culture, of the decades of campaigning against corporal punishment in schools, when its abolition was most vehemently opposed by old men who had been schoolboy sufferers. ('It never did me any harm.') Perhaps there is a natural urge for former child victims of torture to revenge themselves on future generations.

Female circumcision is frequently claimed to be a religious requirement for Muslim families, though some exegetes maintain that the Koran actually stipulates the circumcision of boys only, not girls.

Although banned in Britain by the Prohibition of Female Circumcision Act, 1985, FGM is still widely practised in Muslim communities in this country. Some of the little girls are taken on 'holiday' (often by their grandmothers) to their ancestral homes for the operation; others are illegally circumcised in Britain by traditional male practitioners – including doctors – for whom it is a substantial money-spinner.

Despite the law, those who carry out FGM here are rarely brought to trial – partly because our health and social workers are reluctant to appear 'politically incorrect' by intervening in the traditions of any immigrant culture. Some British health workers even promote 'medicalisation' of the procedures, under clinical conditions, so as to reduce the attendant pain and health risks – but this only legitimises the superstition that underlies this child mutilation.

It was the subject of an exposé on October 7 by the excellent television documentary series on Channel 4, *Black Bag,* which concerns itself with topical issues in Britain's black communities. Though it did not pull its punches, the programme did soften the harrowing details by use of the euphemism 'cutting the rose', not only verbally but also in its visual substitution of roses for human flesh. But the message came across clearly enough. Some of the young women who spoke out against the practice were sufficiently courageous to allow their faces to be shown on the screen; those on the other side, understandably enough, hid behind camera angles and blurring techniques. But some of their dossiers are now to go to the police and, in the case of medical practitioners, to the General Medical Council.

At the end of the TV programme, the address was shown of the campaigning organisation FORWARD (Foundation for Women's Health Research and Development) International, which, 'promoting awareness to counter traditional practices prejudicial to the health of women and children', is also active in the alleviation of suffering from vesico-vaginal fistula resulting from FGM.

[November 1997]

The After-Death Experience
[Book Review]

[*The After-Death Experience* by Ian Wilson (Sidgwick G Jackson, £12.95) and *As In Adam All Die* by S Ramsay Blackley (The Book Guild, £9.50)]

THE author of the first of these two books made his name with books on the so-called Turin Shroud, and told me in a recorded radio discussion on that subject that the evidence he had uncovered for the authenticity of that relic had forced him to convert from agnosticism to Roman Catholicism. (My reply, 'Rather a materialistic basis for faith, isn't it?!' was cut out of the broadcast version.) Though his latest book on that subject is far less certain in its findings than his earlier writings, he has yet to relinquish the faith. Indeed, his selection of historical and scientific facts and theories, and the emphasis he gives them, are always directed towards an apparent conclusion that happens to underpin current Roman Catholic orthodoxy.

The book under review continues Ian Wilson's remunerative production line of popular, glossy, well-illustrated publications that contrive, by blinding the average reader with science in a smoke-screen, to lend a spurious air of academic respectability to religious sensationalism. He always builds up a selective picture, finally discounting most of the alleged evidence he puts forward, but keeping enough of it in reserve for a concluding question-mark at the end of each chapter.

The title *The After-Death Experience* was chosen, he says, by the commissioning publisher; but it is significant that he has kept the sensational title, though in the body of the book he has to employ the more scientific label 'near-death experience' for the well-known out-of-the-body phenomenon for which the title of the book is popularly used. At the same time he suggests, quite absurdly, that these undoubted psychological experiences of the near dead might relate to some real *after*-death state. And because part of his technique is always to include a few Aunt Sallies, he also drags in alleged evidence for both spiritualism and reincarnation – which, of course, he then proceeds to knock down, since these claims run counter to Catholic doctrine. In the course of this exercise, he gives rational explanations and supporting evidence that exposes fraud in many cases, and some of this material could be useful for rationalists dealing with other apologists, though it is mostly available elsewhere.

The 'out-of-the-body' experience is frequently reported by patients who have been resuscitated after a few minutes of cardiac arrest. But it is quite susceptible to rational interpretation. Though the patient may remain half-conscious, and can afterwards often report the things said by members of the medical team, the temporary deprivation of oxygen to the brain prevents him from experiencing his body in the normal way, so it is not surprising if this unprecedented lack of feeling in his body gives him the sensation of floating above it and actually looking down on it. At the same time, it may also (especially in the case of religious believers) include dream-like images of dead friends or relatives in another world, such as paradise.

Any other explanation of the 'out-of-the-body' experience would mean our abandoning the basic known fact that thought is an outcome of brain activity, and repudiating our understanding of the relationship between mind and body and, indeed, of causality itself. But, of course, suspending the normal rational framework of ideas that human beings have built up on the basis of reality is what religion is all about. Among the questions it raises is this: why do we need, for the interpretation of reality, all our elaborate physiological and biochemical mechanisms, including the human brain, if the 'soul', once out of the physical body, can manage so well without them?

One particular give-away of Ian Wilson's selective method and of his personal criteria for belief is his comment (page 153) on the near-death experience of a cockney woman who reported seeing the entrance to paradise, described by her as a nasturtium-lined path leading to the door of a 'nice prefab'. Wilson finds the cockney idea that heaven resembles a cosy post-war prefabricated bungalow as a 'difficult-to-take feature of the cockney lady's story'. And he goes on, 'For the rationalist-minded, including myself, it does seem to be asking a great deal to believe that the afterlife might take such a prosaically earthly form.' No doubt he would have found an ivory tower more credible.

The other book under review, written by a man who himself has had a cardiac arrest, covers much the same area of concern, but from a genuine rationalist viewpoint – and therefore with less expectation of the best-seller status that pays for a glossy production and expensive illustrations. But it is written with wit and robust good humour, and includes some amusing instances of religious beliefs concerning life after death.

[February 1998]

Educational 'Apartheid' on the Taxpayer

[Faith Schools]

TO DENY children a healthy range of nutritional food would be a serious form of physical child-abuse; to deny them contact with a range of views on important issues is surely a form of mental abuse that is comparably serious. Yet the Government is now encouraging this, with the first public funding of Muslim schools in line with those of the Anglicans and Catholics (and a handful of Methodist and Jewish schools).

Though I am as concerned as anybody about the right of minority groups to pursue their own chosen lifestyle, I am also concerned about the rights of minorities within those minority groups (for example, their women and their children), and of the smallest minority of all (the individual). If families settle in this country, surely they should be willing for their children to become part of it?

Freedom of religious belief and practice must, of course, always be defended; but so must freedom *from* religious belief and practice. And in the case of communities which have come into the country fairly recently, pressures are exerted by their more fundamentalist members on the rest to conform to religious and cultural traditions.

I am unable to comment on the two institutions chosen to pioneer the new policy, but Muslim schools in general are likely to be far more restrictive, especially for girls, than Christian schools now are – and the decision opens the floodgates to a wave of applications from all manner of religious groups, which it will be difficult to reject.

215

The Labour Party is generally more conciliatory to Muslim extremism than Conservatives are, partly because the Muslim vote has always almost entirely benefited Labour, and partly because of their commitment to the mythic ideal of 'multiculture' and their genuine concern about legal inequity between one religion and another.

In July 1989, the Labour Party's pledge of appeasement to the Muslim community was enshrined in an official policy document entitled *Multicultural Education*. Even before that, it was foreseen by the National Secular Society and the *Freethinker* that when the Labour Party got to power it would be likely to reconsider the Conservative rejections of specific applications for funding Muslim schools. We have therefore issued public warnings about it many times over the past few decades. We did not, however, foresee the suddenness of it: we naïvely imagined that it would be preceded by a debate in Parliament, or at least discussion in the Cabinet – but apparently there was no such semblance of democratic procedure. It was, it seems, simply a cosy agreement between Tony Blair and David Blunkett.

There has been virtually no media comment on the dictatorial nature of the decision. Indeed, apart from a few readers' letters in some papers, there was very little media comment of any kind on so important a social innovation.

Two exceptions were the *Guardian*, which ran a predictably blinkered article on it by Roy Hattersley, and the *Independent*, which allotted 33 column-inches to the subject but entrusted it to Trevor Phillips, who saw fit to digress from the schools issue, devoting much of his space to a diatribe against a BBC football commentator who had dared to say that he found it difficult to distinguish between one black player and another. It was a storm in a teacup, to be forgotten in a few weeks, whereas religious schools are likely to be causing psychological and social trauma – even violent conflict, as in Northern Ireland – for decades to come.

The Government's dictatorial announcement was made by a spokesman for the Education Secretary on January 9th – 'felicitously on a Friday in Ramadan', as the *Daily Telegraph* commented. On looking at the applications for public funding made in the past dozen years by two Muslim schools and one Hasidic school, Mr Blunkett had, we are told, found no 'reasonable grounds' for adhering to the rejections of them made by his Conservative predecessors. Reasonable grounds were hardly likely to come to light, however, if his considerations were restricted to the applications themselves. Is it too much to suggest that he might also have considered the wider statement which, with the names of 23 distinguished signatories, was published in full on the correspondence page of the *Guardian* on July 9, 1986? Since the signatories included Sir Alfred Ayer, Dr Cyril Bibby, Edward Blishen, Prof Bernard Crick, Lord Houghton, Naomi Mitchison, Dr Joseph Needham, Lord Raglan, and Lord Willis, one might have expected the letter to have found its way into the appropriate official files.

The letter was initiated by the NSS. As its president, I prepared the draft of it, then had to negotiate every word with all the proposed signatories. (Not easy!) Our original intention was to get the letter into all the broadsheets, but some of the Labour signatories refused to let their names appear in *The Times* on account of a compositors' dispute with the owners over redundancies, and we were finally reduced to the one outlet. It was reprinted in leaflet form, for distribution at the NUT conference and elsewhere.

Apart from the introduction since then of grant-aided status alongside voluntary-aided status for schools, the letter remains pertinent today.

We are very concerned about a dangerously divisive factor in our educational system: the large number of voluntary-aided denominational schools that segregate children according to their religious background. The social divisiveness this causes is seen at its worst in Northern Ireland.

Voluntary-aided denominational schools have so far been confined almost entirely to Anglican, Roman Catholic, and a few Jewish schools; but we are now seeing the beginning of a proliferation to include various immigrant religions.

In April this year a recommendation from a local authority (Brent) that a fundamentalist Islamic primary school in its area be allowed public funding, in line with denominational schools in the Judaeo-Christian tradition, was sent to the minister of state for education.

Whatever the decision in this particular case, it cannot be long, in the name of racial and religious equality, before a separate Muslim or Sikh (or Hindu or other religious) school is granted voluntary-aided status, thereby encouraging a general upsurge of immigrant denominational schools.

This may seem, superficially, a progressive step in line with current trends towards multiracial education and bilingualism; but in fact it would mean for

217

many children – especially girls – of immigrant families almost total isolation from the host community and from ideas at variance with those of the home background.

This would not only be a disaster for these youngsters personally; it would also inevitably build up for future generations a greater degree of animosity and violence than we have seen even in Northern Ireland. There, children are segregated on grounds of religious background only; in this case there would be the additional divisive factors of race, skin colour and sex.

And besides driving a wedge between immigrants and the host community, separate religious schools would import to Britain some of the religion-based bitterness and strife that exist on the Indian subcontinent. In the name of equity, however, it is manifestly impossible for the state to refuse Muslims and Sikhs the same right as Christians and Jews to state-subsidised schools of their own.

How, then, can this looming social tragedy be averted without blatant discrimination? Only by Parliament legislating without delay to phase out subsidies to denominational schools of every kind. Besides encouraging integrated schooling, this would make good economic sense: at least 85 per cent of the capital cost and 100 per cent of the running costs of voluntary-aided denominational schools are financed from the public purse, and this dual system of education is notoriously wasteful. We cannot deny, however, that a parliamentary decision to phase out subsidies to denominational schools will need considerable political courage, since it will inevitably lose votes. It demands an all-party determination to grasp the nettle.

Needless to say, Parliament has never grasped the nettle of announcing an end to any new public funding of religious schools, to be followed by the phasing-out of the existing public funding. The inequity between one religion and another in this respect has therefore dragged on, only to be resolved now by extending the right to expand educational apartheid at the taxpayer's expense.

The words 'immigrant' and 'host' in the letter, though approved at the time by our late (Indian) treasurer, G N Deodhekar, sound rather dated, even patronising, twelve years later, since so many of the Muslims and Sikhs living in Britain today were born here. Besides, there is also an increasing number of indigenous converts to Islam, especially (amazing though it seems) among women. The foreboding voiced in the letter, however, is even more urgent and relevant and serious now than it was then.

Two years after the letter appeared, a new law aggravated the situation. This was the 1988 Education Reform Act, the religious clauses of which attempted to increase school religion (predominantly Christian) in the state sector. It faced educationalists with an unresolvable dilemma: on the one hand to force Christian teaching on children of non-Christian backgrounds, or, on the other hand, to provide separate religious teaching and assemblies for these children or to encourage their parents (some of whom would not be able to read or write English) to 'opt' them out in writing – though the legal right of parents to withdraw their children from RE and the religious assembly has proved to be most unsatisfactory.

The former solution would mean complaints of proselytisation and increased pressure from non-Christian religious leaders for their own separate state-funded schools; while the latter would create unacceptable cultural, racial, and religious divisions within the school, as well as condemning many of the girls to lifelong oppression.

Why should the law create this appalling dilemma by forcing religious teaching and worship on our schools in the first place? Most other countries in the Western world have banned religion from their state schools. Parents who want their children to learn the tenets of a particular creed can surely carry out this teaching themselves, or entrust it to their own church, chapel, synagogue, or mosque, outside school hours. There is no justification whatever for making school a part-time place of worship.

Many Muslims saw the 1988 Act as an attempt to christianise their children. To the mullahs, if there was one thing worse than the prevailing lack of religion in the state sector of education, it was the wrong sort of religion. Though their fear was largely unjustified – for most schools contrive to get round the religious requirements of the law and rarely christianise even nominally Christian children – they have played on it as an additional argument for their own publicly funded schools.

Insofar as religion is taught at all in the local-authority schools, then certainly Islam should take its place alongside other world religions: provided, of course, that the teaching is objective and that alternative world views – disbelief (including secular humanism) as well as a range of beliefs – are accorded comparable time and respect. But we have always held that there is no need for a special slot for religion on the timetable: it should simply take its natural place in literature, drama, history, geography, sociology, art, and liberal studies.

As for the corporate act of worship in state schools, that is an abomination to believers and non-believers alike. The original intention behind the corporate religious assembly was, we were told, to inculcate a communal sense of cohesion; but separate assemblies for each cultural and religious community can only have the opposite effect.

Now that the first two Muslim schools have achieved state funding, further applications from denominational schools are to be expected – and not just from Muslim schools. Besides, parents who may prefer integrated schooling for their children and previously had the excuse of high school fees, will now have more pressure put on them by the mullahs to send their children to the Muslim schools, which will then proliferate.

[February 1998]

This Reactionary Pope
[Pontifical Bio-Ethics]

WHILE the Anglican churches were openly debating outmoded sexual restrictions at their international convention in Canterbury in July, and its host archbishop was making a fool of himself on the same subject in the pages of *The Times*, the Pope must have preened himself on having been able to get in first with his recent 'apostolic letter', *Ad tuendam fidem* (In Defence of the Faith) – without any need for public consultation, agenda papers or proposals put to the vote.

The *Guardian* front-paged the document on July 2 under the headline 'Pope turns on liberal Catholics', and it is certainly designed to gag some of the more progressive theologians on these issues. But whether it will make much practical difference is another matter, since not only does the claim of papal infallibility ring increasingly hollow, but the Church no longer has the power to burn dissidents at the stake and there can be few who regard excommunication as a fate worse than death.

Not that the document states anything new – quite the contrary.

It is really no more than a technical device to enshrine in canon law the traditional Vatican stand on such issues as artificial contraception, abortion, voluntary euthanasia, the medical and experimental use of foetal tissue and embryos, priestly celibacy, 'family values', and women priests – a stand which the Pope had already reiterated less formally in his encyclical *Evangelium Vitae* (The Gospel of Life), published in 1995. [See my review of it in the *Freethinker* of May 1995.]

In January 1989, a theological crisis was precipitated by the dissident document known as the Declaration of Cologne, signed by 163 North European (German, Austrian, Dutch and Swiss) theologians, and later supported by many more. It demanded, *inter alia*, a modification of the total ban on contraception, and the 1995 encyclical was partly a put-down of that demand.

Then fifty-thousand women converged on Beijing, for the fourth United Nations Conference on women. As expected, the greatest controversy was on the worldwide campaign for greater access to contraception and for legal abortion, both predictably opposed by delegates from Catholic countries and from a number of conservative Muslim countries – in temporary alliance, as they had been on the same issue at the Earth Summit in Cairo. On abortion, they were also supported by a few fundamentalist Protestants, including two British delegates from the Society for the Protection of Unborn Children. But they were severely trounced by the liberal camp, spearheaded by Platform for Action and backed by a large majority of the delegates, including those of the European Union, with a more responsible attitude towards the world's population explosion.

The Vatican itself sent a large delegation to Beijing – surprisingly headed by an American woman law professor, Mary Ann Glendon. She loudly proclaimed equal rights for women, while aiming to deny them rights over their own bodies.

Homosexuals in almost every Christian sect are made to feel guilty about their own nature, and homosexual Catholic priests particularly so. The next pope might well be less intransigent on this issue than the present one. In particular, the use of condoms by gays, included in the Vatican's blanket ban on condoms – except for the perforated ones used in obtaining semen from husbands for IVF – is obviously crucial in preventing the spread of HIV; but the Pope will not compromise his insistence on total gay celibacy.

How long can the Vatican stand out against the tide of social history? The present pope will never change; but he can live for only a few more years. Younger members of the College of Cardinals, though chosen finally by the pope, are inevitably less reactionary on sexual matters than those too old to have a vote, and are ready for a change of policy; so the next pope is likely to be comparatively permissive.

Early on in the reign of the next pope, the 800-year-old rule of clerical celibacy will almost certainly be made voluntary, if only because Catholic bishops are desperate about the multitude of priests leaving the priesthood. In the USA they are said to number 42 per cent, of whom 90 per cent blame the celibacy mandate for their leaving. Besides, all the recent publicity given to the widespread sexual malpractices of priests, both with women and with vulnerable boys, points to the advisability of making celibacy voluntary. During the pontificate of Paul VI (1963-78), the requests of priests for laicisation so as to marry were received sympathetically, but the present Pope put a stop to this laxity, and made it much more difficult for a priest to leave the priesthood without being excommunicated – apparently failing to predict that this would inevitably mean a rise in the incidence of priestly 'affairs', not to mention child-abuse.

Acceptance of women to the priesthood will not be far behind a relaxation on celibacy for priests, if not for gays. There are several reasons for this – including the shortage of priests, political correctness on sex equality, and the desire for expansion through rapprochement with the Anglican communion.

The acceptance of artificial contraception – at least by certain methods – is also likely to follow closely on the election of the next pope, but the prohibition on abortion, widely disobeyed though it is, will almost certainly persist.

Sexuality has always loomed large in the problems that beset Mother Church – from the neurotic hang-ups of St. Paul, through the sexual scandals of the medieval papal court and of supposedly celibate clergy and monastics, through the Anglican schism triggered by Henry's lust for Anne Boleyn, to the insidious rebellion of millions of Catholic women against the Vatican's continued ban on artificial contraception.

Comparatively flexible as the Anglican communion is, the divergences exposed in the Lambeth Conference last month are making it difficult to hold together the Sea of Faith theologians at the one extreme and some of the fundamentalist African bishops at the other. There was a time when WASPS could afford to ignore African opinion, but now it represents their only strong growth area – as, coincidentally, it does also for the Church of Rome – and most of the African Christian converts, of both denominations, are as reactionary on sexual politics as the Pope himself.

[August 1998]

Muscling In

[Christians and the Millennium: Letter]

THE Archbishop of Canterbury and Cardinal Hume have joined forces to threaten a boycott of the Millennium Dome inauguration unless the programme devotes 'significant time' to Christian prayers. Their specious argument is that the occasion is primarily the 2000th anniversary of Christ's birth.

Does that mean they reject the gospels as a true record? Herod the Great, who figures largely in the nativity story and the alleged 'slaughter of the innocents', is known to have died in the year we now designate 4BCE. So why didn't Christians have their birthday party in 1996, instead of trying to muscle in on the secular celebrations? And what is the Christian significance of midnight on December 31, when they usually celebrate the nativity on the 25th?

[April 1999]

My Week with the 'Enemy'

[Evangelical Confrontation]

THE fly-on-the-wall BBC2 television series, *Living with the Enemy*, brings together extremists on either side of a contentious issue. The issue chosen for the programme transmitted on October 13 [1999] was Christianity versus Atheism, for which I was to be the representative atheist, while the 'enemy' with whom I was to lodge for a week in Surrey was Gerald Coates, leader of the Pioneer Team – a widespread evangelical Christian network of about a hundred happy-clappy churches and several social projects in the 'New Church' movement – together with his wife and colleagues.

A great deal of time and effort is devoted to selecting the protagonists for this series, but at the end of the day the producers are more interested in personal confrontation than in the issues themselves. The editing policy therefore concentrates on trivia at the expense of anything that might smack of an intellectual debate – which, to ratings-conscious television moguls, is anathema nowadays for any programme destined for prime-time transmission.

In fact, there has been a noticeable 'dumbing down' even in the past year, since the previous series of *Living with the Enemy* showed more sustained argument on the issues between the 'enemies' than we were allowed – as the *Daily Telegraph* critic, reviewing the programme I was in, pointed out.

Living with the Enemy (BBC2) obligingly served up a neat illustration of its own decline. In the last series, the religious journalist Damian Thompson spent a week with an evangelical group. There was a difference of beliefs, but the two sides made a decent attempt to understand each other and had real conversations.

'This time', he complained, 'the two people simply shouted across each other until the programme ended'. It is not true that it was all shouting, but certainly any 'real conversations' on theology (as opposed to personal matters) were almost entirely edited out.

Gerald was as long-winded and evasive as any politician, but he was always gentlemanly to me – rather too smooth, in fact – whereas I was my usual abrasive self.

However, I only once really lost my cool. Needless to say, that moment was seized upon by the editors as being good screen fodder. It took place during the only communal dinner of the week, to which Gerald and his wife had invited four of their evangelical activists. So there was I – Daniel in the lion's den, pitted against six of them, and trying to eat at the same time: not the most relaxing of situations. In the end, I turned on one of the four guests, and told him he was weak-brained. Had I simply said that in the sphere of religion he was allowing his emotions to get the better of his reason, it would have sounded less rude.

Gerald protested that the man must be very intelligent, since he earns £100,000 a year – which suggested something to do with serving Mammon. Indeed, as the preview in the *Evening Standard's* 'Hot Tickets' magazine noted, 'the evangelists ... unwittingly reveal their mercenary smugness.'

Most of the previews were reasonably kind to me. 'In keeping with this series', said the *Guardian*, 'both sides remain unconvinced of the other's beliefs. But Barbara knows her Bible and can argue the toss more strenuously than Gerald.'

What an extraordinarily wasteful medium television is today! Though the fly-on-the-wall documentary is by no means the most expensive format, since it saves on studio costs and high celebrity fees, it is by far the most time-wasting. I realised, of course, that they would shoot many times the film footage required, but was amazed to discover that it was as much as sixty times the requirement – that is, some thirty hours of filming, often employing two camera angles, for a programme limited to 28 minutes.

Needless to say, the whole production team, from the executive producer and series producer down the hierarchy to the director of the production team for the particular programme, his assistant producer and various technicians, complain that the programme deserves a whole hour, but the inadequate time at their disposal does not mean that they edit out irrelevances and avoid repetition. What it does mean is that they can choose some funny or disconcerting episode as the main theme of the programme.

In our case, it was the alleged miracle of the sudden alchemical transmutation of amalgam tooth fillings into gold. There had been one such hysterical occurrence during a 'Toronto Blessing' at Gerald's home church the week before my visit, but the ridicule this had attracted in the tabloid press caused him and his colleagues to shield the miracle recipient from any further contact with the media and to ban us from filming in the same church during my resident week. So the director of our production team resorted to showing me a video of the event and filming my reaction to it.

Although this was not, strictly speaking, part of the week that was supposed to comprise the programme, it was used as a running gag – the camera shots inside the woman's mouth being repeated, as though the editors had insufficient material to fill their 28 minutes.

I actually felt quite sorry for the woman for making such a public fool of herself, but I cannot help being glad that she enabled me to get in the best of my quips that was not edited out: I asked Gerald why, even if she was convinced about the gold miracle, she had ascribed it to God, when it would seem more logical to ascribe it to the tooth fairy – to which he solemnly declared that he did not believe in the tooth fairy!

As the *Evening Standard* commented in its write-up of the programme, 'Perhaps God *is* the tooth fairy.'

It seemed to me that God the Dentist made my 'enemy' too easy a target for me, and I would have been better off with a more traditional theologian. After the transmission, however, I scrolled the BBC's Online Forum on the programme, running to 214 messages, and, to my horror, found that a number of the contributors – all, presumably, educated, computer-literate young people – do actually believe in alchemy.

The one head-to-head argument that I would have particularly liked to retain was my attack on the immoral doctrine of salvation through vicarious atonement – which, though the very cornerstone of Christianity, is inexplicably overlooked by most atheist philosophers. (Carefully avoiding hard words like 'vicarious', I used the analogy of the whipping-boy, but it was obviously still too serious for peak-time viewing.) Gerald's response, that the Saviour had willingly accepted crucifixion for love of humanity, hardly makes the scenario either moral or rational; it merely makes Christ masochistic so as to excuse the Father's capricious sadism.

I allowed the kind-hearted ladies who run a weekly 'prayer station' in Cobham to pray over my chronically tingly fingers, in a hopeless attempt at faith-healing – though I did warn them I had no faith whatsoever in their ministrations. Afterwards, interrogated as to what I would have said had my fingers thereupon improved, I had to admit that, deferring to David Hume, I would have put it down to coincidence, which would be so much more credible than the supernatural suspension of natural law – the agreed definition of a miracle.

Since my week's intercourse with the evangelicals I have been asked by several people whether it moderated my atheism. Now that *would* be a miracle.

[November 1999]

Undoing Baptism

FOLLOWING my interview on BBC's 'Woman's Hour' about the National Secular Society's promotion of 'de-baptism' ceremonies, I received a request from a listener for practical advice for such a ceremony and a suitable form of wording. She felt strongly about having been inducted into the Church of England while a helpless infant, and said she 'would like this undone'.

I replied as follows: 'Obviously, it is only a gesture, but one might as well make it a public gesture, which serves as a way of 'coming out' as an atheist. You could hold a party (to which no religious friends or relatives should be invited), and solemnly burn your baptismal certificate. You could also prepare a de-baptismal certificate, for signing and witnessing at the party. If you make it decorative, you could frame it later for permanent display – but not before photocopying it, so as to send copies to the local clergy, if that seems appropriate, and to anyone else you would like to annoy.'

I enclosed a copy of my own de-baptismal certificate, which, though specifically RC, might be adapted for other denominations. It concluded: 'I wish to be excluded from future Roman Catholic statistical claims, except for the statistics of apostasy.'

My correspondent then sent that on to the Archbishop of Canterbury, informing him of her intention. She received a long reply from his secretary, who assured her that the C of E uses current church attendances, not past baptisms, as a basis for its membership statistics. However, I was able to let her know that this is not strictly true, as past baptisms are certainly dragged in when doing so might secure political advantage. By way of evidence, I enclosed two pages from chapter 15 of the recently published Wakeham Commission Report, *A House for the Future*, in which past baptismal statistics are cited to boost claims of church membership, so as to justify retaining religious representation (the Bench of Bishops) in the proposed 'reformed' second chamber.

The next letter I received was so exuberant, I really must quote most of it verbatim (but without names).

The deed has been done: I have been de-baptised. It happened last Saturday, though it hadn't been planned for then at all. My daughter, who has just completed an MA in art and performance art, had prepared, as part of her work for the MA final assessment, a group of about thirty ceramic angels, some eight inches high, in varying poses – haughty, angry, pregnant, and so on – and was asked to exhibit them at a local arts festival. She was given a part of the parish church to show them in – an interesting choice!

Over lunch beforehand, I showed her my de-baptism certificate, as she had been following my correspondence on it with interest and enthusiasm. Somehow it was decided to do it that day, in the church, as the 'performance' part of her exhibit. She and her father disappeared for a bit and we all met up in the church. She read out the short introduction she had written, then the wording of the certificate, and presented me with some flowers and a white mask. Then we went outside for the signing and witnessing.

Though that part of the church had been empty when we started, part-way through the ceremony we realised that there were quite a few people watching. Unfortunately, one of the onlookers was the vicar – in plain clothes. He followed us out, and wasn't too happy. His main objection was that de-baptism is 'impossible'.

Altogether, it was a lovely day and the ceremony was exactly right. I am sending copies of the certificate to one or two people I want to annoy, as well as to some who will approve of what I have done. And I will reply to the Archbishop's secretary with some of your points. None of this would have happened without your support and ideas.

The sample certificate that follows would be suitable for de-baptism from any Christian denomination that practises infant baptism.

Declaration Of De-Baptism

After due deliberation, I, ...,
having been subjected to the rite of Christian baptism in infancy (before reaching an age of consent), hereby publicly revoke all implications of that rite and any pledges made on my behalf. I renounce the Church that carried it out, and, in the name of human reason, reject its creeds and all similar superstition – in particular, the perfidious belief that a baby needs to be cleansed by baptism from alleged original sin and the evil powers of supposed demons. I therefore wish to be excluded henceforth from enhanced claims of church membership.

Signed:

Date:

Witnessed

[January 2000]

Self-Centred Faith

[Believers and Personal Tragedy]

THE Catholic television personality, Terry Wogan, revealed some while ago that he had suffered a loss of faith following the death of his little daughter – though he had obviously known for most of his life that millions of people had seen their children die.

How is it that more distant tragedies can leave religious faith intact? Naturally, we all feel more deeply when someone close to us is struck down, but surely any other tragedy must raise the same theological questions. In fact, show me a god-believer and I will show you someone who has never stopped to think.

Terry Wogan is laudable for devoting much of his time to fund-raising for children's charities, but if, until the death of his own daughter, he managed to absorb all the reported worldwide disasters without ever questioning the alleged beneficence of his God, he must be blinkered and self-centred. And he is by no means alone.

Another showbiz personality, evangelical Cliff Richard, more recently described his crisis of faith (as reported in the October *Freethinker*), consequent upon the tragic murder of 'someone as beautiful, talented and harmless' as Jill Dando, who was a close friend of his. He said he 'screamed and railed' at the deity. But why did it take him so long?

A few weeks later, Sir Cliff had apparently made it up with God (as reported in the December *Freethinker*), for he devoted his usual Christmas single to literally singing the praises of the deity – indeed, doing so in God's own attributed words (as reported by Matthew and Luke), by using the Lord's Prayer, which he updated by renaming it *The Millennium Prayer*. This was a crafty dodge, the words having been out of copyright for almost two millennia. He was able to save money likewise on the music, by using the tune of 'Auld Lang Syne'.

However, the lot of a pop singer is not altogether a happy one: Sir Cliff was faced with another tragedy when his usual record company rejected *The Millennium Prayer* and BBC Radios 1 and 2 refused to play it. How could it hope to reach the charts, let alone Number One? But God was rooting for it.

First, the London-based evangelical radio station Premier Christian Radio took up the cudgels by promising to play the record once an hour every hour for one day and to keep it at the top of their play-list until Christmas. Next, the Catholics showed commendable ecumenism by putting their mighty buying power behind the record.

Their top-selling newspaper *The Universe* gave it a half-page plug on November 14, and followed this up two weeks later with the whole of the front page, continued on page 2 – thus making it almost a religious duty for RCs in this country to buy the record, which went straight into the charts at No 3, and a week later reached No 1.

It's enough to convert Sir Cliff to Rome.

[January 2000]

Freewill v Determinism

[Philosophical Epigram]

COMING down on the side of determinism in the age-old freewill/determinism debate, Barbara Smoker has devised the following explanatory slogan.

> You choose to act the way you wish,
> But do not choose the way you wish to act.

[June 2001]

Subsequently, I expanded this epigram into six lines of rhymed verse, as follows, for publication in the American journal *Free Inquiry*.

> Opposing Hume's deterministic view,
> Freewill for humankind did Kant infer
> To justify God's ire when people err.
> Which view is true? Has Hume or Kant won through?
> While we may choose to do what we prefer,
> We cannot choose what we prefer to do.

Pressing for Definitions

[Letter]

IN HIS letter headed 'Sympathy for the religious' ('Points of View', November), Peter Arnold says that atheism 'would be a more tenable position if one could agree what is meant by a god or God or the supernatural.'

Of course – and we atheists are always pressing believers to give us their own definition of what it is they believe in. Only then can we refute it or go along with it. If they posit an almighty and beneficent creator, this belief is refuted by, *inter alia*, natural disasters and the tragedies of

231

life. If they say their God is the whole universe, I tell them I share in that belief but find it less confusing simply to call it the universe.

Mr Arnold also declares that 'loss of faith' may be psychologically dangerous – which is tantamount to saying that 'cold turkey' could be dangerous for drug addicts. Is that an argument for ensuring that junkies remain addicted for life? Surely we should aim at getting people strong enough to face up to life without dependence on mind-bending drugs or mind-bending religion.

[December 2000]

Religious Terrorism
[New York, September 11]

THE moment we heard about the American disaster we all knew the perpetrators had to be Muslim extremists, for nothing but an unshakeable faith in post-death rewards can turn human beings into suicide-bombers. This was the motivation of the Japanese kamikaze pilots, as it is of terrorists on both sides in northern Ireland and everywhere else.

Yet since September 11 we have been constantly informed that the airliner terrorists in America could not possibly be Muslims – or, at least, not real Muslims – since the greatest crime in Islam is to take innocent life. But, of course, to many Muslims, especially those whose countries have been victims of American state terrorism in recent years, Americans are *not* innocent.

Although the scripture that is the common basis of Judaism, Christianity, and Islam, commands simply 'Thou shall not kill', all three religions have introduced the element of guilt or innocence – which is morally irrelevant. The one salient moral criterion on utilitarian grounds is desire to live.

Intrusion of the extraneous word 'innocent' has enabled all three religions to connive at both warfare and the death penalty, while abjuring abortion (however early) and euthanasia (however late). And it makes 'guilty' America a prime target for Muslim seekers after glory and their promised ghostly houris.

[October 2001]

Bring on the Clones

[Legislation on Human Cloning]

THE lead story of the January issue of SPUC's free paper *Pro-Life Times* hysterically denounced the new legislation to regulate human cloning, because it merely banned implantation in a womb, not the actual production of embryonic clones for research. The Pro-Life Alliance had been successful in the High Court in November in putting a stop to the whole cloning programme, but the new law enabled the Government to get the November judicial decision reversed in the Court of Appeal in January. This was a few weeks before the final report was due from the House of Lords Select Committee on Stem Cell Research. (Stem cells are the master cells that have the potential to grow into any kind of body tissue.)

The *Catholic Herald* of February 22, just one week before that report was published, devoted both its front page and its editorial to the same subject – though bizarrely concentrating on the alleged financial corruption involved in bio-tech funding.

On February 27, despite all this hoo-ha, the House of Lords Select Committee – chaired, surprisingly, by an Anglican bishop, Richard Harries of Oxford – gave the green light to the creation of human embryonic clones for the supply of stem cells for therapeutic purposes.

Licences for such experimentation and use are likely to be issued almost immediately – thus putting Britain in advance of the USA, and every other country with the exception of China, in a very important development of medicine, which will probably enable diseases such as cancer, diabetes, Parkinson's and Alzheimer's, as well as paralysis through damaged nerves, to be treated radically in as little as five years from now.

It is sheer common-sense to meet medical needs in this way, and opposition to it turns either on general ignorance or on the religious superstition of 'ensoulment'.

Embryonic stem cells (ESCs) can be harvested either from fertilised human eggs or from embryonic clones. The great advantage of the latter method for transplantation is that the patient's immune system will not reject self-cloned tissue.

The US Government, which has bowed to religious pressure at home against human embryo cloning (though, illogically, still allowing the destruction of spare embryos in IVF programmes) aims to persuade the UN to ban human cloning world-wide, and is itself concentrating instead on doubtful attempts to obtain patients' own adult stem cells of comparable versatility to ESCs.

The fundamentalist religious lobby opposes any experimentation on, and the ultimate destruction of, all human embryos, whether fertilised eggs or artificial clones.

The first source is embryos left over from fertility programmes. These would otherwise be wastefully destroyed – but pro-lifers are opposed to IVF anyway, unless every embryo, even if defective, is implanted into the mother for gestation. (One wonders how they rationalise the high rate of spontaneous early abortion, for which their god must be logically responsible.) In the second method, doctored fertilised eggs are treated with a chemical to start cell division.

In both methods, after five days (i.e. at the blastocyst stage), the inner cell mass is separated and the stem cells cultured to develop into whatever type of cell is required.

Squeamishness about using human embryos is due to the absurd notion that eggs are people. No one thinks that a chicken's egg is actually a chicken or an acorn is actually an oak-tree, so why confuse a human egg – even a fertilised human egg – with a human being? Since it has no nervous system, it can have no feelings, and an entity without feelings can have no intrinsic rights. Before becoming a human being with human rights, the fertilised egg would have to be given time to develop in the requisite environment – that is, in a womb, or possibly in an artificial womb.

Technically, a cloned embryo could probably be developed into a full-term human baby, but the new British regulations do not allow this.

Even if it were to be carried out one day, would that be so very terrible? There are already millions of human clones in the world – called identical twins – and they are more alike than a clone would be if born into a different environment in a later generation. But of course the exploitative replication of a large number of clones, as in Aldous Huxley's *Brave New World*, is another matter altogether.

A related controversy concerns those parents who, having a seriously disabled or dying child, use IVF to try desperately for another child with the prerequisite DNA to provide the first with a compatible transplant of, say, bone marrow. The one real moral imperative here is that the second child be wanted for itself and be treated equally with the first. However, a common misunderstanding about it is that the intention is to sacrifice the second child for the first. Actually, the new baby would donate nothing except stem cells from the umbilical cord, which is generally thrown away.

In fact, if stem cells were routinely collected from umbilical cords for properly computer-catalogued storage, they would always be available for everyone who needed them.

[April 2002]

What Price a Black Pope Next?

THIS month (May 18) marks the Pope's 82nd birthday, and his visibly declining health suggests that he cannot be lagging far behind our late Queen Mother in the universal race to life's end – to everlasting oblivion or the pearly gates ... or whatever.

The election, in the second conclave of 1978, of this Polish pope, John Paul II, né Karol Wojtyla, was the first election of a non-Italian pope for 455 years. Though it came as a surprise to everybody, this departure from precedent had been facilitated by a significant drop in the proportion of Italian cardinals.

Aged 58, Wojtyla was young for a pope, and he was a very fit athlete. This may well have counted in his favour, as the last thing the Vatican wanted was another untimely papal death followed by yet another expensive conclave.

Less than three years later, however, he was seriously injured in an assassination attempt, and has never fully recovered from the injury. In almost any other high-level job, it would have earned him industrial compensation and early retirement on a good pension; but the papacy is literally a life sentence. Now, his worsening disabilities include not only Parkinson's disease but a particular occupational scourge – arthritis of the knees, said to be aggravated, if not caused, by all that kneeling in prayer. (A self-inflicted addiction malady?)

Next time, the conclave will be less keen on choosing someone young and fit: a reasonably short pontificate is what most of the electors will be looking for. The Italians make no secret of their desire to win back the papacy: the present incumbent has always remained in their eyes a meddling foreigner, and they are not alone in resenting his 'presidential style of government'. (A familiar phrase to British ears!) The decline of collegiality, they insist, can be reversed only by returning to a traditional Italian 'Bishop of Rome'.

Meanwhile, however, the Italian tranche in the College of Cardinals – the source of the papal electorate – has plummeted to the all-time low of 15 per cent. (Half a century ago it was about 60 per cent.) So it would come as no surprise if the Holy Spirit were to pick another non-Italian for the job. But what sort of non-Italian? Certainly not another east European – the political motive for that evaporated more than a decade ago – but possibly a man from another continent altogether. And that continent could well be Africa.

After all, it is in the developing world that Catholicism thrives today, and Africa is top of the league – with a twenty-fold increase in its Catholic population since 1980.

Besides, a black face under the triple crown would surely look politically correct.

The still powerful Cardinal Ratzinger, German-born doctrinal prefect of the Vatican, paved the way for this a month ago by suggesting, in an interview published in the German newspaper *Die Welt* on April 3 [2002], that an African papacy would be a 'wonderful sign for all Christianity', and would be 'to the Church's benefit'.

Since most of the twelve African cardinals are on the theologically conservative wing, they chime well with Ratzinger himself – and, should there be a conclave in the near future, he is, despite his 75 years of age, the most likely king-maker. The African favourite is clearly the 69-year-old ultra-conservative Nigerian, Cardinal Francis Arinze, who (already leader of several of the Vatican congregations, councils, and committees) is the only one of the twelve Africans considered to be realistically *papabile*.

Ratzinger may have become something of a joke among the younger and more progressive prelates of the Church, but they too are likely to favour a contender from the Third World – though they would presumably prefer some liberation theologian from Latin America, or possibly an Asian, to a conservative from Africa. However, a compromise is the best they can hope for – and it is this sort of incongruous alliance that invariably plucks a new pope out of the hat after a number of inconclusive ballots, in which one faction blocks another from reaching the requisite two-thirds majority. (The Holy Spirit moving, as always, in mysterious ways.)

Anyway, theological progressives are under-represented in the College of Cardinals, largely because new cardinals are chosen by the reigning pontiff. While he is constitutionally precluded from nominating his successor, he does choose those who will elect him – and Papa Wojtyla has been distributing red hats like paper headgear from Xmas crackers. So, in spite of the age limit introduced for papal electors, there is at present an electorate of 126 (six more than the rules lay down). However, most of the 126, being diocesan bishops who have lost authority to the curia, are progressive on, at least, the issue of decentralisation, which has been one of the broken pledges of the second Vatican Council.

If Arinze, or any other conservative, is elected to the top job, his conservatism will presumably include immutable opposition to contraception – and the dire social consequences to the Third World of the perpetuation of this policy could endure for decades. Not only is birth-control needed most in the very countries where Catholic influence is strongest, the RC-imposed lack of condoms in Africa is a major cause of the prevalence of AIDS there – so uncannily reminiscent of the plagues to which Yahweh subjected Egypt at the time of Moses.

My research for this article has included approaching leading firms of bookmakers for a price on the next pope being an African. (After all, bookies are the professional experts on applied probability.) But Ladbrokes refused to offer odds for this event at all, while William Hill's were willing only to quote for named contenders – and then very cautiously.

For Arinze, Hill's offered me (after 24 hours' deliberation) only 25-1, with a £50 stake limit. (Perhaps I was suspected of insider knowledge, or even a hot line to the Holy Spirit!) I turned down the quote with derision, but asked to be informed when an official book is opened on the event – which, for the sake of decorum I was told, will not happen until JP II dies.

The huge papacy field will include many dark horses, making a pin-selected bet on the Grand National look like an odds-on certainty. However, there is one conclave certainty: there will be no woman in the line-up – not only next time but for the next half-dozen conclaves.

First, there will have to be a truly progressive pope with collegiate backing to introduce the ordination of women; then pioneer Catholic women-priests will need time for promotion to bishop, archbishop, and eventually cardinal, before there can be even a potential Pope Joan in the betting.

[May 2002]

Fruits of Muslim Martyrdom

[Letter on Paradisal 'Houris']

FURTHER to my February letter, in which I asked the source of the virginal houris promised after death to Islamic martyrs, I am now informed that they are not human virgins at all, but merely raisins!

According to the *New York Times* and *International Herald Tribune* of March 4, a scholar of ancient semitic languages, Christophe Luxenberg, has recently uncovered a Koranic mistranslation, in which the original Syro-Aramaic word for 'white raisins' (or 'white grapes'?) was mistaken for a similar word meaning 'houris'.

My informant comments that, however sweet, the asexual fruit said to await suicide bombers in paradise may prove a bit of a disappointment.

[June 2002]

The Author

BARBARA SMOKER, born into a devout Roman Catholic family in London in 1923, was brain-washed by her convent education, which left her with the ambition to become a contemplative nun. But wartime service in the Women's Royal Naval Service in multi-credal Ceylon gave her the opportunity to re-think her religious assumptions. After the war – unfettered by a university education – she thought and read a lot about religion, and the more she thought and read the less she was able to believe. Finally renouncing Christianity in 1949, she joined the secular humanist movement, later becoming active in the Campaign for Nuclear Disarmament, the Committee of 100, Vietnam and other war protests (including an illicit speech from the public gallery of the House of Commons), prison reform, 'squatting' homeless families, women's equality, and gay rights.

As president of the National Secular Society from 1971 to 1996, she represented the atheist viewpoint in print, on lecture platforms and soap-boxes, in speaking tours, in university debates, and on radio and TV. From 1981 to 1985 she chaired the Voluntary Euthanasia Society, and she compiled a book on that subject (published by Peter Owen). Other writings include *Humanism* – a book for use in secondary schools – first published (by Ward Lock Educational) in 1973, with a new updated edition in 1998; a book of satirical verse, *Good God!* (1977); a cassette script, *Atheism on a Soap-Box;* and a pamphlet on embryo research, *Eggs Are Not People*, which was distributed to all Members of Parliament in 1985. The same year she recorded a radio talk, 'Why I Am an Atheist', for the BBC World Service.

In 1984 she undertook a five-week speaking tour of the United States, as an atheist, and in 1990 a similar tour of India. When Muslim extremists held a march in London on May 27, 1989, calling for the death of author Salman Rushdie, she stood on the route with a homemade banner reading 'Free Speech' – and survived a physical attack by a surge of the demonstrators. In 1998 she visited India again to inaugurate a mass atheist rally, and the following year she featured in a BBC2 TV documentary, 'Living With the Enemy'.

This volume of articles, a personal selection from the journal the *Freethinker,* covers three-and-a-half decades, from 1966 to 2002 (somewhat intermittently) – beginning with the final emergence of the author's mature views on religion and bio-ethics and continuing into her eightieth year.

The contemporary scene on which she comments from that perspective includes unprecedented scientific progress, a remarkable transformation of the supposedly immutable RC Church, the decline of other mainstream Churches alongside the upsurge of fundamentalism, the rise of New Age cults, and the growing threat of multicultural extremism in Britain.